ADVISOR
~ *for* ~
LIFE

ADVISOR ～ *for* ～ LIFE

BECOME THE INDISPENSABLE FINANCIAL ADVISOR TO AFFLUENT FAMILIES

STEPHEN D. GRESHAM

BICENTENNIAL
1807
WILEY
2007
BICENTENNIAL

John Wiley & Sons, Inc.

Published by John Wiley & Sons, Inc., Hoboken, New Jersey.
Published simultaneously in Canada.

Wiley Bicentennial Logo: Richard J. Pacifico

For general information on our other products and services or for technical support, please contact our Customer Care Department within the United States at (800) 762-2974, outside the United States at (317) 572-3993 or fax (317) 572-4002.

Wiley also publishes its books in a variety of electronic formats. Some content that appears in print may not be available in electronic books. For more information about Wiley products, visit our web site at www.wiley.com.

Library of Congress Cataloging-in-Publication Data:

Gresham, Stephen D.
    Advisor for life : become the indispensable financial advisor to affluent families / Stephen D. Gresham.
        p.   cm.
    Includes bibliographical references and index.
    ISBN 978-0-470-11233-5 (cloth)
    1. Financial planners.   2. Investment advisors.   3. Affluent consumers—Finance, Personal.   I. Title.
    HG179.5.G738   2007
    332.024—dc22

                                                                2006037890

Printed in the United States of America.

10 9 8 7 6 5 4 3 2

To the most important people in my life:
Jane, Rachael, Meggie, and T.J. Gresham

Contents

Acknowledgments

Writing a book is like taking a long journey: You start out with a pretty good idea of where you're going and what you'll do and see along the way. But as in any trip, it's the surprises—the unexpected and wonderful sights and experiences along the way that happen only if you keep your eyes and ears open—that make the voyage memorable. And having friends along for the ride makes it all the more fulfilling.

Described in these terms, *Advisor for Life* was a great journey. The process of capturing the best practices of top advisors uncovered some terrific new tactics. Some advisors I have known for years revealed new aspects of financial advice that are exciting concepts for today's competitive markets. I also found new thinkers who helped me better frame my observations.

A first-class team of professionals joined me for the journey and provided the support and camaraderie required to complete the trip in style. Their contributions added both balance and deeper meaning to my words, and I'm indebted to them.

First, the advisors I have met over the years provided the inspiration for *Advisor for Life*. These are the classy professionals who embody the values sought by affluent families. Kerry Bubb, Peter Burton, Louis Chiavacci, Mary Beth Emson, Scott Finlay, Ken Gordon, Steve Grillo, Brian Kelly Sr. and Brian Kelly Jr., Bill King, Leon Levy, Robert Levy, Bill Lomas, Greg Miseyko, Jim Pratt-Heaney, John Rafal, Mike Simon, and Trisha Stewart all gave generously of their time and selflessly offered their insights to the community that is the financial advice profession.

Many industry colleagues encouraged me to update my past work with fresh insights for the current marketplace. Frank Campanale of Campanale Consulting Group; Rose Cammareri of AGF Funds; Bob Cunha of Market Metrics; Chris Davis of the Money Management Institute; David

Geracioti of *Registered Rep.* magazine; Hannah Grove of Hannah grove.com; Brian Lord of Premiere Speakers; Steve Geist, Tom Williams, Ginny Macdonald, and the team at CIBC Asset Management; Eric Sondergeld of LIMRA; Cami Miller of Financial Forum; Len Reinhart of Lockwood Advisors; Julie Segal of *Institutional Investor;* Toshiya Shimizu and Yasusuki Annen of Nikko Cordial Advisors in Tokyo; Victor Dodig and Tom Monahan at CIBC in Toronto; Susan Moloney, Mona Bisson, Jane Wolff, Anne Steer, and Norman Malo of National Financial; and Evan Stewart of Zuckerman Spaeder are just a few of the countless supporters and contributors to my career.

Some genuine superstars provided additional inspiration and insight from their unique perspectives. Ken Dychtwald was generous with his time and research information. Coach Mike Krzyzewski of Duke University blends leadership insights with humility and compassion to get results. And mountaineer Laurie Skreslet is a fascinating authority on human nature, as well as a wonderful teacher.

I was especially fortunate to receive contributions from several industry authorities whom I sought out for their special knowledge and experience. Ron Surz of PPCA is one of the industry's brightest and original thinkers. Walt Zultowski is the guru of the perennial Phoenix Wealth Survey and read much of the text, adding key facts along the way. Leo Pusateri and I have worked together for nearly 20 years, traveling the world in search of best practices and advisor value. He has taught me more about value and life than almost anyone. He and his business partner, Giles Kavanaugh, delivered a key part of this book in Chapter 12 that could stand alone. Jeff Marsden of PriceMetrix joined the team at Giles's urging and provided additional perspective to the tricky topic of demonstrated advisor value. Tim Welsh was a valued collaborator while at Schwab Institutional, and his chapter on valuation brings clarity to a complex subject that will continue to be a hot topic for the rest of our careers. Russ Alan Prince of Prince and Associates has both tremendous knowledge and unerring candor. Finally, my father and fellow *Registered Rep.* columnist, Dr. Glen Gresham, offered a great deal more than his few credited words on the financial implications of health care events.

My editorial team made me look a great deal better as a writer than I am. The folks at John Wiley & Sons, led by David Pugh, were patient and supportive. Todd Tedesco, senior production editor, ably guided the manuscript through production. The staff at Cape Cod Compositors grabbed the composition task with energy and diligence. Joe Finora worked on several chapters and contributed the section on using the media in Chapter 16. Mike Lynch was a valued ally when we worked together at Phoenix Investment Partners, and he brought energy and technical expertise to the project—especially Chapters 6 and 7. My assistant at Phoenix, Susan Ingvertsen, pitched in at key moments to bail me out of countless logistical logjams and kept the train running.

Two key players require special notice. I am especially indebted to my editor of many years, Evan Cooper, who took charge as the project neared completion and created significant additional value out of my collected writings. My longtime friend and accomplice, Arlen Oransky, helped manage the overall project from start to finish as the ultimate utility player concerned with everything from the checkbook to top advisor interviews. Thanks to you both.

And no one but a hermit could write a book without sacrificing considerable personal time that should be reserved for family. My wonderful wife, Jane, never complained and helped make time on the weekends and early mornings for me to write without interruption. My terrific children, Rachael, Meggie, and T.J., all gave me space and even prodded me back to work when I wanted to take a break. All three are still hoping I'll write a "real" book someday.

Finally, thank you for taking the time away from your practice and your family to explore ideas that I hope might make a difference in your business. Let me know what you like, what you'd like to hear more about, and where I can improve. You are *my* client.

—Steve Gresham
www.greshamcompany.com

PART I

The State of the Advice Industry and Your Opportunities

INTRODUCTION

Buicks and Big Macs

What the Financial Advice Industry Can Learn from General Motors, McDonald's, and FedEx

I recently participated in a workshop for top advisors of a leading wirehouse brokerage firm. My topic was "Catching the Baby Boomer Retirement Wave"—specific tactics for tapping the historic opportunity of 77.5 million Americans hurtling toward retirement with (generally) insufficient funds. I was interrupted along the way by an advisor who admitted the importance of the boomer wave, but shared that he just doesn't see anyone from that generation. Our dialogue follows:

> *Gresham:* How old are you?
>
> *Advisor:* Forty-two.
>
> *Gresham:* So you're a boomer yourself and you don't encounter boomer-aged people in your practice?
>
> *Advisor:* Not as clients.
>
> *Gresham:* Have you purchased or leased a car in the past couple of years?
>
> *Advisor:* Yes—but why?
>
> *Gresham:* Did you choose a Cadillac?
>
> *Advisor:* No.
>
> *Gresham:* Why not?
>
> *Advisor:* No reason—I just didn't.
>
> *Gresham:* My grandfather saved for years to get a Cadillac, and he was so proud of it—he showed people he had finally succeeded.

3

You're more financially successful than he was, so why no Cadillac?

Advisor: I have nothing against Cadillacs, but buying one never occurred to me.

Now you know how a lot of baby boomers feel about full-service financial advisors—once a status symbol of the elite, they are largely out-of-mind for the current generation.

Cadillac was for many years the epitome of postwar American success—even its name came to symbolize success and status, the standard-bearer for an industry with commanding worldwide market share. In the same era, having your own stockbroker usually implied your sophistication about money and a macho ability to take risks in search of outsized riches. But just as Cadillac lost its luster when it failed to court the children of its most loyal customers, the full-service brokerage industry now teeters on the brink of its own mortality. Is it too late—as it was for Oldsmobile—or will the wirehouses reinvent themselves to avoid being trumped by a financial Lexus?

LOSING THE LIMO MARKET

Surveys of millionaire households confirm anecdotal reports that many members of the baby boom generation are going it alone as investors. Buoyed by a sea of information and online tools, the boomers can sail seemingly without fear toward retirement. At work, most of them are given that role without choice as 401(k) plans replace the defined benefits of their parents' generation and a shifting economy creates job changes and new rollovers. Try Googling "mutual funds." You'll find Morningstar.com, a site at which a bevy of powerful analytics and provocative research ideas are but a few clicks away. Combined with a robust history of seemingly every known fund, what more could an investor need for assurance?

NEW TIMES, NEW BRANDS

Companies like Charles Schwab, Fidelity Investments, and Vanguard have become far more than just financial services companies—they are well-known consumer brands. Each company has declared its value proposition and has attracted a substantial following. Schwab provided the first popular platform to hold securities and funds from different companies; Fidelity is among the largest providers of retirement plans; and Vanguard has championed low-cost mutual funds. By contrast, what is the unique strength of Merrill Lynch or Smith Barney? An early attempt by one firm to distinguish itself in the marketplace was the dramatic but hollow line, "We make money the old-fashioned way—we earn it." A similar smugness was revealed by General Motors when its ads challenged, "This is not your father's Oldsmobile." If sales are any guide, the answer soon became clear.

The baby boom marketplace (Americans born between 1946 and 1964) is much larger than that of the earlier generation. At 77.5 million strong, the boomers outnumber the Silent Generation (born 1926–1945) by nearly three to one. The sheer population increase can support more choices and more providers. Indeed, Detroit's Big Three have seen their competition spring from seed during the boomers' car-buying lifetimes. But population alone does not guarantee demand, forcing many brands to either focus on a market niche, be overwhelmed, or become extinct (remember Oldsmobile).

Volvo's first U.S. imports were ugly but offered safety. Toyota and Nissan delivered reliability and value, while their Lexus and Infiniti divisions tapped an upscale desire for luxury—in addition to unprecedented quality. Porsche and BMW have delivered performance, and Mercedes has toppled Cadillac as the world's prestige brand, while at the same time acquiring former Big Three player Chrysler.

Where go Merrill Lynch, Morgan Stanley, and Smith Barney? Le Cirque or McDonald's? Will they follow the path of Oldsmobile into history or will they forge new identities?

One of the great challenges to the full-service advice business is the enormous dispersion in its service delivery. The client experience is highly varied in almost all touch points with an advisory firm. There is, of course, an argument to be made in favor of personalized solutions and that no two clients are identical—therefore their results will differ. But I'm talking about the entire service offering.

Consider the quality of advice created by the very best advisor at a wirehouse firm and that of the very worst. Without arguing for the moment about what constitutes "best" and "worst," let's make the judgment simpler. How many clients of the brokerage firm outperformed the market? Better yet, how many clients are on track to achieve their retirement goals?

Dig a bit deeper. It's clear that there is no quality control of these (to me) basic issues. Imagine the trouble that would be created for FedEx if it attempted to manage an international delivery service in which some packages arrived before 10:30 A.M. the next day (as the firm promises), while others were entrusted to drivers with their own agendas who didn't deliver until after lengthy lunch breaks or afternoon rounds of golf? Hold on, you say—the client of a brokerage firm is in part a determinant of success or failure. Clients will often direct investments that may be too risky and end up losing. Okay—but beware of the economic reality of competition.

FedEx is able to charge a premium price not because it surprises clients with an 8 A.M. delivery (instead of 10:30), but because on any given day most of its clients are *not* surprised. FedEx has many competitors, most of which succeed by charging lower prices or by serving more personally a market not frequented by FedEx (such as the U.S. Postal Service, which will pick up your Express Mail nearly everywhere). The consistency may not be quite as good—I frankly don't know—but it's certainly good enough for a great many consumers. The market sustains the perception that it is not.

Now apply the same standards to the full-service advice industry. Ultimately, the consistency of results will determine a firm's ability to attract and retain affluent investors. The more consistent, the more successful due to the maintenance of a reputation for consistency. That's how a brand is built. An additional dynamic is how much people will pay for that service. The more consistent and the more successful, the higher the price. In addition, the more outstanding the service, the higher the price. The more personalized the service, the higher the price—for a certain clientele that's willing to pay.

Perhaps a more accurate industry comparison for the full-service advice business is the similarly fragmented restaurant world. McDonald's attracts more customers to its individual restaurants than do most local coffee shops or diners, allowing it to continue investing in new products, quality control, manager and franchisee training, and, importantly, specific and compelling advertising. Consistency is its hallmark—McDonald's is not attempting to land atop some Zagat's list of leading culinary experiences. Le Cirque, by contrast, has no interest in drawing a crowd. It has limited seating and covets the reputations of its superb chef and manager. The CEO, top management, and franchisees of McDonald's can all do well by making a lot of people a little bit happy (kids are easier to please!), and the owners of Le Cirque are not suffering, either, as they delight a limited clientele. The business models are distinct, and the organizations reflect the differences.

What to do with a full-service brokerage firm in which the largest client eats regularly at Le Cirque and a great number spend weekends at McDonald's? Beyond their taste in restaurants, these folks likely have very different financial needs. And just like the restaurant industry, there are business models to accommodate the specific needs and interests of each patron. The secret of success is to understand your target market and consistently deliver services appropriate to that market at the right price: Marketing 101.

The trouble today is that too many firms are trying to service Le Cirque patrons inside of a fast-food chain while also claiming to offer Le Cirque–quality cuisine to slightly above-average Americans at fair prices. The closest I've seen to capturing the entire spectrum of tastes is Disney's two domestic theme parks. But there the model is simpler—just two parks, plus two more overseas. How do you do it in an international company with hundreds of offices and thousands of financial advisors? The success of the model depends more on the skills of the individual employees—the advisors—than it does on the company itself. It is in fact the advisors who determine most of the client experience (with the exception of Web offerings and monthly statements). The products—like the food created by the restaurant—are one aspect of the relationship, and their performance is critical to the client's success. But just as exceptional service can overcome an average meal and make the evening a night to remember, so too can the skills of a first-rate advisor offset the ubiquitous product offerings of large financial services firms—none of which have maintained an edge in product delivery or pricing for any extended time period.

Back to Detroit. What are the lessons to be learned by full-service financial advice firms from the experiences of the automotive industry, so humbled by the boomers? And is it too late? Consider the various aspects of managing a business, and consider the challenges and potential solutions of each.

> ### Learning from History
>
> The most detailed chronicle of Detroit's decline—and the rise of
> Japan as a global automotive player—is certainly *The Reckoning* by
> distinguished storyteller David Halberstam. This 1986 classic is now
> out of print, but copies can be found on eBay and Amazon.

Quality

Is the advice good? Detroit confronted the quality issue in several
ways, but some lessons are clear:

You need more than a slogan—"Quality is Job 1" made for a great
lapel button but it didn't convince anybody. Changing perception is a
longer-term process of deeds, not words. Compounding Detroit's issues were not just that quality was not rewarded anywhere in the company, but also that multiple, vertically integrated layers provided all of
the product components. The Ford Motor Company was actually quite
a substantial miner and smelter of iron ore at one time. Full-service financial advice firms are no longer entirely reliant on closed architecture using their own products—that wall has fallen. But many other,
more subtle forms of vertical integration persist at the largest firms.
One is technology, where legacy systems have prevented the most important client-service requirement to date—the ability to hold all of
your investments in a single account. Many discount brokers popped
up as commissions were deregulated in May 1975, but Schwab became
the largest—not just because its trades were cheapest, but in part because it was an innovator in allowing clients to consolidate their stocks
and funds in one account. Almost 20 years later, full-service firms were
still working to match the capability.

Detroit's competition that stole the quality prize included Acura
and Lexus. One way those organizations competed with Detroit was
a TV commercial in which the announcer rolled a ball bearing down
the side seam of a car's hood—between the hood and the car
body—to prove the accuracy of the hood's fit. An American car's
seam was so gapped that the bearing rolled off or literally fell inside
the car. Oops.

For the full-service advice industry, the lesson is to make sure the quality of the service is indeed sufficient. What constitutes valuable advice? Is it the same test as when a stockbroker provided a quote and access to the New York Stock Exchange? That same generation as car buyers tolerated the "planned obsolescence" scheme cooked up by the finance guys who got control of Detroit in the 1960s and 1970s.

At the highest end, quality differences are the most glaring. As a result, most comparisons of product or service are unnecessary—the winner is clear. Cadillac, the icon of American success and status, lost its crown to Mercedes in a breathtakingly short period of time. So complete was the victory that Daimler-Benz swooped lower into the price lineup, ultimately capturing buyers with models below $30,000. I recall a status-seeking friend who bought one of the first 190 models in 1987 because, as he said, "I can now own a Mercedes." But it drives terribly in the snow!

High quality has not left the full-service advice business, although what passes for high quality has many interpretations. The very best advisors are not determined solely by the products or services delivered; neither are they identified by their form of compensation. Unfortunately, some firms have tried to increase quality using both strategies. A terrific advisor might sell only securities culled from research augmented by the advisor's own expertise. Saying that person is "just a stockbroker" is not relevant if in fact the performance achieved is superior to others. Similarly, an advisor who sells managed accounts and is compensated by an asset-based fee could actually be a product pusher. More specific measures are required to spread quality throughout a firm.

Reliability = Consistency

You can create a high-quality product or service, but if it has problems in manufacturing, the quality is only as good as the model the client receives. This is the automobile recall factor (or the FedEx delivery time promise). For Detroit, the reliability issue remained a thorn in its side—even after the Big Three began creating cars people liked. And the affliction was not entirely theirs—I remember the old line about a British-made brand, "You have to own two because one is always in the shop." For the full-service firms, the problem is actually more acute because the product (advice) is being dispensed across a far broader platform of individual advisors. The difference between the best and worst is profound. How can a national advertising campaign have any impact when there is such a huge disparity among expertise levels and advice quality? FedEx drivers who can't get their packages delivered on time do not stay employed at FedEx. Franchisees at McDonald's who substitute ingredients or don't serve french fries will hear from someone—quickly.

Toyota and Honda played the reliability card against Detroit and won big. Both companies continue to raise prices while the Big Three became caught in a death spiral of discounts.

Value

Competition based on value has many different aspects. Value is a highly personalized concept. What constitutes value for one person may not fit another person. Take the value of performance. While one investment may produce greater absolute returns, the required volatility may not be acceptable to your client. How then to measure value? I think each person has an inherent sense of what he or she considers value. Value can also refer to the services rendered. For example, does your client value your advice? This is an important and basic question. And what is your client willing to pay for that service? At least two dynamics are at work in the advice industry—what services are valued and whether they are provided at a fair price.

Auto manufacturers lost their dedication to value when they eschewed quality for short-term profits, when they provided models that did not match the public's needs, and when they failed to produce cars for a reasonable price. Competitors soon filled the void.

What is your value? Thoroughly consider again what you do—are those services truly valued by your clientele? Do they result in referrals? Just as importantly, are clients willing to pay you for them?

One great concern about financial advice is that it must reflect changing requirements and the reality of stronger competition. Consider the impact of defined contribution/401(k) plans. In the previous generation, the first purchase of a mutual fund, stock, or municipal bond was typically facilitated by a financial advisor or broker. Clients would make that initial purchase and at some point might be lured to a less-expensive alternative source like a discount broker or direct provider, but they seldom cut the tie to their advisor, preferring to check in from time to time to see if they remained on the right course. Researchers call these folks "validators"—clients not requiring full-time assistance (from their perspective), but unwilling or unable to entirely rely on their own decision making.

Enter the 401(k). Many baby boomers in particular have their first investing experience by choosing within the protected environment of a defined contribution plan. What had once been an experience conducted with taxable monies through an advisor is now first conducted with the assistance of information about capital markets, asset allocation (AA), and a limited array of investment choices—not the confusing universe of all investment products but a significant enough selection in most cases.

Clients of the current generation have therefore begun one step ahead of their parents—or have they? More importantly, the new folks are also entering within the context of investor education and with exposure to critical maxims like diversification and AA. Increasingly, these new retirement investors can opt out of decision making and select an AA fund tuned to their risk parameters and/or time horizon. A growing percentage of 401(k) plans now default participants to a life cycle fund if the participants have not made selections from among the plan options.

Advisors promising to provide diversification and AA were once offering a better strategy than that of the investor who had simply purchased several unrelated bonds, stocks, and funds. But 401(k) plans have raised the bar. Why will clients pay for AA and diversification if their retirement plan experience tells them they can do it on their own via a mutual fund company's web site or—even simpler—through an AA fund? The growth rate in AA funds should serve as a warning to advisors—people can and will do it themselves. But this change has brought an opportunity. Offering such a fund can be a terrific way to acknowledge the benefits of investing and rebalancing—freeing you to work more on the substantive issues confronting your client's household.

Ultimately value will be determined—as it always is—by the marketplace. My suspicion is that like most other industries, the advice business will retain its profit margin primarily through the delivery of services that cannot be provided over the telephone or via the Web and that require a greater level of expertise. What you can only do in person is what will determine your value—what your unique value will be—and what clients will pay for are the more sophisticated and sometimes even intangible services that clients cannot approach on their own. Investors can select securities, build portfolios, and even rebalance online through multiple providers. But can they accept the discipline of investing in a market sector as it falls in value relative to other investments? Can they prepare an estate plan? Can they build a legacy? How are they made aware of new products? Who will explain risk to them or help them plan for the next generation? As Warren Buffett notes, "Investing is simple, but not easy." It is simple to accept the laws of physics. Each of us knows that much of what goes up is destined to fall, but it is another matter entirely to put your money on that fallen star.

So if the millionaire households will pay for what they value, the questions become: What will they value and how do we market it? We explore this topic more in the following chapters, as we focus our discussion more on life issues than on investment topics.

In the pages ahead, we explore the wealth management issues that are most relevant to your clients. These are the same issues that led *Money* magazine to completely remake its monthly product from a publication favoring investments to one now organized around five specific aspects of wealth management. Sensing a change of interest in its subscriber base (nearly two million copies of *Money* are distributed each month), Time Warner (publisher of over 150 titles) spent about $1 million to research its offering. The results were startling. Readers were overwhelming in their opinion: *Money* devoted too much space to the discussion of investments. Who'd have thought that a magazine named *Money* could be guilty of talking too much about investing money? But what the researchers heard was a plea for advice that was still about money, but also what to do beyond investments.

Money was relaunched with the April 2005 edition divided into five separate categories—Start, Plan, Home, Invest, Spend. "Start" is just what you'd expect—a section devoted to simply getting started with a lifetime financial plan. "Relevance" was the word mentioned most often as I listened to the *Money* team describe their new baby's focus. Is your practice relevant? Refreshing? Do yourself and your clients a favor and subscribe. A "professional discount" subscription set me back $10 at the time of this book's writing. In his great book, *Marketing to the*

Affluent, Tom Stanley advised: "Read what your prospect reads." Good advice. Don't just buy the magazine. Do what *Money* did—ask your clients basic questions. What are they seeking beyond investments? What are their concerns beyond retirement? What are their fears? Then think of how you can help them. There is no shortage of basic questions that could be asked that could lead your practice to a new, refreshing, and rewarding direction. All good advertising makes a promise to improve the customer's life in some way. Are you doing at least this?

Niches

If asset allocation and the diversified approach to investing are no longer points of differentiation, are all advisors destined to go the way of the dinosaur? Not necessarily. Look again at the automobile industry's travails. Several important players have found niches around the mass-marketing machinery determined to pump out ubiquitous sedans, minivans, and SUVs to a shrinking customer base. Porsche has been experiencing record sales, driven in part by a boomer craving for performance—even in the family car. BMW is selling a record number of SUVs, as is Mercedes. By making a commitment to a specific aspect of automobiles—performance—all three manufacturers have retained and grown market share while protecting profit margins by giving customers what they want. Listening to the customer is not rocket science; it's just basic marketing and it works.

Of course the parallels between automobile performance and investment performance are too easy to miss. Thousands of mutual funds and a similar number of hedge funds are managed with the hope of beating market indexes for clients who "don't want to drive 55." Advisors with the rare ability to consistently deliver strong returns will always attract clients willing to pay for the thrill. The fickleness of the performance buyer is of course the risk accompanying any marketer offering performance—a true performance aficionado is always seeking more speed, but speed also kills. If you cannot maintain your edge, you will lose out to another player. And there is always someone gunning for you—indicating that this is a risky road to take.

But the call to think (and act) outside the box can be compelling. Other niches have been successfully built around less exciting aspects of personal transportation. What about Volvo's appeal to the safety-conscious? There will always be opportunities for those willing to adjust to individual needs. Value is personal, but the ball is always in play and to succeed you need to be where the ball is going—not where it's been.

So what will be the road next traveled by those in the advice industry?

It's hard to say. We do know it will be a crowded thoroughfare and there will be many ways to make the trip. Along the way the models will change and the prices will fluctuate, and the only certainties will be those of change and variety. And, oh yes, it will be an interesting journey, one you probably will not want to miss.

This book is about successfully making the trip. We will explore the alternatives to building an appealing, profitable, and enjoyable business that surprises clients with its ability to create consistent value. When the trip is more successful and enjoyable, it should be more fun as well. Let's get started, because to reach your destination you'll need a map.

CHAPTER 1

The Value of Advice

Which Advice Is Most Valued by Affluent Households—And What Should It Cost?

- *What services are today's clients willing to pay you to provide?*
- *What can you offer—and what do you want to offer?*
- *What five words can help guide you to provide a consistent offering of services valued by affluent clients?*

If other service professions can be a guide to financial advisors, they reveal that the most reliable long-term profits can be earned from those services that cannot be easily delivered via nonhuman means, such as over the telephone or via the Web.

There is an incredible, once-in-a-lifetime opportunity for those advisors willing to engage those who need long-term financial help. The most lucrative segment of the industry will remain for those advisors who can deliver what clients will pay for—real advice for real issues. That advice will require you to determine for each client household its greatest:

Needs—the requirements of daily living, including household income.

Concerns—issues that worry a household based on current conditions, such as the care for an aging parent.

Fears—potential problems, such as the chances of contracting a major illness or being confined to a nursing home.

Risks—vulnerabilities—financial, emotional, or otherwise.

Goals—what people hope to accomplish.

Dreams—the things people hope to do, but typically do not as circumstances catch up to them and realities or lack of motivation outweigh the potential to do them.

WHY THE AFFLUENT WANT YOU

Now save yourself a lot of time. Here's a simple exercise to determine if you have the right stuff to be an Advisor for Life:

Think about your own life and family. What do you need to live on right now? What level of income is required by your current lifestyle? If you are a successful advisor, you earn a six-figure annual paycheck—or more. So what is that annual number? Now ask yourself: What would you do if your income fell by 50 percent this year? Where would you turn? Who would you ask for advice?

Consider that the loss of a high percentage of current income is the precise concern of many affluent households. According to *Cultivating the Middle-Class Millionaire* by Russ Alan Prince and David A. Geracioti (Wealth Management Press, 2005), 88.6 percent of millionaires surveyed are "very concerned" about losing their wealth. A "significant financial reversal" is uppermost in the minds of those who have achieved financial success—the fear of losing is what drives so much of what we in the advice industry call risk tolerance. Translate that into your life.

What would you do? Initially you might want some sympathy, but sooner or later you'd want someone to give you advice about what to do—lay out your options, help you decide how to adjust to the situation.

THE ACID TEST—CAN YOU SHOW TRUE CONCERN?

The point of exploring this scenario is to see the client's side of financial advice and financial advisors. The emotions that I trust ran through you as you contemplated the income loss are the same as those surging through your clients and prospects. Here's the true test—can you summon empathy for others? Can you be truly concerned for your clients as they confront life's real challenges? This is the primary test of the Advisor for Life.

The reason I earlier urged you to "save yourself a lot of time" is that if you do not feel concern for your clients, you will not be happy (or successful) as an Advisor for Life.

You can't fake concern. (Warning—you haven't heard the last from me on this topic.) As this book progresses, I will continue to challenge your ability to accept your clients, probe for their concerns and fears, and deliver a consistently superior and surprising level of service. This will maintain your value no matter what the markets do and is the essence of the Advisor for Life.

THE FOUR COMMANDMENTS

My longtime colleague, Don Berryman, has a marvelous way of phrasing important principles so they become impossible to forget. An old branch manager friend of Don's summarized the role of the financial advisor in four words that are appropriate for us to use now to frame the role of the Advisor for Life:

1. Be available.
2. Be concerned.
3. Be informed.
4. Have an opinion.

These four simple but powerful commands capture the meaning of Advisor for Life. While you may intuitively appreciate their importance, here is my perspective.

Be Available

To be truly available to your clients you must be ready to give your time—the most valuable resource. The same is true of how you choose to spend your time away from your role as a financial advisor. To be available to your family—spouse, parents, growing children—is to give the most precious gift you can provide. Busy and successful people constantly lament the shortage of time, yet most don't take a moment to determine where their time is best and most valuably spent. A consistent complaint of many millionaire households is that their advisors are "not proactive" and are "difficult to get hold of." They don't freely offer their time. They do not make contact on the client's terms instead of their own. (See Figure 1.1.)

Most advisors to millionaire households get pretty good reviews from their clients—successful people don't tend to suffer poor service from anyone for very long. But surveys indicate a consistent 20 percent of clients working with a primary advisor are actively looking for a new one or thinking about doing so. Given the rich supply of millionaire households in the United States today—roughly nine million—that is a hefty list of prospects for advisors willing to provide better service!

The opportunity for prospecting millionaire clients by being available—better proactive service—is even greater than indicated by the preceding numbers. The percentage of millionaire households using a primary advisor is only about 70 percent—a number that has been consistently falling as the bull market helped buoy the confidence of investors. Digging further into the data reveals that *many of these self-directed households are interested in finding a primary advisor.* Data from a recent survey found that of the respondents who reported keeping the bulk of their assets with a well-known discount commission firm, 38 percent of those households are interested in finding a primary financial advisor. What gives?

FIGURE 1.1   **What Clients Don't Want**
Source: 2006 Phoenix Wealth Survey.

Change Brings Opportunity The self-directed household population draws heavily from two groups—both of which represent opportunity for the Advisor for Life. First, the baby boomer demographic is rife with so-called self-directeds because the generation has grown up with more information and confidence managing its own financial affairs, which to this point have consisted largely of investments. But now boomers are having to confront more complex needs. Estate planning, disability, parental care—each requires knowledge of legal structures, trusts, taxation, insurance, and other issues that are beyond the realm of simple investing. When these issues unveil themselves, even the most confident investors are suddenly in uncharted waters—and they generally don't like it. Figure 1.2 is a chart I'll refer to several times in this book that can help provide perspective (and life preservers) for these investors.

The life cycle shows both the phase of client household financial development and the advisor's role in each phase. Note that the early stages of investing create little or no opportunity for the advisor to add value—indicating where the financial advice marketplace has evolved to support the self-directed client. As discussed in the Introduction, within the relative safe haven of a 401(k) plan, a client can select investments and build a diversified portfolio—a Phase II strategy. In the

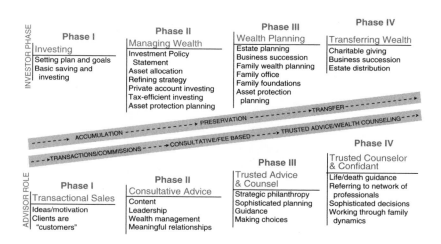

FIGURE 1.2 The Advisor for Life Cycle
Source: The Phoenix Companies, Inc.

late 1980s, the innovation of managed account programs was to help investors who owned a grab bag of individual stocks, bonds, and funds to build a managed solution with structure and purpose. Now that advantage has been taken away and provided to the average defined contribution plan investor. The opportunity for the Advisor for Life to make an impact has been moved to Phases III and IV.

The others who are ready to accept the value of the Advisor for Life are those households unable to navigate the financial markets since the bull market lost its steam. For them, the thrill of making their own decisions has worn off through the unexpected shock of the tech wreck in 2000–2001, or, even more likely, the flat market of 2005—the second flattest in modern market history. Down markets followed by flat markets are especially frustrating because nothing good seems to be happening while investors are hoping to make up for earlier losses.

Allocating the Advisor's Time The final aspect of availability is the numeric reality of time. A survey of top advisors examined their allocation of time among a number of activities. And while "administration" and "business processing" garnered much of the advisors' attention, the largest segment was devoted to "client service." (See Figure 1.3.) I believe client service to be the most important and therefore the most lucrative activity for top advisors, so the ranking is appropriate. But

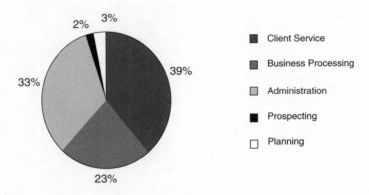

FIGURE 1.3 Where Advisors Spend Their Time
Source: Advisor Impact.

consider the numbers—39 percent of top advisors' time is allocated to client service. Is it enough?

Let's now test the time commitment to affluent clients and see if advisors are allowing enough of it to provide the needed service(s). A 50-hour workweek over 48 weeks a year would give 2,400 working hours per year.

Now consider the amount of time required to provide effective service to a millionaire household. From a Phoenix Wealth Survey, an annual survey of millionaire households (net worth minus value of primary residence) conducted by the Phoenix Companies, Inc. with Harris Interactive, we know that a large percentage of millionaire households think monthly contact with their primary advisor provides the right balance for service.

Take it a step further. What does the total year of service comprise? Is each contact an hour? What about the more complex work? What about reviews? Preparation? If the time commitment to your affluent clients is one hour a month, that's 12 hours every year. If you devote two hours per month, that's 24 hours each year. For the sake of this discussion, call it 20 hours. Based on a 39 percent slice of your 2,400-hour year, you can provide adequate service to just 47 households— more only if you reduce the service time.

You probably have more than 47 clients—the average Series 7 registered rep has over 500 accounts, according to the Securities Industry and Financial Markets Association (SIFMA)—and you don't want to limit yourself to that number. What's the result? Some clients get more of your time than others. That's what's happening across the industry. Millionaire clients aren't going to tolerate shoddy service, but neither do most advisors intend to provide less than expected results. The problem is mathematical—there is only so much time in the day and only so many days in the year. The amount of time we have is finite, yet client concerns are infinite. The major complaints about service are based on the pure reality that few advisors have adequate time to spend with clients. Based on other commitments and the structure of their responsibilities, most advisors don't spend the time they should with clients.

There are two observations here—first, that much of this book is dedicated to helping you determine and deliver the most valued services in limited time. Second, we will examine ways to recapture time—

primarily by eliminating from your routine those services that can be provided by others or even eliminated. A great motivator and coach, UCLA's John Wooden, was fond of saying, "Don't let something you do well get in the way of something you do great." Your time is precious—use it for what no one else can do and for which you will reap the greatest reward.

We'll revisit availability later on, including service strategies that reflect client needs and concerns—especially in the context of the all-important communication opportunity, the client review.

Be Concerned

Concern is what top professionals show their best clients, and it pays dividends for them. They do not provide a superficial worry. Instead they offer a real empathy for their clients' situations. Some may call this the human factor or the personal touch. At the end of the day it's about simple and honest caring.

Consider this scenario. How successful would any physician be without having at some level a genuine interest in taking care of people? The same could be said for a teacher who didn't honestly love children. The difference between accomplished professionals and those who spend a lifetime doing "ordinary work for ordinary pay" is that the very best care about their profession and their clients, patients, or students. The difference between an average restaurant and a fabulous one is the chef's passion to put art on a plate and an unmatched service commitment from the maitre d'. If you aspire to these levels, your concern for clients will be noticeable, appreciated, and, best of all, reflected in your work.

How to Get There   The question then becomes: "How can you best exhibit concern?"

Start with the order in which most people make financial decisions. The list provided earlier is a good framework. Most people focus on satisfying whatever current, perceived *need* they face. They then consider their goals and, finally, dreams. The financial advisor's role is to follow the emotional path as indicated by the client. Help ensure that needs are met, and that goals and dreams won't be compromised by risks along the way. At the same time, the Advisor for Life will probe for concerns and fears to make sure they do not spoil your client's quality of life.

Concern's Two Dimensions There are two dimensions of concern. The first is "what"—what could happen to a household that would derail its ability to achieve its goals? This calls for my favorite financial planning tool, the Wealth Planning Overview (see Figure 1.4). This one-page chart summarizes the big issues for affluent households.

Which risks may threaten your clients' current and future existence? Knowing that most people want a comfortable retirement, which issues revealed by the Wealth Planning Overview could prevent this? One advisor uses this chart to find for each client where his or her blind spot is for risks. Another longtime practitioner is more dramatic. He likes to say he's looking for the "bullet" that could "take out" the household's financial plan.

We'll return to the Wealth Planning Overview in Chapter 5. Consider it for now a tool to help show your genuine concern for clients—an inventory of potential risks.

FIGURE 1.4 The Wealth Planning Overview
Source: Stephen D. Gresham, *Attract and Retain the Affluent Investor* (Dearborn Trade, 2001).

The second dimension of concern is timing. Timing is the difference between an issue being a concern, risk, or fear—and how we act upon it. The more time you have to deal with a problem or objective, the more likely you are to resolve or achieve it.

Consider the basic issue of retirement. Retirement is easier to fund for the person with more time to save and invest. If you suddenly had to retire tomorrow, would you have the same flexibility? Of course not. Similarly, many concerns can become fears if the time line to their appearance is shortened. Being concerned about a potential health risk can quickly become a fear once that risk surfaces. The person who acts early to address that risk usually has the best chance of managing it.

To manage time in the context of concern I often refer to a chart given to me by a wise minister in upstate New York. He had struggled for years to find a way to counsel couples contemplating marriage. Optimistic and in love, and mostly young, his parishioners wanted to plan their weddings, not their futures. The minister found himself offering a vision of the future that was not so rosy as he asked tough questions such as: What will you do if and when you have children? Do you have enough income? Will both of you work? What if your folks become unable to care for themselves?

Though he was showing genuine concern for these young people, the betrothed couples most often dismissed or minimized the minister's queries. He found himself lecturing and sounding more like a worried parent than a spiritual counselor. His solution was to lead the couples into a discovery process called the Fantasy Trip. Only by having them come to their own conclusions could he hope to open their eyes to the risks ahead.

The Fantasy Trip is a simple exercise with profound value and clarity. The minister would ask the couple to list the 10 most important people in their lives—present and future. By that he meant for them to include relatives, future children, even business partners. The list itself can be interesting in that showing which people are most important is a value judgment unto itself. To use the chart with financial advice clients, the Advisor for Life can determine the people for whom each client feels the greatest responsibility or dependency. In this aspect, the Fantasy Trip chart (see Figure 1.5) has value for any household at any stage.

The Fantasy Trip is a journey into the future. After listing the 10 most important people in the client's life, have him list the ages of

			Current Year	Plus 5 Yrs	Plus 5 Yrs	Plus 5 Yrs	Plus 5 Yrs	Plus 5 Yrs	Plus 5 Yrs	Plus 5 Yrs
Client's Name	Charlie Smith	Client's Age	46	51	56	61	66	71	76	81
Spouse's Name	Lisa Smith	Spouse's Age	44	49	54	59	64	69	74	79
Relative's Name	Jessica Smith	Relative's Age	10	15	20	25	30	35	40	45
Relative's Name	Joseph Smith	Relative's Age	7	12	17	22	27	32	37	42
Other's Name	Amos Smith	Other's Age	78	83	88	93	98	103	108	113
Business Partner's Name	Bob Patrick	Business Partner's Age	40	45	50	55	60	65	70	75
Other's Name	Barbara Jones	Other's Age	70	75	80	85	90	95	100	105
Other's Name	Patrick Jones	Other's Age	68	73	78	83	88	93	98	103

FIGURE 1.5   The Fantasy Trip

Source: Stephen D. Gresham, *Attract and Retain the Affluent Investor* (Dearborn Trade, 2001).

those people today. Then for each name, we add the current age of that person. Once the ages are in place, the chart prompts you to fill in the ages of each person in future time periods—in this case every five years over a 35-year horizon. Once completed, the Fantasy Trip provides a simple picture of a family's future, projecting what life might be like at any time.

We'll return to the Fantasy Trip and discuss the issues created by this vision of the future. No substitute for formal financial planning, the Fantasy Trip is a prospecting and communication tool for helping you connect with clients—and for them to identify real future issues. The topic of this chapter is to determine what affluent clients are willing to pay you to do.

Next, combine the dimensions of concern—what might happen and when it might do so. Baby boom expert and visionary Ken Dychtwald of AgeWave.com interprets his research of baby boom clients to mean that they seek an advisor who can help them "visualize and fund their future." The future holds challenges for any household. These two tools can help bring focus to a wide array of potential issues and provide the basis for more valuable conversations with both prospects and clients. These tools can help with the far more involved conversations about what you can do to help them avoid trouble—dodge the bullet—and also realize their goals.

Be Informed

What millionaire household would pay for advice from someone who is uninformed? How can you prove you are well-informed?

How would someone know you are a good financial advisor? What evidence do you have of your skill or experience? Physicians and professors can show you their walls of diplomas and scholarly awards. If you work for a brokerage firm, you might have a plaque or a nice statue that identifies you as a member of a recognition club, such as the Chairman's Club or President's Council. I have one of those—exactly 20 years old at this time. When I still had my advisory practice I proudly displayed that plaque until the day a client asked how I earned it. I was forced to reveal that it was my annual income from client accounts that warranted this recognition—not my top account performance or rave reviews from clients.

How can you show that you are informed? Affluent households regularly respond in surveys that they seek someone who knows how to take care of people like themselves. They seek evidence to provide comfort that their professionals have been there, done that. Who wants to be the first patient of a new Lasik surgeon? At the doctor's office, you see diplomas and licenses. What's on your office wall?

On an easel in the offices of one metropolitan New York financial advisory practice I know, there is a chart that represents a lifetime of diagrams created on cocktail napkins and envelope backs, as well as in careful office deliberations—all seeking answers to real-world problems of clients and their families.

Pointing to the easel, team members can show prospective clients evidence that indeed they have been there before and have seen everything. As quintessential Advisors for Life, team members seek to give prospects comfort in advance of their first meeting. Each team member will probe for a family's needs, concerns, risks, and fears. The team terms the process a search for "vulnerabilities"—a more comforting approach than an examination of potential "bullets."

Evidence that you have worked with similar clients is comforting to the prospects as well as to potential centers of influence, such as accountants and attorneys. Openly share that evidence.

Another way to illustrate your problem-solving history is to have handy a number of case studies depicting issues confronted and resolved by your practice. We'll talk more about case studies in Chapter 16, as well as the role of another credibility-enhancing tool, the professional designation. Marks such as CFP (Certified Financial Planner) or CIMA (Certified Investment Management Analyst) can help distinguish you.

Have a Professional Opinion

Real professionals provide recommendations for action. Think of other professionals you admire—your doctor, college professor, or CPA. Do you admire the physician who tells clients what they wish to hear rather than explaining their need for strong medicine? The prescription may not be something they want to hear, but it is the result of the characteristics I've described so far—being concerned and being informed. Having a professional opinion is the obligation of every true professional, and it is what will earn you respect. It is the point at which training, experience, and judgment manifest themselves in a course of best action designed for the client.

We'll examine the work of institutional investors later in Chapter 6, but I refer to their role as that of being *responsible* investors. Because pension fund and endowment trustees carry the burden of investing on behalf of others—retirees, university students and faculty, hospital patients and staff—the institutional investor is never free of the responsibility to work on behalf of others. Therefore they are never free of the need to have an opinion about how the assets are to be managed. They can't dodge the responsibility to engage with the public securities markets and make choices about investment managers. They have a fiduciary and moral duty to serve their organization and its beneficiaries.

The Advisor for Life must have a professional opinion. No affluent household will long tolerate an advisor who asks what the client wants to do. Where is the value in that approach? Top advisors have an opinion because they are informed, whether through experience or training or both. A solid opinion is the result of doing one's homework and exercising sound judgment. This combination provides the confidence to have an opinion. In this book, you can see more examples of how to have opinions without having to forecast the stock market or make some other outrageous claim. While you should rely on personal experience when providing opinions, keep personal opinions out of your discussion. Remain objective. Many opinions are those about how to approach a situation—they provide a game plan or strategy like diversification and show why you're recommending this course to obtain a comfortable retirement. They are not just vague predictions or general pronouncements.

BE INSPIRATIONAL—THE FIFTH DIMENSION

Credit for adding a fifth dimension to our four principles goes to Dan Lampe in St. Louis. Dan heard Don Berryman recount these four principles and immediately observed that even the most available, concerned, and informed advisors will often fail to get clients to accept their opinions because they express them without a compelling level of conviction.

Saving and investing for retirement can be a difficult and often abstract concept—especially to a young family. Dan rightly urges advisors to make their opinions inspirational as well. Don't just recognize your role as a coach to help your clients achieve their objectives—savor it. Look forward to the challenges.

The Advisor for Life is like those very good coaches who are unyielding and demanding in their principles, but also are supportive. And the team's best interest is always at the top of the list. A good coach also makes sacrifices in the drive to the championship, not just the players. To get the most out of even a top player, a good coach may have to challenge that player to be better, to make adjustments, to work harder, or to be smarter—spend more time studying the playbook. The player may have to sacrifice—eat better and spend more time in the weight room. The Advisor for Life has the unpopular task of being a conscience about spending and a stickler on process issues like rebalancing portfolios. It's the job of the Advisor for Life to take a sharp pencil to the bottom line and draw a direct route to the finish line.

At the end of the day, inspiration is a differentiator. You're surrounded by smart, competitive professionals with similar products and services. You may be able to prove superior knowledge versus another advisor, but can that message stand out in a crowded field? A good preacher leaves the congregation with more than something to think about. He inspires them to reach for that elusive next level. Your job is no different. The power to help people take action is as important as the recommendations themselves. In a recent World Health Organization (WHO) survey, it was found that among various prescription drug patients, less than half of those afflicted actually took their medicines as instructed by doctors. Even in the case of life-saving drugs like beta blockers for heart trouble, the majority of patients did not follow their doctors' recommendations. Why?

Good financial health is just as much a chore and an effort as good physical health. The devil in your mind says, "Spend today, save tomorrow" while the savings angel pleads for a long-term view. The Advisor for Life must not only be available to clients, be concerned for their futures, be informed about effective strategies, and have an opinion about what to do now—the Advisor for Life has to be inspirational to clients so that they will take the necessary actions.

This chapter has focused on answering the question: What will clients pay you for? The answer can be found in the five simple words from Don and Dan:

1. Available
2. Concerned
3. Informed
4. Opinionated
5. Inspirational

We will now get more specific with each area and dig deeper into those services that will help earn you a lifetime of clients.

PART II

Investment Counsel Advice for Life

CHAPTER 2

How to Develop a Compelling Investment Philosophy

- *What do you believe is the best long-term investing strategy?*
- *Do you have the greatest confidence in buying undervalued assets and waiting for them to appreciate (value investing) versus seeking out companies with great future potential (growth investing)?*
- *Do you favor use of multiple-manager styles or a core-and-satellite array?*
- *When selecting investments for your clients, do you utilize active management or a passive approach?*
- *Is it more important to fund specific client liabilities, or do you favor a total return goal?*
- *What role does tax efficiency play in your investment philosophy?*

Whatever your philosophy, you must be able to articulate it with clarity and conviction to current and prospective clients and they must *share your vision.*

COMMON VALUES AND YOUR SUCCESS

Critical to the success of any long-term relationship—personal or professional—is the concept of common values. Scratch the surface of any healthy marriage and you'll find a couple who may appear to have many differences, yet they share similar philosophical views and

---

Investors First

Sam (not his real name) and his team of financial advisors sum up their commitment to the investment process: "We are first and foremost investors ourselves. We are constantly seeking education and valuable information in an attempt to become better investors and wealth management advisors; . . . our primary mission is to intelligently and opportunistically allocate capital." When presenting his investment approach to prospective clients, Sam uses examples of specific investment solutions created for clients based on their unique requirements.

---

identical objectives for their lives together. Such is the bond of a shared game plan that can make any relationship more fulfilling and sustaining.

Often overlooked by otherwise savvy financial advisors is the importance of a *shared investment philosophy*. In its most basic form, an investment philosophy reflects the fundamental approach to profiting in the markets. There is perhaps no more emotional topic in financial advice, save that of an individual's personal concerns about the future. Here are gathered the multiple dimensions of moneymaking.

TIME HORIZON—IS TIME ON YOUR SIDE? BETTER YET, IS IT ON YOUR CLIENTS' SIDE?

Time horizon is the period governing the investment process and the hoped-for returns to finance one's lifestyle and other objectives. The longer the time horizon for an investment process, the greater the flexibility and—statistically—the likelihood of success. When examining investment philosophy from the angle of time horizon, call this aspect the "patience" factor.

But the time horizon has additional aspects to it that can become part of your philosophy. No other aspect of investment philosophy is more abused by clients and advisors than that of time. We've each encountered a client who was ostensibly a long-term investor but, after just six months, was suddenly nervous about the market and seriously considering the termination of the investment manager.

Markets are by nature humbling, and the recent history of equity markets has provided a lifetime of variations in just the period between 1995 and 2005, in which the Dow Jones Industrial Average rose from 3,834 (December 31, 1994) to 11,338 (May 21, 2001)—a gain of 195 percent—then collapsed 36 percent to 7,286 (October 9, 2002), only to top 11,000 again in late 2005, a return of 50 percent from the low point of 2002. (See Figure 2.1.)

Plus, investor confidence is a function of prices. "Don't confuse bull markets with brains" is another market adage with statistical validity. The Phoenix Wealth Survey of millionaire households conducted over the years 2000–2006 reveals the relationship between stock market performance and investor confidence. When asked in early 2000, when the market was at its tech bubble best, only 30 percent percent of millionaire investors claimed to be confused about how to invest their money. Surveyed again in early 2003, when the stock market was still languishing near the bear market low, the percentage of "confused" investors had risen dramatically to 47 percent. By early January 2006, after the Dow had again passed 11,000, confidence had returned and only 29 percent of millionaire investors said they were confused over how to invest.

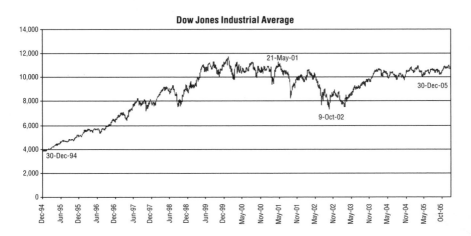

FIGURE 2.1 Dow Jones Industrial Average, 1994–2005

BULL MARKETS AND BRAVERY

Yet the effect of the bear market was lasting, according to the survey. In very early 2000, 56 percent of respondents said, "It is important to get a substantial return on my capital, even if it means taking some risks," while the other 44 percent chose to answer, "It's important to preserve the safety of my capital, even if it means accepting a lower return."

As the market crumbled, so did investor confidence. One year later, after less than a year of falling prices, the sample was split 50–50 between substantial return with risks and safety with a lower return. By early 2002, the sample had reversed field to 46 percent favoring higher returns with risk versus safety (54 percent), and the safety players have held the field since then—most recently 55 percent to 45 percent in early 2006 (2006 Phoenix Wealth Survey).

One of the great Advisor for Life challenges is to help clients realize their objectives by becoming the Client for Life. The best advisors educate their clients, knowing that benefits accrue to both clients and advisors. Long-term investing success is dependent on a long-term mind-set. But that kind of perspective is an affront to human nature. Remember how missing the best days over virtually any market period has a seemingly disproportionate impact on investment return? The most recent version is shown in Figure 2.2.

I've always found this particular investing lesson to be especially vexing to clients, since most simply cannot believe that with all the trillions of dollars under management and billions spent on market research that the investment industry can't identify at least some of the bad days and some of the best! Surely there must be a way. And that hope is the central marketing proposition of market timers and traders—an enormous and growing segment of the investing population.

Given a choice between the patience required of a long-term strategy and the ability to influence results with action in the moment, most people will choose the latter course. It is both instructive and interesting that during both bull and bear markets in the years 2000 to 2006, nearly half of respondents to the Phoenix Wealth Survey of millionaire households declared their willingness to take advantage of short-term opportunities in financial markets. Does anyone see a conflict here?

It instead shows the ability of investors to have both a core long-term strategy and an interest in short-term actions. What is more inter-

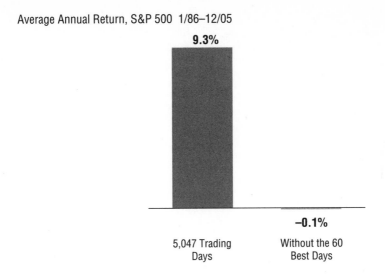

Average Annual Return, S&P 500 1/86–12/05

Returns cited exclude dividends.

FIGURE 2.2   The Risk of Market Timing
Source: © 2006 Mulberry Communications.

esting to me is how many good advisors are threatened or concerned about this dichotomy instead of encouraging it—or at least facilitating it. Which diet would you choose—one that allows you to occasionally snack or have dessert, or one that forces compliance at all times? Don't fight human nature. Success is determined over the long run, and the Advisor for Life has to help clients live that life in a sustainable way.

The implication of multiple investing interests and needs suggests the potential for more than one time horizon per client. That reality is stretched further by the multiple needs of affluent households—different objectives require different time horizons. For most families, college expenses arrive sooner and are paid for faster than retirement costs. The Advisor for Life must juggle these multiple objectives and help clients to stay the course by assigning different "maturities" to each obligation.

One of the most common mistakes made by both advisors and clients is to lump assets together into one pile, managed altogether

Holding on to the Real Money

Gary, an experienced and savvy independent advisor in Ohio, accommodates clients who want to "have a little fun on the side." He helps them establish a trading account with an online discount firm. There the clients can make their own trades while Gary concentrates on the core of their investment strategy. The main goal of this separation is to emphasize to the clients the difference between casual investing and his more serious role as the steward of the bulk of their money. The trading account has a budget of usually not more than $30,000. Just like with a young child, "When it's gone, it's gone!"

with an often hazy and probably inappropriate aggregate benchmark. Institutional investors, by contrast, separate assets—at least through specific accounting—for different needs. Often, separate investment policy statements and risk profiles are created for those different accounts, reflecting the variations. For example, a hospital endowment may have a long-term endowment fund, a shorter-duration pension account for employees, a more liquid fund for operating expenses, and a buildings and grounds account with multiple tranches reflecting the depreciation of specific buildings and new construction plans.

Advisor question: Are you including time horizon in your investment philosophy?

RISK—WALL STREET'S FOUR-LETTER WORD

Risk is usually expressed as intraperiod volatility. I'm going to change the definition for the purposes of this book to reflect the more realistic view of the Advisor for Life. *Risk is not relative in the long run—it is absolute.* Success is determined only by achieving objectives. "Beating the market" is a hollow victory if the market goes down and the investment manager's performance is better but still negative. So risk will be true for our discussion and volatility will have its own place in the sun. Here we'll discuss absolute, not relative returns. No one can spend relative returns.

For the purposes of developing an investment philosophy that is attractive to clients and prospects, I hope you will choose absolute returns and absolute risk. This is the only time I won't offer you a choice of how to include a topic in your philosophy! Calculating the amount of risk is then not much more than determining household expenses during retirement (or other goal) and how much of a reduction in quality of life can be tolerated. That test is the most realistic projection of true risk. Since most surveys indicate that funding a comfortable retirement is by far the number-one goal of millionaire households, it should not be a surprise that the top concern is not being able to fund a comfortable retirement.

The 2006 Phoenix Wealth Survey gives more details about what represents a comfortable retirement. Fully 81 percent of respondents expected to live in retirement with at least 80 percent of current income. A good portion of the participants were already retired at the date of the survey, but there was nonetheless a healthy expectation that income could be maintained. Some 40 percent said they expected to have consistent earnings throughout retirement—no decline. Income levels are pretty healthy for this crop of millionaire households, with 77 percent at $100,000 per year and above, and 43 percent exceeding $150,000. Given that 68 percent of the respondents claimed net worth (net of the value of their primary home) between $1 million and $2 million, there is little margin for error—and some fairly aggressive assumptions about returns. Risk as I define it—in absolute terms—will become very real very quickly if the household suffers a serious market reversal or unexpectedly large medical bills.

Advisor question: How will "risk" be defined in your investment philosophy?

VOLATILITY—CAN YOU WEATHER THE STORM?

Volatility is the dynamic within investing that leads to premature manager terminations and fund redemptions when they appear to have lost their performance edge. Rather than risk holding on to a failing story, too many investors will scrap even the most lauded portfolio manager. Also known as the "quality of the ride," volatility must be communicated to clients to avoid unhappy experiences and poor performance.

As a rule, the most aggressive management styles have the most volatility—the proverbial trade-off between risk and reward. Blended appropriately with other investments, these more volatile results can actually improve risk-adjusted returns, depending on how the path of returns correlates with other management styles. In other words, volatility is not uniformly bad; it should be applied in appropriate measure and not only reflect your investing approach but also match your clients' emotional fortitude. Another aspect of volatility is style. To the average investor, the failure of a manager to follow a distinct path may seem like volatility. I'll address style in the next subsection, but it is very important to separate the two concepts at the client level. For the moment, consider specifically the challenge of explaining an investment manager's history of volatility and what that history suggests may be the future path relative to specific types of securities and their benchmarks.

The old question "Are you unhappy about the manager—or the asset class?" refers to the difference between volatility inherent in a particular style and the current state of affairs for the asset class itself. An aggressive mid-cap growth manager's performance can seem volatile—even erratic—in absolute terms, but how much of the differential is consistent with simply being a mid-cap growth manager? Volatility is a tricky concept to communicate, especially given its long-term positive relationship to performance.

A branch manager I know uses a remarkably simple illustration to educate clients about volatility: the quarterly account values for his own account with an investment manager he has used in his asset-allocation solutions for clients. The actual account value, net of additions and withdrawals, is on a spreadsheet (not a graph or mountain chart). He includes not only the account value, but also the amount of appreciation or depreciation for that quarter. Although the long-term history of the account is positive, he pauses when showing the bear market periods to emphasize how difficult it can be to stay the course.

Advisor question: How will you incorporate volatility in your investment philosophy?

STYLE—IS YOURS FLEETING OR STEADY?

Investment manager style—typically growth or value—reveals a personality that can be matched with clients of similar orientation to sustain a relationship through the most difficult market periods. Clients who truly understand their investment managers and appreciate disciplines are able to maintain confidence and commitment during those inevitable times when a style is out of favor. The most resilient clients are able to capture additional gains by rebalancing into an out-of-favor manager or investment style while the less objective ones are often chasing current winners.

A second aspect of style is the natural fit with a client's psychology. For example, a client whose road to financial success was a function of saving and restrained lifestyle—same car, same house, same spouse—may be more comfortable with a buy-and-hold manager who is long-term focused with several core positions, rather than a more aggressive manager trading in and out of positions. The more active trader may not reflect the values and mind-set of the long-term "millionaire next door." For the same investor, a value style of management, investing in companies currently out of favor but with good prospects, may be more appealing than a philosophy that pursues the latest and greatest technologies—more a growth style. Compatibility with a manager's style is one of the most important drivers of long-term client relationships—and may be the most basic.

Advisor question: Style and rebalancing should be included in your investment philosophy. How will you address both from the client's perspective?

INVESTMENT VEHICLES—HOW DO YOU EXECUTE YOUR INVESTMENT PHILOSOPHY?

A client seeking long-term capital growth with income may be comfortable with stocks and bonds that she can see in her account. If she instead owned shares in a mutual fund, she would not have that clarity of the underlying investments. Would she be comfortable with the fund's management if she could see what they were buying and selling?

For a great many investors, the transparency of a separately managed account may be too much information; they "want to drive the car but don't want to look under the hood." Strategies utilizing small companies or even derivative instruments may appeal to aggressive, active investors and terrify others.

History also plays an important role in a client's investing preferences. Asking for such history is a very important part of determining your compatibility with prospective clients. Learning of a prospect's bad experience with a certain type of aggressive bond fund, for example, would be helpful before recommending its use—even if the interest rate situation is much different today. In other words, your knowledge and perspective are superior to the expertise of most clients. Don't mistake a bad impression of an investment for its poor timing. The memory of an investment mistake and the attendant embarrassment and loss of capital can forge an indelible memory that is not easily overcome.

More survey information is helpful to gain insight into millionaire-household preferences. The most common financial products owned by this group are stocks—80 percent of respondents to the 2006 Phoenix Wealth Survey replied that they or someone in their family owned equities in early 2006. (Of note is that in early 2002 stockholders made up 92 percent of the sample.) Mutual funds held outside of an individual retirement account (IRA) or 401(k) were second at 64 percent, and bonds were third at only 52 percent. Among these millionaire households, there seems to be a preference for packaged solutions without regard for contents; for example, IRAs, listed as a financial product owned by 72 percent of the sample, almost certainly contain funds, stocks, and/or bonds. Some 54 percent said they participated in a 401(k) and 11 percent have 529 plans.

Funds are a comfortable choice, with 92 percent of respondents with them stating their commitment to keep the same (or more) money in them for the next year, and 48 percent planning to add to their investment by the same (or greater) amount as in the previous year. One in five households that do not currently own mutual funds say they will likely buy them within the next year. A full 29 percent said they own a separately managed account, and only 6 percent own hedge funds.

Distinct preferences for financial products pervade the advice industry. Despite all entreaties by advice firms and the clear impression that clients seek results and don't so much care which vehicles are used to obtain them, many advisors remain trapped in silos of their own making. Be flexible!

Advisor question: Which products do you use in creating investment solutions, and how do they figure in your investment philosophy?

COST—A TOUGH ISSUE TO SOMETIMES JUSTIFY

Fundamental to the psychology of many investors is the issue of how much investment counsel should cost, and the very existence of fees is a philosophical issue for the Advisor for Life.

In the millionaire survey, cost was cited by 25 percent of clients who were planning to find a new advisor. Just as an individual may emotionally favor value stocks over more adventurous (and pricey) growth issues, a thrifty client will be drawn to a low-cost structure.

While we examined cost in Chapter 1 in the limited context of investment philosophy, expenses are directly related to returns. What is an appropriate fee for results achieved? Consider the range of fees and returns represented by the investment industry. At the high end, hedge funds commonly sport a "one-and-twenty" structure representing a 1 percent value of assets under management, plus a retention of 20 percent of annual profits. This rich arrangement has created many wealthy hedge fund managers, with the top advisors earning in excess of $100 million—and some topping $500 million—in annual compensation. And while many investors are delighted to share a generous slice of total return in order to achieve better results, the fat absolute cost of hedge fund fees is abhorrent to many others. In Barton Biggs' book *Hedgehogging* (John Wiley & Sons, 2006), he quotes Chris Davis, president of Davis Funds: "Never in the history of financial commerce has so much been paid to so many for so little."

More traditional growth and value strategies have historically annually charged 1 percent of assets under management, creating an incentive for managers to increase portfolio value. Fees typically decline in percentage terms for larger accounts and reduced complexity of management style. High alpha generators, such as the most active small-cap philosophies, have limited capacity. The managers of such portfolios can earn higher fees than those of large-cap investors. Passive strategies have significantly changed the investment management landscape through both the philosophy of their index or sector approach—eschewing active management by a team of analysts and managers—and also by dramatically reducing fees. Some index funds for large-cap market indexes offer their largest clients participation in the equity markets for less than 10 basis points. Exchange-traded funds have become an intriguing and powerful new force offering unprecedented diversification potential as they expand into the nooks and crannies of public markets, but also by providing lower costs and tax efficiency superior to index funds. At this writing, the relatively high costs associated with mutual funds and some separately managed account programs are under greater scrutiny as clients seek better returns from markets now offering normalized returns of 10 percent or less after the heady bull market run of 1982 to 2000. Look for more pressure as the mutual fund scandals wane and simple economics take over.

The 10 Percent Rule

I've always considered fees to have a gravitational center for the broad marketplace at about 10 percent of expected returns. For example, the old 1 percent fee is about 10 percent of the long-term equity market return of just over 10 percent. Fees for bond portfolios have typically floated at about half the rate of equity portfolios. Fees for packaged portfolios, such as separately managed accounts, followed the same 10 percent rule during their early years as bull market returns of 20 to 30 percent per year supported rates of up to 3 percent per annum for all services including investment management.

As market returns normalized after 2000's tech wreck, fees continued to decline to levels more similar to those of mutual funds. Should market returns remain in single digits, look for fees to continue their fall as single-digit net returns force greater investor scrutiny. Fees are at once a potential bond between investor and advisor, creating an incentive to work together for mutual benefit as account values increase, but also a point of practice-management leverage. The fee structure also exposes the portfolio to market forces beyond the manager's control, resulting in unearned gains when the market rises and depreciation when it falls. When properly invested, both manager and investor can obviously prosper from successful guidance and rising markets, providing the leverage for so-called fee-based investment services. However, performance-oriented fees, while becoming more commonplace, will come under greater scrutiny as investors increasingly question the validity of a fee structure that rewards an advisor even when the account value does not rise.

Your philosophy must include your opinion about the value of what you do. While this sounds obvious, it can be easily overlooked. How do you charge for your investment results, and does your pricing reflect your overall philosophy? Hedge fund managers seek high absolute returns, so a fee including a profit percentage is consistent with that aggressive posture. By contrast, consider the value proposition of index funds; rooted in a low-cost structure and passive strategies they sit at the opposite end of the spectrum from high-flying hedge funds. Costs and the types of vehicles you employ in your investment solutions speak loudly about your philosophical approach to markets and investing.

Advisor question: Is your fee structure reflected in your investment guidance?

PASSIVE VERSUS ACTIVE—CAN YOU JUSTIFY EITHER APPROACH?

Just as investment vehicles and costs reflect the core of a philosophy and their appeal to specific clientele, you make a further fundamental decision by choosing your basic approach to the markets. Specifically, do you think active management can beat the returns of unmanaged indexes or market segments? The argument in favor of active management is as old as the markets. It is simply unacceptable to resourceful market entrepreneurs and many academics that value cannot be added to a static market, and billions of dollars have been and continue to be invested by individuals and organizations in the pursuit of market-beating strategies. Most people of wealth and accomplishment believe that the creative human mind should be able to beat the market, dominated by the masses. This latent elitism has of course not been borne out by the experience of most investors, whose returns typically lag those of the markets and top institutional investors.

A new entrant in the passive investing space is the exchange-traded fund (ETF)—a potentially exciting low-cost and tax-efficient vehicle offering the ability to invest in significant markets like the Standard & Poor's 500 or Japan's Nikkei 225, as well as narrow slivers like certain fixed-income maturities, commodities, or pharmaceutical stocks. Combining the benefits of a publicly traded security with those of index or sector funds, ETFs represent a breakthrough for investors seeking a convenient method of participating in specific markets. Their status as a publicly traded security gives them tax efficiency through their internal management that is not available with traditional mutual funds.

Index funds and ETFs permit you and your clients to create portfolios at low cost with the built-in advantage of always representing the market. Beating the benchmark is not the objective of passive strategies—gains are achieved through the time-honored role of asset allocation. Instead, the passive strategy is designed to avoid surprises, such as manager style drift or other underperformance. Alpha is achieved at the portfolio level, not by individual managers. In addition, ETFs in particular allow clients to participate in very limited segments of the market, even individual industries, without the added risk of investment manager stock selection. Consider the following, from the *2006 Investment Company Fact Book* (Investment Company Institute):

- At the end of 2005 ETFs accounted for approximately 3 percent of the total investment company assets compared to mutual funds, which managed over 94 percent of total investment company assets.
- ETF assets have grown by approximately 350 percent since 2000 compared to mutual fund assets, which have climbed by about 27 percent.
- The net new issuance of ETF shares was over $54 billion in 2005 compared to $192 billion of net new cash raised by stock, bond, and hybrid mutual funds combined.
- Although ETFs accounted for only 3 percent of the total investment company assets, they raised over 15 percent of the net new cash raised by mutual funds, money markets, ETFs, closed-end funds, and unit investment trusts (UITs) during this period.

As a philosophy, passive versus active investing is determined by your most basic beliefs about how to earn money, which are generally influenced by your experience, education, and skills. Can investors beat the market? Can you? What is more important, asset allocation or investment manager skill? Where are the acceptable risks for investors? Such a foundation is critical to establish long-term rapport with clients. Clients who have suffered a manager's futile attempts to beat a benchmark may prefer to end the quest and give in to the passive strategy. Analytical types who know the statistical challenge of beating the markets over an extended time period may prefer passive investing due to their appreciation of the scholarly data. Finally, there is a cost advantage to most passive strategies that appeals to the thrifty client who decries the active managers' costs.

Notwithstanding all of the benefits of passive investing and its undeniable appeal to many types of affluent clients, human nature will trump analysis in favoring some form of active management for most clients. The idea of "passive" anything is an unlikely state of affairs—especially for households whose success has been the result of a skill or tenacity (or both) applied to a business or profession.

Advisor question: Have you articulated the strengths and weaknesses of active versus passive investing to your clients and prospects?

STYLE BOXES VERSUS CORE AND EXPLORE—*IT'S UP TO YOU*

A former colleague said it very well when he outlined the appeal of a core strategy versus that of a shifting mix of asset classes and styles. Citing the tendency of many millionaire households to be savers and regularly frugal in their lifestyles, he suggested that in keeping consistent with their practices, these people would most likely not desire a constantly shifting investment portfolio.

While this is a good suggestion, there are additional considerations to weigh when describing your philosophy to clients and prospects that can involve this aspect of investing. Transparency is one issue briefly touched on earlier that reveals a level of change. That issue can be overcome with products such as asset allocation funds or managed accounts that automatically rebalance themselves. Asset allocation funds account for 26 percent of the new fund sales in 2005 compared to 2 percent in 1999, according to Investment Company Institute data as reported in *BusinessWeek* Online, June 26, 2006. Tax implications have been cited by several advisors as a reason to prefer core investing over a more complex rebalancing strategy. Intraperiod volatility can be greater with a style strategy, depending on its complexity and your willingness to create a more diversified portfolio. Finally, consider the potential for client involvement, which can be accommodated easily in a core-and-explore philosophy in which clients may choose some of the "explore" components as their contributions to the plan, either separately with additional assets or with your participation. Again, ETFs and some specialized funds offer ideal vehicles for these explorations.

A Core and Explorer

For the last four years Greg has designed a core-and-satellite approach for clients, referencing the work of Dr. Burton Malkiel, author of the industry classic, *A Random Walk Down Wall Street* (W.W. Norton, 1985). When Greg advises clients, he pretends that Dr. Malkiel gets copies of his client's statements. "He is my invisible conscience from Princeton." Greg says, "When you structure a client's portfolio, the satellites must respond to the core. The satellites must pay attention to tax efficiency *and* the client's investment objectives." Greg uses a four-quadrant grid to address both concerns. The left side includes investments subject to a lot of tax, and the right side holds only tax-efficient items. The top row seeks high returns, while the bottom row promotes risk reduction. That means the northwest quadrant holds the high-return "tax-ambivalent assets." The southwest quadrant is the "risk reducing without concern for taxes" quadrant. The northeast quadrant represents tax-efficient high-return investments, and the southeast quadrant represents tax-efficient assets included for risk reduction. The left side would be owned in tax-exempt entities such as IRAs and 401(k)s, and the right side in accounts subject to taxation. Greg blends the four quadrants for each client to individually address risk, return, and tax efficiency concerns. Greg's team creates a monthly performance report comparing their returns to the benchmark.

Advisor question: How will you use the concept of a core or style strategy in your investment philosophy?

INFLATION—FIGHTING THIS "HIDDEN TAX"

I served as a financial advisor to affluent families in the early 1980s when inflation was a very real and destructive force just being tamed by Paul Volcker, the celebrated and valiant Federal Reserve chairman. Interest rates fell so far in 1982 that the 30-year Treasury bond total return blew away all competition from other asset classes, up over 52 percent for the year. Any investor from the mid-1970s on had a healthy respect for the ravages of inflation and its effect on property values,

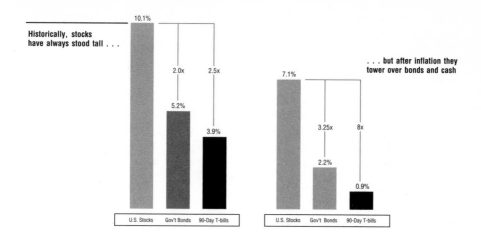

Data since 1926. Stocks: Wilshire 5000. Bonds: 10-year government bonds. Cash: 90-day T-bills.

FIGURE 2.3 Combating Inflation
Source: Global Financial Data, Inc.

product prices, and investment returns. (See Figure 2.3.) Remember the administration of President Gerald Ford, which produced the "Whip Inflation Now!" lapel buttons?

With the inflation beast much subdued most of the time during the past 20 years (through 2006)—at least relative to the intermediate past—many advisors and their clients have underestimated inflation's potential impact. Beware. Make sure portfolios are inflation tested, but don't hide the process; promote it in your investment philosophy. As these words are written in mid-2006, gold and silver are cresting 20-year highs (nominal prices, not adjusted for inflation), while natural resource stocks and nondollar assets are also climbing. Long-term trends have a way of resurfacing, and savvy advisors will help prepare clients—and portfolios—for them.

Advisor Note: The market has evolved and there are now readily available tools to help combat the effect of inflation on a client's portfolio. According to the *Wall Street Journal,* mutual funds that invest in Treasury Inflation Protected Securities (TIPS) experienced an increase in

Filling Up on Inflation

John Rafal says inflation is an important issue, but because it has not been a factor in recent years it is sometimes hard to get clients to quantify its impact. The best example today is gasoline prices. John tells clients that gas prices may seem high, but adjusted for even the modest inflation of the past 30 years, they are still lower than they were during the gas crunches of the 1970s.

assets from $4 billion in 2002 to $34.4 billion at the end of May 2006 (reported by the *Wall Street Journal* Online, June 23, 2006).

Advisor question: How do you incorporate rising prices and inflation concerns into your philosophy?

TAXES—THE BANE OF INVESTORS

Other than a comfortable retirement and not running out of money, the top concern of most millionaire households is the burden of taxation. Those who work hard are all too familiar with the impact of taxes, yet another shock is often in store for even the most educated retirees as taxes creep into the picture with unexpected force.

There is much debate about the benefits of so-called tax-managed or tax-advantaged investment strategies, and the appeal of the concept is understandable. However, it is best said that *the ideal after-tax strategy begins with the most significant and consistent pretax results*, offering many ways to interpret success. Advisor Greg makes sure that every client is tax aware. "Every return will be taxed some way, somehow," he says.

Long-term capital gains rates are attractive relative to those imposed on marginal income, but the balance is to earn those capital returns versus the prospect of deriving a more certain revenue stream from income-based investments. Bringing taxes into the picture of investment philosophy is vital, but since the rest of this list has so many less conspicuous (and capricious) issues, I ended with this one.

Advisor question: Are you helping clients to minimize their tax liability?

FOR THE MANY OTHER CONSIDERATIONS—ASK!

There are many investment philosophy aspects that invoke interest, concern, and even passion among investors and potential clients. Oftentimes you will lament the loss of a client—even though you thought you had provided terrific service and results. Sometimes there are other issues that transcend the investment dimension—such as social or personal concerns.

The best approach to revealing areas of specific importance is to ask clients and prospects. Unresolved issues fester under the surface of a relationship, and many are afraid to ask questions for fear of appearing unsophisticated. Draw them out with regular probing and questioning, while also taking the time to explain your methodology and rationale. Naturally, you will often be confronted with the "new discovery" made by a client of some alternative approach or philosophy, and you should be prepared, as you likely are already, to accommodate the questions and help the client understand how you feel about the suggestion.

A great question to baffle rookie brokers years ago was to ask during a role-playing session about no-load mutual funds. Many an intense and otherwise intelligent trainee would be caught off guard by what is now a very common aspect of investing. Today's potential pitfalls for advisors who don't have a well-articulated investment philosophy include index funds, life cycle funds with targeted maturity dates, some annuities, bond ladders, and ETFs. You can develop opinions and rationales for including or excluding any product, but the best defense against a varied and constantly changing competitive landscape is to develop and maintain a well-conceived and effective investment philosophy of your own and deliver it with Leo Pusateri's "confidence, passion, and speed" (more in Chapter 12). Challenge prospects and clients—and their advisors—with the intelligence of your approach, but be constantly vigilant for signs of those who don't understand or don't share your most important investment beliefs.

RECRUIT OTHERS TO YOUR INVESTMENT PHILOSOPHY—AND TURN AWAY SKEPTICS

Be the champion of your investment philosophy. The greatest investors over time have been passionate spokespersons for their processes,

Write one sentence representing your investment philosophy for each of the following 10 dimensions:

1. Time Horizon

_____

2. Risk

_____

3. Volatility

_____

4. Style

_____

5. Investment Vehicles

_____

6. Cost

_____

7. Passive vs. Active

_____

8. Style Boxes vs. Core and Explore

_____

9. Inflation

_____

10. Taxes

_____

FIGURE 2.4   Worksheet for Developing a Compelling Investment Philosophy

which has no doubt helped them better articulate what they do as well as create a following that helps them stay the course—consider Vanguard's John Bogle. Most philosophies are not complex and intuitively make sense. That's the best test.

Are your ideas a good fit with your personality? You will be a better judge of a good fit for your approach than most prospective clients will be of themselves. You have perspective and years investing on behalf of other, seemingly similar believers. And since much of what you do is really investment consulting—not actual portfolio management—

you need to recruit like-minded teammates to the process. This should ideally include investment managers and wholesalers who can help your practice thrive. Each should have a written copy of your investment philosophy, understand their companies' roles in helping you reach your goal, and support you in client meetings, appreciation events, and prospecting efforts. (See Figure 2.4.)

Consider your 10 sentences. Which are the most important aspects of your investment philosophy? Save these sentences to use in Chapter 3 as you apply them to your investment process.

Creating a Defined, Effective Investment Process

- *How do you invest for clients?*
- *How do you achieve sustainable, repeatable results?*
- *Can you articulate your process to clients and prospects?*

Once you are clear about *what* you believe about investing—your investment philosophy—you can then develop a process—the *how*—of implementing those beliefs. The primary goal of a process is to produce performance relative to client objectives and to do so in a consistent, repeatable way. If philosophy is the mother of process, consistency is the father of success. Benefits of having a solid advisory process include:

- Being able to more easily market your services because clients and key referral sources can understand how you achieve results.
- Being able to create a systemized work flow that helps you and your associates define jobs, measure results, and free up time for the most valuable activities.
- Creating an ongoing business of which you are an important part, but not necessarily the entirety. Through process, you are creating equity that can be monetized in a variety of ways.
- Standing apart from other advisors who can provide little justification for the steps they take on behalf of clients.

In Chapter 2, we examined investment philosophy—the core principles upon which you approach the securities markets in search of returns for your clients. To be effective, that philosophy must be deeply felt and truly reflect your innermost convictions about investing. Passionately sharing your philosophy with clients and prospective clients creates a kind of defensive shield over your practice or business, protecting it through the inevitable market downturns. Those rough patches, which often drive less committed advisors to follow the latest fad, provide the Advisor for Life with a stage on which to demonstrate his or her long-term outlook and value.

Because it is based on core convictions, your investment philosophy is not a sweater that you wear or remove depending on the way the wind blows; it is a way of life. In the best book I have read on the topic of investment process (*Investment Policy*), Charles D. Ellis, the longtime managing partner of consulting firm Greenwich Associates, appropriately refers to investment philosophy as "an enduring investment commitment—through cycle after cycle in the stock market and in the business economy." Ellis dryly observes that the only way for an active investment philosophy to be successful in a marketplace where information is plentiful and competition intense is to "depend on the errors of others." He writes, "Whether by omission or commission, the only way in which a profit opportunity can be available to the active investor . . . is that the consensus of other investors is *wrong.*" It takes courage to hold on to your principles when others are saying and doing something different. So how do you put your principles into action? By building an investment process.

Because they follow a formal investment process, institutions tend to outperform individual investors. You can emulate their success by establishing a formal process to guide your investment decisions for your clients.

FROM WHAT TO HOW—THE INSTITUTIONAL METHOD

Let's look at how a few leading mutual fund managers describe their process. For example, Harris Investment Management, Inc. describes itself as an organization that "manages money according to a long-standing tradition that combines discipline, focus, knowledge, and state-of-the-art informational resources." Its investment process "focuses on active portfolio management that incorporates quantitative modeling and fundamental research. By balancing the strengths of statistically sound quantitative analysis and broad-based, fundamental research, Harris is able to evaluate current investment trends while focusing on long-term results. This disciplined approach helps Harris manage the challenges inherently associated with investment decisions."

Seneca Capital Management, a San Francisco–based investment management firm, uses this explanation to describe its investment process in managing its small-cap growth portfolio:

> Seneca screens the equity universe for earnings surprise and earnings acceleration. We further screen for earnings quality and sustainability, and the surviving companies are subjected to rigorous fundamental analysis to determine overall quality and potential return. We select stocks of companies which are growing at rates which place them in the top ranks of the universe we screen, which are producing quality, sustainable earnings; which have high quality management; and [which have] strong financial characteristics. We meet with management prior to a company's inclusion in the portfolio.

Duff & Phelps Investment Management Co. approaches investing in real estate investment trusts (REITs) this way:

> We believe that the value of a REIT extends beyond the value of the underlying real estate. Through fundamental research, we can uncover and exploit inefficiencies in the market. Ours is a four-step investment process.
>
> - *Step 1—Macro-Economic Analysis:* Regional economies, demand and supply relationships, demographics; all determine sector target weighting (expressed relative to the benchmark). This process typically yields 150 securities to consider.
> - *Step 2—Screening Process:* Create target list by utilizing a) market cap screen, which narrows the field to 125 securities, and b) fundamental factors screens, which narrows targets further to 60 to 70 securities.
> - *Step 3—Fundamental Research:* Analyze REITs based on management strength, property, financial and performance review, and target valuation relative to peer group.
> - *Step 4—Portfolio Construction:* Using 25 to 45 securities.

NOW IT'S YOUR TURN

As you notice from the way institutions explain how they invest, articulating a process requires sensitivity to the needs of the human ear and brain. Frame your process in such a way that people can more easily grasp its important components and then explain that process to others. How many steps or building blocks are there to your process? An opening line of any good process says you are organized around fundamental beliefs and principles that guide the success of your clients. A well-defined process also answers the primary questions all prospective client households raise (whether overtly or in their thoughts): "Does this advisor share my outlook on life? Has this advisor worked with people like me? Has she walked this path before?" Just as a physician guides patients through life-saving treatments by creating a clear path with definitive action steps, you can lead clients through retirement planning and other frightening and uncertain issues by developing a process statement that offers a clear-cut explanation of the route you'll be taking on their behalf.

Since the way you carry out your unique investment philosophy also must be specific to you, offering a boilerplate process would be presumptuous and, ultimately, unworkable. But most advisor process statements should take into account at least the following eight dimensions or elements. I've also included some sample statements advisors have used to explain their investment process in each of the areas:

Cost

- We charge a fee based on a percentage of our client's assets under management. This puts our financial success in line with our clients' success—as they prosper we prosper.
- We are a fee-only financial planning firm and are compensated only on fees paid by our clients. We do not accept commissions or compensation from any other source.
- We are registered investment advisors and charge our qualified clients performance fees based on a percentage of the capital appreciation in the client's account in a given year and an annual asset management fee.
- We charge an annual retainer and hourly fees.

Inflation

- The purchasing power of a portfolio can be destroyed if its component investments do not provide the appropriate real return. When constructing client portfolios, we strive to strike a balance between future growth and current income.
- We strive to select investments that will deliver real rates of return of at least 3 percent.

Investment Vehicles

- We rely on professional money managers through what are known as separately managed accounts and other so-called wrap programs to invest our clients' assets.
- We incorporate hedge funds and private equity to reach our clients' long-term investment objectives.
- We utilize a combination of mutual funds, stocks, exchange-traded funds (ETFs), and bonds to diversify our clients' portfolios across various asset classes, including small- to large-cap domestic and foreign equities, fixed-income securities, real estate, and commodities.
- We utilize multidiscipline accounts (MDAs) managed by institutional money managers.
- We utilize a "portable alpha" approach to investing by purchasing low-cost derivative contracts that track certain market indexes and using the freed-up capital to invest in hedge funds and private equity funds that seek returns uncorrelated to the equity markets.

Passive versus Active

- Like many professionals, we believe that active management, or trying to select investments that will outperform the market as a whole consistently, is a "loser's game." Therefore, we manage our clients' portfolios exclusively through passive investment vehicles consisting of index and exchange-traded funds.
- We believe markets are not efficient and that it is possible for a skilled portfolio manager to outperform the market over time. We therefore select experienced portfolio managers with track records of superior performance.

- We use a combination of active and passive management because we believe that while the large-cap market is efficient, it is possible to add alpha in the less efficient small-cap, mid-cap, and international asset classes.

Risk

- While risk is inherent in everyday life, we take no more risk than is necessary to achieve our clients' objectives.
- We define risk as the failure to achieve your objectives. We therefore will make no investment that we believe will jeopardize the attainment of investor objectives.
- Because there is a certain amount of risk in all investments, we educate clients so they understand the risk-return trade-offs we make on their behalf. In order to construct a portfolio that will incorporate both the long-term goals of our clients and their risk tolerance, we carefully evaluate each client's ability and willingness to take on risk.
- We have incorporated modern portfolio theory into our practice and the concept of portfolio perspective, which is the notion that individual investments should be analyzed not on their own risk but on the additional risk they add to an entire portfolio.

Style Boxes versus Core and Explore

- Like most institutional investors, we believe that our clients' assets should be allocated across the asset spectrum and be periodically rebalanced.
- Our core investment strategy is to allocate client assets according to institutional-style parameters, yet retain the flexibility to accommodate special-situation investing that can yield above-market returns.
- We seek to invest opportunistically, rather than be bound by rigid asset-class distinctions.

Taxes

- We believe that investing without regard to the effect of taxation is malpractice.

- When selecting portfolio managers, we place greater weight on the after-tax returns as opposed to the pretax returns. It is more important to analyze what you keep as opposed to what you earn.

Time Horizon

- We create investment programs that provide the income necessary to fund the retirement of an investor's choice.
- We are long-term investors—our clients share our vision that successful investing is a function of patience, not hasty judgment, and that investment choices must be provided time to reach their potential.
- Buying the shares of growing companies is a time-honored investment approach, requiring an investment horizon of 10 to 20 years or more for success.
- Our clients have multistage time horizons, reflecting both short- and long-term liabilities. We take these into account when investing in order to properly fund all future liquidity events, including college education for children and income in retirement.
- In our role as portfolio advisors, we do not try to time the direction of the market by making short-term bets. We strive to keep our clients fully invested according to the guidelines set forth in each client's unique investment policy statement.

YOUR ASSIGNMENT

Define your investment process. Review the material in this chapter, and consider the three to five issues most important to you and the way you approach investing. Develop an investment process statement. Once it is complete, review it with your immediate team to determine whether it resonates with them. Then begin implementing it with your clients, explaining that you have now put into tangible form an approach that you have been doing informally for quite some time. Incorporate your investment process statement into written materials and share it with current clients and prospects.

CHAPTER **4**

Setting Goals:
What *Really* Matters?

- *How do you set client goals?*
- *What real-life objectives are held by your best clients?*
- *How do you work with them to determine the objective and subjective criteria for success?*
- *How will you measure your progress to help keep the plan on course?*

"**H**ow are we doing?" is probably the most common question asked by clients to their financial advisors. There is always an element of trepidation—or confidence—depending on the client's mind-set and the history of your relationship. Yet maintaining the client's confidence is perhaps the most important goal of your practice and a benchmark of business success. Let's explore the concept of client confidence from your perspective as an advisor—and from their perspective as clients. How are you *both* doing?

TIME TO START COUNTING

Virtually every millionaire household seeks a comfortable retirement as its primary objective. We've explored how investment process can be created to address this goal, but now it's time to be very specific about what the clients want to achieve.

Very few households have calculated how much money they'll need in order to fund that comfortable retirement. Even fewer have a written plan to achieve their objectives. Akin to their interaction with the medical profession, many amble through life with a vague notion of what they need to do, but are undermined by procrastination, apathy, or even outright denial that they need to take action. A few well-meaning but less educated folks may even believe their current level of saving and investing is adequate—just as they can assume that a healthy diet alone can remove the need for regular checkups.

In a 2005 article, Ashvin Chhabra of Merrill Lynch ("Beyond Markowitz") stated that one in three American households is a single event away from bankruptcy. It's important to have specific goals to be sure an adequate plan is in place—and it's equally important to know how to monitor a plan in order to make adjustments along the way.

BEGIN WITH THE END IN MIND

In one of the great life guidance books, *The Seven Habits of Highly Effective People*, Stephen Covey declares what should be obvious: You have a better chance of reaching your objective if you take the time to determine exactly what that objective is. Most millionaire households have multiple objectives, none of which will surprise you, led by a "comfortable retirement." (See Table 4.1.) Take it a step further, though, and ask what that means. One family's comfort is another's luxury. "Comfort" is highly personal and subjective. It reflects expectations of lifestyle and quality. Since we know from surveys that few millionaire households have calculated the actual expense of their

TABLE 4.1 Most Important Financial Goals

Assure a comfortable standard of living in retirement	46%
Assure I will not run out of money in retirement	20%
Protect my estate from the impact of taxes	8%
Leave an estate to my heirs	7%
Minimize my income and capital gains taxes	6%
Finance my children's college expenses	5%
Provide long-term care for myself and/or my spouse	5%
Begin transferring wealth to beneficiaries	2%
I do not have any financial goals	1%

Source: 2006 Phoenix Wealth Survey.

TABLE 4.2 Estate Plans

Yes, it was put in place in the last year	7%
Yes, it was put in place in the last 1–5 years	23%
Yes, it was put in place over 5 years ago	28%
No, but I plan to establish one in the near future	34%
No, and I don't plan to establish one in the future	8%

Source: 2006 Phoenix Wealth Survey.

retirement vision, we have to help bring them to that reality before we can employ our investment philosophy and process.

Preparation is sorely lacking for the millionaire households, especially the newer families of the boomer generation. According to the 2006 Phoenix Wealth Survey and Phoenix Marketing International 2006, only about one-third of millionaire households have written financial plans. Fewer still have current estate plans, although about 60 percent claim to have current wills. In one survey among affluent baby boomer households aged 50 to 59 with an average net worth (exclusive of primary residence value) of $1.7 million, 62 percent did not have a written financial plan for retirement and one in four had not met with a financial advisor. The younger households showed similar results, with 64 percent aged 41 to 49 and possessing an average net worth of $900,000 failing to have a written plan and only 31 percent having met with an advisor. (See Table 4.2.)

IT'S NEEDS FIRST, GOALS SECOND

As mentioned earlier, a focus on goals is not necessarily the best way to begin connecting with an affluent household. I credit skilled industry observer and author Mitch Anthony (*Storyselling for Financial Advisors* and *Selling with Emotional Intelligence*) with the observation that people can focus on the future and their more lofty goals only when they are confident their basic requirements have been met. And the difficult job of creating a successful retirement income program for a millionaire household begins with determining the cost of that "comfortable" retirement. I suggest a two-step approach that first covers the basics and then tackles the luxuries. Most clients will appreciate the separation and as they learn more about the process will be better participants.

GREAT EXPECTATIONS—EVERYONE HAS THEM

Through surveys we've learned that most millionaire households know their current income and have a pretty good idea of what percentage of it will be needed in retirement. In an across-the-board national sample of millionaire households, 48 percent of whom are already retired at least part-time, the expectation is high for retirement income to be a large percentage of current income. (See Tables 4.3 and 4.4.)

Now apply the reality check of their current assets. *The income expectations of most millionaire households cannot be met through the investment of their investable assets.* However, before we go any further, first consider the assets declared by the millionaire households. (See Table 4.5.)

TABLE 4.3 Current Income

	% of Total Sample	Fully Retired	Full-Time Employed
<$50,000	2%	3%	1%
$50,000–$99,999	21%	35%	11%
$100,000–$149,999	34%	30%	37%
$150,000–$199,999	12%	7%	15%
$200,000–$249,999	9%	4%	13%
$250,000+	14%	7%	20%
Declined to answer	8%	14%	3%

Source: 2006 Phoenix Wealth Survey.

TABLE 4.4 Expectations of Comfortable Standard of Living in Retirement

	% of Total Sample	Fully Retired	Full-Time Employed
<80% of current income	19%	20%	19%
80%–<100% of current income	40%	43%	41%
100% of current income	28%	27%	25%
101%–120% of current income	7%	7%	7%
>120% of current income	6%	3%	8%

Source: 2006 Phoenix Wealth Survey.

TABLE 4.5 Net Worth Distribution

$1 million–under $2 million	68%
$2 million–under $3 million	18%
$3 million–under $5 million	8%
$5 million–under $10 million	3%
$10 million or more	3%

Source: 2006 Phoenix Wealth Survey.

These figures reflect the estimates made by the households themselves of their current assets, net the value of their primary residences. Nonetheless, this data may be misleading. While the totals reported are generally high, consider what assets might be on the list. Retirement plans are likely to be included at their current value, not their after-tax value. That impact can be as high as the household's marginal tax rate (combined federal and state). Many other surveys estimate that investable assets comprise only about half of the net worth reported by millionaire households. Vacation homes, rental real estate, and business interests can be included in the net worth list, but many of these assets are not liquid because of personal preference, lifestyle choices, or real illiquidity, such as that of a family business. A good "financial X-ray" may reveal that most millionaire households think their assets are worth more than they actually are.

But by staying with the income goal relative to assets, it is clear that most millionaire households cannot sustain their income expectations with current assets. That's a tough place to start building goals into a retirement plan. Instead, address the need by exposing the true costs. Then you'll have a better likelihood of achieving common ground to plan further with your client. This will surely be tough medicine for some, but those who are serious about meeting their goals will appreciate this no-nonsense approach.

LIFE AFTER WORK: WHERE TO LIVE

Try this exercise: The most basic decision that must be made by a preretiree household is the location and style in which they will live during the early stages of retirement. This is the most immediate goal. Of millionaire households not already retired, the average time until retirement is generally a little less than 11 years, so it's conceivable that most folks have at least thought about their first few years after working full-time.

The majority of households will not move from where they presently are, though they may add a vacation home, renovate their current residence, or trade to a different type of home in the same area—for example, house for condominium. Have a discussion with the client (preferably both spouses) early in the relationship about retirement living plans and map out the costs. (See Figure 4.1.)

For clients who are still employed, point out to them how expensive their house may be. The timing of these expenses is important as well since very few have the discipline to remain within a budget ("After all, we're going to live there for the rest of our lives, so why not

Principal Investment $ _____

Cost of Home   _____

Renovations   _____

  Less: Proceeds of Previous Residence Sale   _____

  Net Cost of Home   _____

Ongoing Expenses

  Maintenance and Repairs   _____

  Taxes   _____

  Mortgage Interest and Principal (if any)   _____

  Utilities   _____

  Insurance   _____

    Total   _____

  Estimated Annual Growth Rate in Expenses   _____

  Adjusted Annual Expenses   _____

FIGURE 4.1   Worksheet for Retirement House

TABLE 4.6 The Compounding Effect of Inflation

	Annual Inflation Rate			
	3%	4%	5%	6%
5 years	1.159274	1.216653	1.276282	1.338226
10 years	1.343916	1.480244	1.628895	1.790848
15 years	1.557967	1.800944	2.078928	2.396558
20 years	1.806111	2.191123	2.653298	3.207135
30 years	2.427262	3.243398	4.321942	5.743491
40 years	3.262038	4.801021	7.039989	10.285718

Example: $2,000 current housing expenses @ 3% inflation rate in 10 years = $2,687.83 and in 20 years = $3,612.22

$2,000 × 1.343916 = $2,687.83
$2,000 × 1.806111 = $3,612.22

Example: $2,000 current housing expenses @ 6% inflation rate in 10 years = $3,581.70 and in 20 years = $6,414,27

$2,000 × 1.790848 = $3,581.70
$2,000 × 3.207135 = $6,414.27

make it nice?") and most simply won't want to. As expenses for the initial residence start-up can be quite high, they can impact the long-term ability of the retirement plan to make up the difference. Inflation can be a factor as well. (See Table 4.6.)

If the retirement home funding example is effective, your client will have a renewed appreciation for the specifics of retirement planning or become completely depressed—even angry. Be prepared to brace yourself! But if you are able to move on, the seriousness of your task soon becomes even more apparent.

HEALTH CARE—THE REAL MONEY PIT

Health drives the cost of retirement—from two perspectives. The cost of health care is for many retirees their single biggest expense. The wild card is the quality of the client's health and the length of any chronic or terminal condition. Health care expenses for many otherwise healthy people can be concentrated within the final years of life in the event of a prolonged illness.

The second dimension of health and its impact on retirement is longevity—how long will retirement last? The irony of planning a comfortable retirement is that few can roughly estimate its cost because they lack hard answers to the two most important variables—longevity and health. Imagine being the bank that gives a loan with no specific payoff date! Because no one knows how long they will live, they cannot determine how much they will need to fund their lifestyle. Add in the uncertainty of health and you have at best a vague target based more on your client's family medical history than on capital market returns.

To assess and estimate the costs of health care expenses during retirement, we've created five categories. While some of these calculations are pure guesswork, much of the cost can be assessed from the perspective of risk. As stated before, to completely eliminate risk is beyond the financial ability of most affluent households, so in these cases a little prevention can go a long way and a little planning can make it stick.

1. Medical insurance premiums—Medicare, medigap.
2. Treatment expenses, principally co-payments for examinations and prescription medications.
3. Long-term care expenses—LTC insurance premiums, home health care, nursing home care.
4. Wellness plan—exercise classes and programs, personal training, fitness center membership, dietician services.
5. Noncovered lifestyle and treatment expenses—such as an elevator or ramp added to the home or over-the-counter medications.

Some data is helpful to begin nailing down specific expenses. Two March 2006 surveys (by Fidelity Investments and the Employee Benefit Research Institute) indicate that a 65-year-old retired couple faces out-of-pocket medical expenses of about $200,000 during retirement. However, another study estimates that expense total for only the first two items listed, insurance and treatment. According to a 2006 study by Genworth Financial, the average annual national cost of a private room in a nursing home is $70,912.

Because life expectancy used in the study is 82 for men and 85 for women, these numbers may be conservative for a generation whose members may live much longer.

The Employee Benefit Research Institute extends its estimates to

History Rules Health

Consideration of the family's medical history is critical to helping clients assess their own mortality and health risks. It is a no-brainer to recognize that a millionaire couple with a deep family history of stroke, heart disease, or cancer might be at greater risk than another family with great cholesterol genetics whose members have routinely survived past 90. In my household, my wife's family suffered from Alzheimer's and cancer, while my two grandfathers lived well into their 80s and their siblings made it past 90 and one even to 101.

greater longevity with a predictably negative impact. EBRI data reflect a $216,000 expense for a couple without company health benefits if they live to 80, but a jump to $444,000 if they reach 90. If the couple reaches 100, the cost is $778,000!

While considering a family's medical history is critical to helping clients assess their own mortality and health risks, longevity is grossly underestimated by most families, making the health care cost calculation difficult and emotionally charged.

The updated longevity calculations suggest that today a 65-year-old man has a 50 percent chance of living to 85 and a 25 percent chance of reaching 92 (American Society of Actuaries, published in *Financial Advisor*, March/April 2006). A 65-year-old woman has a 50 percent chance of reaching 88 and a one-in-four shot at 94. Couples at 65 only improve the odds, as 50 percent of couples, both aged 65, will see one of the pair make it to 92 and there is a 25 percent chance of a survivor at 97.

Medical insurance premiums are an especially thorny issue for millionaire households because some of them are based on income. Families with higher retirement incomes are responsible for more of the Medicare premium expense. As I write this in 2007, the high earners in the millionaire surveys mostly have income expectations that surpass the threshold under which the enrollee is responsible for only 25 percent of the Medicare premium. At $80,000 (single, $160,000 for a couple), the premium share jumps to 35 percent and at $200,000 a couple would pay 80 percent. Another piece of bad news for the relatively successful retirees is that demographics indicate only one direction for these expenses—and the taxes associated with them—*up.*

Long-Term Care Coverage—Pros versus Cons

Depending on the level of preparation desired by your clients, you should of course discuss the potential role (versus the expense) of LTC insurance. Long-term care insurance is an area requiring special expertise and—like many topics in your practice—should be delivered in consultation with a product specialist. For this phase of planning, address the topic from the perspective of relative risk.

According to many of my fellow advisors, the number-one reason why clients do not acquire LTC insurance is that they believe they have enough resources to protect themselves—they are self-insuring the risk because they frequently view it as an unreasonable and unnecessary expense. Given the numbers related earlier by EBRI and others, complete self-insurance begins with the $200,000 current value expressed at the low end for a 65-year-old couple potentially aging to their early 80s. It reaches to over $750,000 for those approaching 100. For clients with adequate resources, self-insurance can be an economical choice, given that LTC premiums are high and rise with age.

Traveling up the Hierarchy of Life

Once you have discussed the expense of the primary retirement residence, the most basic of human life needs—shelter—has been met. Health care is the second consideration and a far more challenging one due to abstract and emotional factors. Most health risks to clients are a function of either family history or personal lifestyle. Neither topic is easy to address even with the most detached and rational client. At some level this discussion can get very difficult. Yet the Advisor for Life cannot ignore this most significant element of life quality, which is also by far the greatest retirement life expense. A strategy for delving into health risks can help you gain critical insights to help your clients.

Evaluating Health—An Approximate Science

If you succeeded with the exercise to determine the cost of a retirement residence, then continue with a similar approach to health expenditures. The more you can utilize worksheets and other objective tools with clients, the more you'll be able to create a forum to facilitate the open exchange of important information with minimal emotion. Consider the health analysis, which begins with the basic client questions:

- *Family history.* Does the family medical history indicate any areas of potential concern? Are cancer, heart disease, stroke, high blood pressure, or Alzheimer's disease prevalent? Whereas these are significant risks, also consider the lifestyle ailments that can be almost as damaging—if only from an emotional perspective. These risks include diabetes and arthritis, as well as other circulatory and nervous system conditions. Are the couple smokers? Is there a history of alcohol abuse or of mental illness?
- *Lifestyle.* The second health risk issue is lifestyle—those habits, current and historical, that impact health. It has been my experience that highly successful corporate executives tend to approach health from one of two extremes—weekend triathlete or anti-exercise workaholic. I know CEOs from both camps. Both types are well aware of their decisions and comfortable with their approaches. As the Advisor for Life, beware of an air of superiority from the aggressively fit compared to the relative defensiveness of the physically passive.

In Chapter 5, we'll talk in greater detail about risks. For now let's consider the proactive side of health issues since we are still assessing preretiree household goals.

Establishing (and Sticking to) the Health Budget

So if the client/couple has sufficient reason to expect at least moderately good health in retirement, how will it be maintained? Considering our five categories of health expense, the lifetime health budget is as much a financial issue as a strategic one. Attitudes about health acquired early can make a world of difference as clients age and challenges arise. Preparations like renovating a home so it's suitable for long-term care needs can help clients and their families meet expensive and emotional struggles at perhaps the most difficult stage of life.

Caring for Others—A Hidden Expense

After shelter and health, the goals of the affluent household begin to shift. While lifestyle is probably the next area for goal setting, with topics including occupations, hobbies, charity work, travel, and leisure, for many clients the next area of concern is the responsibility of caring for aging parents or in some cases adult children.

Care for others is a highly personal issue. Surveys compiled over the years by my friend and colleague, Russ Alan Prince of Prince and Associates, cited in his and Karen Maru File's book *High-Net-Worth Psychology*, indicate that among the many personalities of affluent clients, the most common is that of the family steward. The family steward considers care for his family a primary savings and investment goal. Such responsible clients are very concerned with planning and usually maintain a long-term view of investing. Working with the family steward is the ideal deployment of the Advisor for Life, as it's generally easy to discuss numerous planning aspects with a willing participant. Investment policies, trusts, long-term care, insurance, and succession plans each factor into this equation.

Direct and Contingent Liabilities

Planning for whatever responsibilities may be in store for your clients is a key service. While the more acute issues presented by the needs of a dependent parent or disabled child top the list, also be aware of future risks that may not be readily apparent. These *contingent liabilities* can arise with little or no warning and often at difficult times. For example, what would happen to the household if a parent or sibling suffered a life-altering stroke? Would the care needs require altering your client's retirement lifestyle plan? What preparations have you made for an event like this? We consider risks in greater detail in Chapter 5; let's focus now on the direct expenses and responsibilities.

Stewardship Expenses

There are three primary categories of caregiving expenses. (See Figure 4.2.)

1. *Acute care*—expenses related to current or certain future needs of a dependent relative or other person. Examples include aging parents or a disabled child.

Direct Care Responsibilities

Name of care recipient(s)
_____

Type of care
_____

Financial support
_____

Other support
_____

Special concerns
_____

Legacy

Basic Question: How do you want to be remembered by your family?

(Note: This can be a good conversation starter but it's also a sensitive issue—proceed with caution.)

Heirs (names)
_____

Type of support
_____

Conditions of support, (e.g., maintaining
family values, managing the family business)
_____

Charity

Basic Question: How do you want to be remembered by society?

Organizations, beneficiaries
_____

Type of support
_____

Conditions of support
_____

FIGURE 4.2   Caregiving Expenses

2. *Legacy*—a level of financial support for relatives or significant others. A trust is an example of how to provide for the educational or life expenses of adult children. Parents may want to restrict a trust's benefits for adult children until they are older to encourage independence or a work ethic.

3. *Charity*—gifts to organizations and causes outside the family.

It's important to note the many emotional aspects of these issues. Caring for an aging parent is an act of love that also requires significant energy and fortitude. Leaving money to a spouse can be comforting to the family steward, but the same feelings can do harm if, say, a gift is left for an adult child who then loses incentive to develop a career or who is otherwise irresponsible. Charitable giving can be complex as it usually entails a blend of truly charitable feelings along with some ego gratification, but is generally done only after family needs have been secured.

What are your clients' acute care responsibilities? What will be involved—and how will it change over time? What are the expected levels of support—both financial and physical—and how will those levels evolve and interact? And be sure to consider each expense with reference to its long-term potential cost, as shown in Table 4.6.

Legacy is complicated. Who requires support if the client prematurely dies or becomes disabled, and how will that support get to them? What support levels are possible given the client's resources? Should the support be structured to provide a level of guidance, such as with a trust for minor or young adult children? How will your clients pass on their feelings about family and wealth if they die prematurely?

Charity is perhaps the most straightforward. What organizations and causes are important to the client, and what size gift is desired? Is there a way to structure the gift to minimize taxes while preserving values, such as a planned gift?

LAST CHANCE TO MAKE A DIFFERENCE

When discussing the future, it is always important to strike a balance between expectations and reality. Bring up the past. Clients are often willing to talk about how they got to where they are today and about what they expect of their children and grandchildren. Encourage frank dialogue but be ready to guide it in a constructive manner. Understand that very few clients have the ability to objectively evaluate and address the multiple needs of a retirement without becoming overwhelmed. The expenses mount quickly, and demands can be downright depressing. It can pay to balance discussion of the heavy responsibilities with some positive ideas. One method is to solve a problem. Make sure there is a win in your discussion of goals. There is substantial benefit to having achieved or funded an objective. Make sure you can lock down a goal, like funding the retirement residence or securing long-term care, and use that success to prod the client forward into more complex issues.

Ask them about their hobbies. If one is a hunter, encourage him to make a gift to a wildlife or open-space preservation organization. For those who have been teachers, perhaps a scholarship or gift to a local school would appeal to them. Remind them that gifts do not have to be large to be effective.

HAVING FUN YET?

The second phase of goal setting is to turn toward more positive topics. Consider the recent Merrill Lynch survey of baby boomers, conducted by Ken Dychtwald of AgeWave.com, which indicates their visions of retirement. (See Figure 4.3.)

What's missing from the picture? *Retirement!* Fewer than one out of five boomers is predicting a retirement devoid of work for pay. Their predecessors, the Silent Generation, likely had a much greater interest in an old-fashioned retirement—days filled with golf or fishing and taking it easy—in sharp contrast to the active, work-filled choices of the boomers. Query your clients on their retirement vision. Emphasize the various stages of retirement while showing clients this chart and asking them about their aspirations.

Retirement Is a Full-Length Play, Not a One-Act

Effective counsel requires a focus on retirement realities. The sheer length of retirement can result in dramatically different interests and vocations as your clients age. For appreciation of retirement as a journey, not a destination, look no further than your own family. As the oldest of four children, I was fortunate to know my grandparents prior

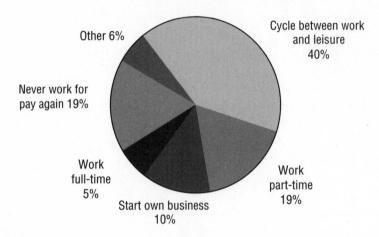

**"Which represents the ideal plan for
how you will live in the next stage of your life?"**

Other 6%

Cycle between work
and leisure
40%

Never work for
pay again 19%

Work
full-time
5%

Start own business
10%

Work
part-time
19%

FIGURE 4.3 A Cyclic Retirement in the New Paradigm
Source: The 2006 Merrill Lynch New Retirement Study.

to their retirements and to enjoy them as they transitioned to a lifestyle of their own choosing.

One grandfather retired early at 63 from a professional career as a chemist and moved immediately to Florida, where he became active in the Service Corps of Retired Executives (SCORE), city politics as an elected official, and commander of the Coast Guard Auxiliary. Each was a dramatic departure from his working life. My other grandfather was president of Bethany College in West Virginia and served on a number of academic and corporate boards. His retirement was mandated at 65 by the college, yet he went on to write several books and travel the globe. His wife lived to 101 and was "retired" for 34 years. During that time, she lived in three different locations. In the first few years, she and my grandfather lived in the college town and remained active in the academic world. They traveled, played golf, and wrote books together. After an unfortunate incident involving a break-in at their home, they began dividing their time between Bethany and North Carolina, where they lived in a new, upscale retirement community surrounded by other successful—and very realistic—people who sought the comfort and security of a closed facility with the amenities of a country club. Upon the death of my grandfather in 1994, my grandmother remained in the North Carolina community, embraced by longtime friends and throwing parties for other 90-year-olds. But the loss of her eyesight as well as many friends sent her back with her family. She spent her final years in an assisted living facility with a nursing wing.

The Retirement Variable: Health

As these experiences illustrate, the differences in retirement for most people are largely driven by the state of their health. If clients suffer from ailments that compromise their mobility, no amount of free time can compensate for this hurdle. My father, a retired physician now living mostly in Florida, often complains about the advertising in his local newspaper portraying platinum-haired retirees cavorting on golf courses and dancing into the night at swanky country clubs or on cruise ships. Having suffered knee-replacement surgeries and coping with other age-related maladies, he says the advertisers paint a picture of retirement that is for many more hope than reality. According to *The Age Wave* by Ken Dychtwald and Joe Flower, 80 percent of individuals aged 65 and older suffer from at least one chronic ailment, and nearly two-thirds require assistance with the basics of daily living.

I address health issues and risk in Chapter 5. Let's now look at the happier side of retirement—what do your clients want and hope to be able to do during their golden years?

The Three Phases of Life

John Shad was the CEO of EF Hutton. After a long and storied career on Wall Street he went on to provide a terrific view of a complete life. Although I heard it early in my own career, his simple guidance was to live his life in thirds: a third to learn, a third to earn, and a third to serve. Consistent with that plan, he left Wall Street to become commissioner of the Securities and Exchange Commission (SEC). Arthur Levitt followed a similar path to the American Stock Exchange as CEO and then to the SEC. Levitt, with whom I once had the pleasure of sharing a transatlantic plane trip, used his youthful vigor to return once again to private industry as a partner in a private equity firm. During that plane ride, Levitt chastised me for selecting the egg and bacon entrée while he nibbled on fruit and cereal that looked to me like chopped cardboard. Was there a method to his madness? Did he know something I did not?

The Three-Item Retirement Shopping List

Despite all the warnings, many fail to make a realistic retirement plan. Help them simplify the process and increase the chances for success by asking them to list three goals that they'd like to accomplish or experience when they have more time. You'll learn a lot about your clients and what matters most to them while learning about how much they've contemplated their retirement. Many have specific plans and can't wait to put them in place, and others are happy to allow their retirement to evolve more gradually (meaning they probably like their current lifestyle and envision only a few minor changes). Still others will find that health or a specific health event requires an adjustment (plan B) and that their attitude will determine their enjoyment and adaptability level. Each of these can lead to productive planning.

Start with yourself. Think about three goals and how they'd guide your retirement. Challenge clients to select one primary goal for each of three distinct avenues of retirement living, what Ken Dychtwald has called the "cyclic" retirement—education, work, and leisure (from the Merrill Lynch New Retirement Survey 2005 and *The Power Years* by Ken Dychtwald and Daniel J. Kadlec, John Wiley & Sons, 2005). Pick an objective for each path. Examples of education choices don't have to be as lofty as "complete a doctoral dissertation." They can be as accessible as an Elderhostel trip to another country or researching family genealogy (my great-aunt, a retired schoolteacher, was in her 80s when she completed the first Gresham family history since we arrived from England).

Work can be a consulting business, a sales job, or a not-for-profit directorship. Leisure should be exactly that, possibly involving a hobby, like gardening or woodworking, to use time that was not available when working and raising a family. Others may want to focus on a sport like golf or tennis, or just sit on a beach and read a book. There should be time for family and an active social life. When given the free time, most retirees develop interests they didn't know they had. Think of retirement as a special time that provides an opportunity for all kinds of growth. The pursuit of these goals may be the true essence of retirement—the freedom to finally do what one has put off for so long—provided we have the health and money to afford to do so.

Your Job—Funding Fun

Can you build a budget for the cyclic retirement? What costs come with education, work, and leisure? Consider that the major goals often provide the base from which to construct a more specific (and sometimes more realistic) plan. Try to scan the horizon for big-ticket items, like a country club membership to support a leisure goal of playing more golf, or the cost of outfitting a home workshop. Watch for adjustments to the plan, which are inevitable and potentially dangerous. Always prepare for the unexpected. My parents developed a very modest plan for acquiring and renovating a small retirement dwelling in Florida. After sweating through a year without a pool, they revised their original budget as the need for a pool became apparent. Likewise, the expense for hurricane shutters and blinds, which were not in the original plan, can suddenly become an urgent necessity. Last-minute financial terms are usually not the most favorable to the borrower. Frequently, such repairs or renovations can be made while one spouse is still working— easing the pain of the outlay with a steady income.

Like a new car, retirement often comes with its own adjustment or break-in period. It can begin with a heady mix of freedom, fun, and cash as clients realize they can sleep late, skip the commute, do what they want, and roll over years of previously untouchable savings. But for most, retirement quickly becomes a balancing act as the reality of finite savings and growing obligations sets in. These early days are particularly treacherous when you consider the Fantasy Trip age chart (see Chapter 1) and what big-ticket expenses can confront the new retiree. The squeeze placed on retirees by adult children, aging parents, and possibly grandparents can disrupt the most carefully crafted retirement plan. And it's not all bad stuff, like supplementing medical bills or regularly driving someone to and from doctor appointments. Weddings, educational costs, and "getting started" gifts place potentially huge financial burdens on the new retiree and represent even greater risk to the plan because they usually appear early in the payout phase. Seek out these contingent liabilities when planning for clients' cyclic futures.

Recommended Reading

A great book to help you help your clients meet their cyclic retirement future is *The Power Years*, by Ken Dychtwald and Daniel J. Kadlec. The prolific author of *The Age Wave* and *Age Power* turns his sights on the popular vision of retirement, which is a long-term exploration of activities, vocations, and vacations. Dychtwald provides numerous ideas and helpful web site addresses for in-depth information and creative conversation.

SUMMING UP

The Advisor for Life is at his or her best when discussing life goals with clients and prospects. When doing so, keep in mind the fine balance between meeting needs and fulfilling dreams. It can pay to remember Mitch Anthony's structuring of the life hierarchy. Make sure their needs are met before allowing clients to fantasize about what they want to do with their extra time. The balance you achieve will frame a family's retirement years—the greatest responsibility an advisor can ever face and a challenge each of us should aspire to meet.

CHAPTER 5

Defining Risk

Or, Is Risk Management a Contradiction in Terms?

- *How do you evaluate your clients' vulnerabilities?*
- *Is risk the reduction of interperiod volatility, or is it the failure to achieve objectives?*
- *Are your clients more concerned with beating a market index or with having enough money to enjoy a comfortable retirement?*
- *What role is played by various forms of investment risk?*

L ife is full of risks and, like it or not, the Advisor for Life's job is to minimize them. Even dedicated investment professionals will admit that risk is not the volatility of the markets; it is instead the failure to achieve their clients' objectives. Risk is not the chance the market goes down; it is the inability to finance your lifestyle.

"The trouble with risks," goes the old saw, "is that you never know when they are going to happen." The example in our children's world is that there is no point in wearing a helmet (for anything) if you're not going to fall.

DO YOU WORK WITH ANYONE LIKE ME?

Among other things, "Advisor for Life" means counseling on what might happen during your client's lifetime. Perspective based on experiences of others is among the most important criteria cited by clients for why they selected their financial advisor. "Have you ever worked with anyone like me?" is the dominant query. When I was an advisor in the early 1980s, I managed the endowment fund for a prominent church in a nearby community. One of the many referrals I received was to a successful group of proctologists. Although I was already known to them from my work with the church, the first question was whether I managed money for any other proctologists and any other local proctology practices. I lost the competition for this substantial retirement fund because I lacked the specific professional referral and perspective they were seeking as well as a local presence. Don't underestimate the value placed by clients on your ability to understand their situation and empathize with their objectives.

EMBRACE RISK (BUT NOT TOO TIGHTLY)

Too often, advisors unconsciously project a preference for one side or the other of a client's balance sheet—a view observed by most clients, where a lack of questions about their real-life issues is interpreted as a lack of interest. Investment advisors tend to focus on growth strategies. Insurance professionals generally suggest scenarios in which a client's family may incur liabilities. Asking advisors from the different professions to trade roles has historically failed, with the exception of "wealth managers"—those with a total balance sheet view of the client household. Currently comprising less than 10 percent—my guess—of all financial advisors, true wealth managers remain a scarce (but very profitable) group. Rather than solve the global issue of wealth management, let's simply relate risks to your practice—no matter its orientation—and consider the potential gains to better addressing the true risks faced by your affluent clients. The true wealth manager is the Advisor for Life.

THE RISK LIST

At some level, all risks contribute to the big risk, not being able to achieve financial independence. For the independent-minded baby boom generation, the loss of this independence is unthinkable. In a recent survey conducted by *Age Wave* guru Ken Dychtwald, the greatest fears held by baby boomers are over losing independence. Being unable to afford medical insurance, contracting a major illness, and being confined to a nursing home each rank ahead of death itself. "The market falling" didn't make the list. So if everything comes back to the risk of losing independence, what might so-called real-life risks be? Are they those things that are beyond the control of your clients or you?

MEDICAL RISKS—DON'T IGNORE THE ISSUE

Consider the chart in Figure 5.1, taken from a recent survey of baby boomer households. Note the thread running through the list of fears. Health care worries reflect lifestyle issues; they are not fears unto themselves.

What are you talking about in your initial meetings or ongoing reviews? The information from a survey by Tiburon Strategic Advisors, as reported in the June 2006 issue of *Financial Advisor*, is invaluable reconnaissance—these are the issues on the minds of clients but many are not taking action. The survey found that only 6 percent of consumers own long-term care insurance, 70 percent of whom are women. Knowing that, what an advantage you have to help people address these fears. The flip side is also true in that failure to surface these primary concerns can mean trouble for an advisor.

Talk with your existing clients—especially those approaching retirement. As they near a time when these issues will become more important, their awareness changes and they can develop concerns they

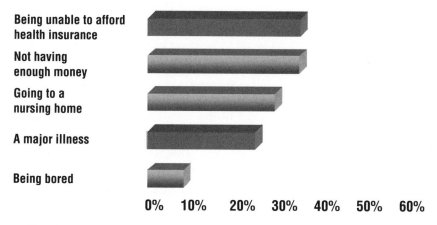

FIGURE 5.1 Boomers' Biggest Retirement Fears
*Source:*The 2006 Merrill Lynch New Retirement Study.

Know What's Important

In a recent "Letters to the Editor" section of a magazine written for clients of a discount brokerage firm, readers poked holes in a previous column on the subject of retirement planning. One reader was especially blunt in her criticism, saying that if the company really wanted to help people plan for retirement, then it could not ignore health insurance. And because the article did ignore this important topic, she said the advice didn't fit her at all. Of course, the fact that the company printed this harsh rebuke is testimony to the fact that it does care.

didn't have even a few months earlier. Be acutely aware of developments with your clients' parents. The loss of independence is highlighted through the lives of aging parents. Some form of the refrain "That isn't going to happen to me" is a common line heard countless times in hospital waiting rooms and nursing home hallways. Health issues are the top concern of most retirees, and the Advisor for Life will find a way to help clients evaluate this tricky issue.

Talk with people about health—show them the chart in Figure 5.1 and query their personal concerns. What do they worry about? Do they have an aging relative or friend whose experience has helped shape their current opinions? Ask if they worry about someone else. The message is clear—the boomers fear a loss of independence. To ignore the issue is perilous if advisors want to hold on to their clients.

LIQUIDITY RISK—ASSETS YES, MONEY NO

Real estate equity, closely held businesses—even partnership investments like hedge funds—can lead to bloated balance sheets but insufficient cash. The liquidity comfort level for each household is different, but advisors often suggest that nothing calms clients like having a year's income available within a few days if necessary. Watch this issue grow in importance as real estate accounts for a greater proportion of affluent household wealth and as more investors buy illiquid alternative investments.

Debtor Nation: It Is Us

One cause for concern expressed by social commentators and economists is the amount of debt carried without apparent concern by the baby boom generation. Match this with the first negative savings rate since the Great Depression, and you have the ingredients for a potential economic crisis. According to Professor Niall Ferguson of Harvard University, as reported by the *New York Times*, U.S. home mortgage debt increased nearly $3 trillion during 2000–2005, and over the past 10 years consumer credit has increased from 13 percent of gross domestic product (GDP) to 18 percent. Meanwhile, Americans' personal savings rate has fallen from a high of 7.5 percent in 1990 to less than zero.

The national addiction to debt has not spared the millionaire household. The unflagging optimism that has defined the boomer generation has spawned unprecedented spending. Facing the occasional audience of investors in my travels, I can't resist asking those in their 70s and 80s how they view their children's spending habits. "Disgusting," commented an otherwise delightful lady from Dallas in a public seminar for well-to-do retirees. I've also noted the sheepish looks from a few much younger participants, but also a few glimpses of righteous defiance from others. To gain the same perspective, consider the size of homes when you were growing up compared to the current national boom in McMansions (according to the National Association of Home Builders, the average home size in the United States was 2,330 square feet in 2004, up from 1,400 square feet in 1970), and try to remember if your parents picked you up from soccer practice in a Mercedes or a Ford station wagon. Freed of the economic and security concerns that governed the Silent Generation (those born between 1926 and 1945), boomers have made consumption a national pastime and we're #1 in the world. So there's little debate about the facts that Americans spend too much and save too little and that having more money often means simply spending more. We can create an entirely separate risk category for "consumption risk"—afflicting the household that can't stop spending.

Liquidity is personal choice like each of our risks. My father has believed for years that a certain amount of cash should be held in the local bank to provide a comfort level. Nick Murray, master commentator and coach for clients and advisors, observed in his 2005 book, *The Value-Added Wholesaler in the 21st Century*, that a prudent professional should have one year's income in a money market fund at all times to help relieve any stress from being boxed into a job or other negative situation.

Yet other factors can drive liquidity concerns. Business owners often have seasonal cash-flow requirements or liabilities that require greater protection. The Advisor for Life will be certain to evaluate not only each client's personal preferences for cash security, but also any contingent liabilities like a business liability risk requiring insurance or additional resources. Be especially aware of the impact of changing property valuations to collateralize debts. And I don't refer solely to the potential for a markdown in real estate prices and its impact on interest-only mortgages favored by so many recent buyers. Consider the impact of reversals on a private equity investment, market declines in variable insurance funds, and the impact on premiums—even lower college savings accounts.

How much does the household need to get by given the worst-case scenario—job loss, disability of the primary wage earner, or health event of an aging parent? Think short-term cash needs—we'll delve into longer-term issues later.

PURCHASING-POWER RISK (A.K.A. INFLATION RISK)—WHAT HAPPENS WHEN YOUR ASSETS ARE DEVALUED IN CURRENCY TERMS?

How quickly much of the investing public has forgotten the devastating impact of inflation on retirement savings. Younger clients won't appreciate the risk, but older ones often talk about bad memories of inflation and how it can destroy purchasing power. When I was a new advisor in 1983, my biggest competition was from a new financial phenomenon called the money market fund sporting rates in excess of 15 percent. I couldn't budge most clients to invest in the stock market (the Dow Jones Industrial Average was at 800 versus 12,000+ at this writing). Federal Reserve Board Chairman Paul Volcker then led an attack on inflation that was ravaging the U.S. economy and began a decade-long interest-rate plunge. The rate drop was so profound that the long Treasury bond soared over 50 percent in total return in 1982—outpacing all other asset classes.

What to do: Stress test your clients' portfolios for inflation risk. Beware of the impact on retirement income payments if there are annuities or other payout options without protection (such as cost-of-living adjustments to annuity payments). Where are the risks? Referring back to liquidity risk, how many of your client households hold adjustable-rate debt? While not necessarily a bad idea, the risk of increased interest costs is a reality check worth taking as it's likely to be your clients' most significant debt.

PREMATURE DEATH—ITS IMPACT ON A FAMILY, ESPECIALLY IF A BUSINESS IS INVOLVED

This seems like an obvious topic, yet only one-fourth of all millionaire households have a current estate plan, *according to the* 2006 Phoenix Wealth Survey. And although most likely they own life insurance, the chances are good that the proceeds are woefully inadequate to maintain the current lifestyle and are possibly also subject to taxation if the death benefits swell the estate's total value and are not sheltered in a trust.

Adequate life insurance protection for a typical millionaire household with aging parents and growing or adult children can be expensive, especially if the breadwinner (the insured) is in less than ideal health or is older. Lifestyle quality is also expensive to insure—expenses for education, health care, and the eventual retirement of a surviving spouse rapidly add up. When planning for premature death, boomers' optimism usually works against them. For many households the trade-off is preparedness for an unlikely risk versus the current expenses required to pay for other immediate items, such as housing.

Since most millionaire households require a death benefit that can send total estate values well into the taxable category, you need to determine what is adequate protection and how to provide the insurance to minimize taxation.

DISABILITY—ALWAYS A POSSIBILITY

A top wirehouse advisor in Southern California had a terrific business-owner client for nearly 18 years. The advisor was fired by the client despite incredible, market-beating investment performance. Why?

The business owner was in a bad motorcycle accident resulting in a prolonged recovery period in which he was unable to manage his business. Like so many entrepreneurs, he had not made provisions for another person to fill in for him. The business was in trouble and the owner was distraught over the prospect of seeing his life's work—and net worth—crumble. He took out his frustrations on the advisor, who he complained had not counseled him to get disability coverage.

Before you argue that there is probably no commercially available disability policy to cover the enormous expenses associated with a Southern California lifestyle, plus sufficient cash to offset the loss of a company founder, the advisor might have played a more subtle role. How about counseling the client that motorcycle riding is a fairly high-risk activity and there is no way to insure against the potential disability? The Advisor for Life will ask for permission to make observations and point out risks. The most obvious answer would have been to advise the client to consider another hobby.

The life insurance industry has a lead on the rest of the advice-giving crowd in that it routinely asks lifestyle risk questions prior to approving a policy. My last insurance policy application asked if I was a recreational pilot, a rock climber, or HIV positive. From the perspective of an underwriter, these are all legitimate questions and it is part of your job to ascertain such risks and help clients avoid them.

According to a Tiburon Strategic Advisors report, disabilities are responsible for over 48 percent of mortgage foreclosures (June 2006 *Financial Advisor* magazine). If your client has a business, there is almost no coverage that can come close to making up for potential losses. Second, who do you partner with that can provide quality service and a very good disability policy? Since this is a specialty item, you should bring in a specialist.

IT'S LEGAL OR IT'S A LIABILITY—*LEGAL ASPECTS*

Surveys of the affluent often indicate their concerns about litigation—especially if they own a business. Of special note, consider your retirement plan clients. Are they conforming to the Employee Retirement Income Security Act (ERISA)? What a great time to prospect self-trusteed retirement plans to ask the same question. Begin to incorporate a few questions into your reviews and dialogue with prospective clients about their legal liabilities and preparedness. Many affluent people have no idea where to turn if they (or a family member) were to become involved in a lawsuit or other civil action. What would they do if they got sued?

MARKET RISK—MANAGING TURBULENCE

Market risk should be incorporated into your investment portfolio work because the perspective is critical to a complete view of a household's net worth. A favorite question of life insurance agents is to ask prospects what would happen to their net worth if the stock market dropped 10 percent or 20 percent. Most clients can't answer but they still worry about it. In the recent book *Cultivating the Middle Class Millionaire*, by fellow *Registered Rep.* columnist and friend Russ Prince (with editor-in-chief David Geracioti), most high-net-worth clients reveal their concern about suffering a severe financial reversal. They do not want more risk.

Great Stock Market Reversals

- Great railway mania 1850
- Florida real estate 1926
- Wall Street crash 1929
- The Great Depression 1930
- Fall of France 1940
- Technology " 'tronics" equity bubble 1962
- Arab oil embargo 1973
- President Nixon's resignation 1974
- Gold rush 1978
- Black Monday October 1987
- Lloyds of London 1988
- Japanese real estate 1991
- Bond market crash 1994
- Barings Bank 1995
- Asian markets 1997
- Long-Term Capital Management 1998
- Technology stock market bubble (AOL/Time Warner, Lucent, eToys, etc.) 2000
- Corporate malfeasance (Enron, WorldCom, Qwest, Cendant, Adelphia, Arthur Andersen, Tyco) 2001

FAMILY CARE RISK—DIVIDING RESOURCES AMONG ADULT CHILDREN AND AGING PARENTS

Each family has concerns about how to care for aging parents, but the most prepared know the roles of the involved individuals. Geography and financial well-being are important, but the burdens of care can fall disproportionately on the closest and/or wealthiest children—or not—fueling rivalries and hostility. What are your best clients' future plans? Have family meetings and advance directives prepared everyone? What happens if some children move away or have their own health issues? What are plans B and C?

Mary Beth Emson has an additional take on this risk, citing what she calls "dependency risk." This is the risk that the executor or the one who holds the power of attorney is not up to the task. As her team has learned, it can be devastating to families when the client's true concerns and preferences are not understood and communicated.

A nagging additional issue of the boomer generation is the potential to care for adult children. Job layoffs, economic pressures, broken relationships, or prolonged job searches can lead to big expenses and poor household timing. Not to be overlooked are happier times that require a financial outlay such as weddings or down payment assistance for a new car or house. Happier, but still expensive. What are the plans? Are you ready to help everyone articulate their wishes?

Finally, consider the importance of advance directives. The tragedy of Terri Schiavo's battle with terminal illness brought to the national stage the importance of having a definitive plan in the event of catastrophic disability. The Kelly Group at Smith Barney in Florham Park, New Jersey, uses the Schiavo story to warn clients of the risks faced without advance directives. Far from the legal fireworks of this high-profile case is the daily misfortune of ordinary people who suffer for years because no one created a set of legally binding instructions to guide otherwise well-meaning caregivers and family members.

LONGEVITY RISK—LIVING TOO LONG?

Setting aside questions of life quality, what protections are in place to guard against the demographic risk indicated by rising longevity rates? As discussed in Chapter 4, one member of a couple may well live well beyond 92. Will the money run out? Health often deteriorates rapidly during the later years.

Family history (i.e., genetics) provides the greatest guide here, but lifestyle factors also play a role. If your client's parents and grandparents lived to old ages, get ready for the potential that they have the same time horizon. What is the plan?

Are they agreeable to long-term care coverage? Often the next generation is more open to this suggestion if their parents' golden years were financially strenuous. A large nest egg can easily be depleted by a few years in a nursing home. Many of us do not want to talk about long-term care needs; it's often easier to discuss one's death.

Simply stating that a long-term care policy can protect and preserve wealth may not be enough to move a client to sign. Consider that having to unwillingly sell assets can hurt from a financial as well as an emotional perspective and can be a major obstacle on the road to financial freedom. Each of us naturally wants to protect and preserve what we've probably spent a lifetime earning for ourselves or for future generations. This is something that should not be overlooked by the Advisor for Life.

REPUTATION RISK—FOR THOSE WHO ARE PERSONALLY, PROFESSIONALLY, OR FINANCIALLY VULNERABLE

Human beings are flawed creatures often ruled by emotions rather than reason. Some of our most memorable characters are those directed by mankind's lesser traits. Consider William Shakespeare's Othello, Charles Dickens' Scrooge, and ancient Greece's mythic King Midas.

Pure human emotion can give rise to envy or jealousy manifested in hostile and hurtful actions. When asked, peers and colleagues have revealed similar issues in their lives that I never would have known about had I not asked. Query your clients. They'll likely tell you more than you ever thought possible on this topic.

What can the Advisor for Life do to circumvent any threats to a client's professional or personal reputation? Business communities tend to be very small worlds. Be sure your clients have met each of their obligations. That succession plans are in place and partners and their families fully understand business relationships. Similarly, be sure wills and estate plans are in order and each family member understands what has been decided.

THREE RULES FOR DEALING WITH RISK

First: Mary Beth Emson says, "Addressing risk is a continuum—you have to evaluate how great the risk is to each household as well as the cost to eliminate it." The cost-benefit analysis of some risks may show they are too expensive to completely avoid while giving the client a better picture of how much risk can be eliminated.

Second: Clients evaluate risks based on personal experience. Consider the long-term care prospect: Was he financially and emotionally hurt by his parents' lack of planning or is he the type who likes to take his chances? It's probably best to discuss the topic, show a sample policy, and leave a copy in the client's file in case the next generation ever comes asking why you didn't offer long-term care coverage.

Third: Everything is a question of priorities. Lay out the risks and have clients help you prioritize for them what they worry about the most, then discuss possible strategies and what it will cost to mitigate the risk to a tolerable level. Determine what kind of risk plan you can provide to your best clients to give them and their families peace of mind.

What's in It for You: Compensation for the Soul

Too often I hear from advisors that working on challenges like the ones we've examined is a waste of time—they say they "don't get paid" for solving such problems. Consider this story related by an outstanding life insurance agent and estate planner with over 50 years of experience.

The advisor had a client who was not 30, yet was a successful entrepreneur with four young children. The advisor pushed the young man to establish an estate plan, which was finally completed after a long process. Very soon afterwards, the man was killed in an accident. Had he not executed an estate plan, his family would have been in terrible financial condition. It's easy to see why this advisor is proud of his work. As tragic as the story is to hear, it has served as a constant reminder to him of how much good he can create by solving problems that clients may not be aware they have. This perspective has kept him motivated. No wonder he calls it "compensation for the soul."

Tools and Process

The very best advisory practices have tools to make the uncovering of risks simpler and easier for clients. The ability to consistently use them in an objective, demonstrable, and repeatable form is the essence of profitability.

Easy-to-use tools and an understandable, transparent process can help clients zero in on their greatest risks. Process has the additional benefit in client referrals, because those who have participated in a good process will talk to others about it with a sense of accomplishment. Contemplate the value of having solved a problem for a millionaire household and how quickly that story might make the rounds among a client's friends. This can be the best business promotion of all.

CASE STUDY: Using What and When, Two Dimensions of Risk

Building a retirement plan with conscious attention to minimizing risks means accommodating the two aspects of it: *what* might happen and *when* might it happen. In Chapter 1, I introduced my two favorite financial planning tools, the Wealth Planning Overview (what) and the Fantasy Trip chart (when). Every household needs a tool to easily pinpoint concerns and risks as well as a format in which to frame the potential time horizon for each one. Let's bring those two tools back now and have you work with a prototypical baby boomer household, the Smiths.

Meet the Average Boomer Household

The Smiths are a typical late-stage boomer household, a family reflecting most of the national trends spawned by the boomers. They have two children, 10 and 7, reflecting the trend of having children later in life (the Smiths are now 46 and 44). They have three living parents— more parents than children, another boomer trait. There is a business partner who could also be a co-worker or other colleague on whom future revenue for the family might depend.

Until you determine your clients' appetite for introspection and discussion of their most personal issues, it is best to stay at arm's length. For now you are like the canary in the coal mine—a warning, not a solution.

Figure 5.2 uses one chart to illustrate a household's primary planning issues. Oversimplified? Sure, but it's a good place to start—there will be lots of time for more detailed discussions later. Consider this part of the discussion to be like a view of life from 50,000 feet up.

As the Advisor for Life, you are visiting the Smiths and suggest an open discussion about their lives. Starting with concerns—remembering the hierarchy I attributed to Mitch Anthony in Chapter 1 suggesting we first solve problems and then discuss goals with the more relaxed client—what issues on the chart draw the Smiths' attention? Like most boomers, they seek a comfortable retirement and aren't likely to have a current estate plan, but these are not the burning current issues.

The closest expenses are those that most concern people. Retirement planning is the largest single expense on the chart, but it is a "later" expense, meaning there is some time to work on it. College

FIGURE 5.2 The Wealth Planning Overview
Source: Stephen D. Gresham, *Attract and Retain the Affluent Investor* (Dearborn Trade, 2001).

expenses for the 10-year-old are eight years away. Private school tuition could be a current expense. Aging parents may require support, and that can be both a later and a current cost. Facing family needs in the present, people typically let estate planning and retirement planning slip into the later category. Your job in this round with the Smiths is to find which areas of the chart of their life provoke the greatest fears and concerns. What do they most worry about? Where is the real ticking financial time bomb threatening the family?

For the Smiths—as it is for most boomers—the most significant and most likely unplanned expense is that of care for aging parents. So what have the Smiths done thus far to prepare for that risk? Can they talk about the topic without getting upset? What steps can they take today to begin a process of coping with the risk?

Farther in the future are the needs of adult children. Playful and dear though they may be today, the Smith kids each represent an enormous potential expense. Education, sports, music lessons, and braces each contribute to the expense of raising a child. But the chart also includes adult children. This means that parents are not relieved of the financial planning implications from children until much later in life. Failure to find jobs, broken relationships, weddings—each may lie in store for the boomer household forced to cope with the long-term needs of the younger ones. Again, what worries the Smiths? Where do they see trouble ahead? How concerned are they?

Use the chart's simplicity to limit the conversation. Even this simple chart betrays an enormously complex array of issues and emotions. Circle issues and place numbers on the three most important concerns. Which is number one? That should be the focus of your immediate work together—to provide relief from the most pressing issue. With that resolved, or at least the subject of a real action plan to eliminate it, what's the next project? After that? Use the feeling of accomplishment to propel the Smiths into problem-solving momentum as you train them to cope with reality's challenges.

Check in with timing of these issues as well. The Fantasy Trip chart from our upstate New York minister provides a startlingly clear vision of interrelationships among key family members. When viewed in conjunction with the Wealth Planning Overview, Fantasy Trip data helps further prioritize family concerns and facilitates goal setting.

Consider the Smiths' Fantasy Trip chart (Figure 5.3).

			Current Year	Plus 5 Yrs	Plus 5 Yrs	Plus 5 Yrs	Plus 5 Yrs	Plus 5 Yrs	Plus 5 Yrs	Plus 5 Yrs
Client's Name	Charlie Smith	Client's Age	46	51	56	61	66	71	76	81
Spouse's Name	Lisa Smith	Spouse's Age	44	49	54	59	64	69	74	79
Relative's Name	Jessica Smith	Relative's Age	10	15	20	25	30	35	40	45
Relative's Name	Joseph Smith	Relative's Age	7	12	17	22	27	32	37	42
Other's Name	Amos Smith	Other's Age	78	83	88	93	98	103	108	113
Business Partner's Name	Bob Patrick	Business Partner's Age	40	45	50	55	60	65	70	75
Other's Name	Barbara Jones	Other's Age	70	75	80	85	90	95	100	105
Other's Name	Patrick Jones	Other's Age	68	73	78	83	88	93	98	103

FIGURE 5.3   Fantasy Trip: Destination Unknown
Source: Stephen D. Gresham, *Attract and Retain the Affluent Investor* (Dearborn Trade, 2001).

Note their current list of key family members and consider the dynamics of having youngsters and hopefully fairly robust parents, as the oldest is 78. Of course, you can't know from looking at this data whether the 78-year-old Amos Smith suffers from Alzheimer's disease or if he can shoot his age in golf. Likewise, Barbara and Patrick Jones may be completely self-sufficient and terrific babysitters, or they might reside in a faraway state and be dependent on part-time caregivers. So what can the Smiths tell you right now about their current situation?

Begin looking forward in time across the chart to the right. Watch the aging process impact the family dynamic. By the time Charlie and Lisa Smith are in their 60s, their kids have grown up and become financially self-sufficient. But the odds are that a 30-year-old and a 27-year-old are still working on their relationship and employment issues and may very well require help. Their grandparents are at the same time becoming more likely to need care and less able to fend for themselves. The circle indicates a time when these forces come to a head, sandwiching Charlie and Lisa Smith between competing needs.

Blending these two simple exercises creates the basis for a personal retirement plan. The process—that of determining future expenses and their timing—is of course identical to the calculations used by actuaries to build defined benefit retirement plans. Since retirement planning is the most urgent boomer need and a comfortable retirement is the most desired financial goal of millionaire households (according to the 2006 Phoenix Wealth Survey), the most important job of the Advisor for Life is to help fund that retirement. And funding that retirement plan means identifying and dating the greatest known risks of the family.

Very few of us truly like to discuss our future risks and liabilities, but as the Advisor for Life, very often your true value comes by opening a discussion on these future shocks so when (and if) they do appear, they're a lot less shocking than they could be.

A comfortable retirement remains the Holy Grail for boomers, but other needs get in the way: caring for aging relatives, raising a family, health, job changes, and so forth can each take a toll on one's ability to reach long-term financial goals. The fact that our lives are stretching longer and Social Security is at best questionable only strengthens the case for long-range planning. Consider that by not discussing the sensitive issues you'd actually be shortchanging your client and providing a disservice.

Best of all, keep it simple. Good solutions do not need to be complex. They need to be sensible and easily communicated. Be sure your clients understand the reasons behind whatever it is you're recommending. Truly aiming to be the Advisor for Life can result in receiving clients for life.

CHAPTER 6

Diversification

Helping Clients Reap the Benefits
of Institutional Investing

- *What are the inherent advantages of the four-step institutional investing process?*
- *How does rebalancing impact returns?*
- *What strategies can improve portfolio diversification in the current markets?*

How do you define diversification and educate your clients about its value? Here's a way to explain asset classes so that clients understand and embrace diversification as part of the overall solution you provide. Fresh from prodding clients about their goals and assessing their real-life risks, we turn now to implementing investment strategies to help realize those goals. If long-term wealth creation through investing is part of the plan, the secret to success lies in diversification. A portfolio of complementary investments across many asset classes will power your client's future.

In "Sources of Return," David Swensen, the wildly successful chief investment officer at Yale University whose skills have added more than $12 billion to Yale's endowment over a decade, writes about the value of portfolio diversification. He says,

> From a strictly financial perspective, diversification improves portfolio characteristics by allowing investors to achieve higher returns for a given level of risk (or lower risk for a given level of returns). Generations

of economic students who learned that "there ain't no such thing as a free lunch" may be surprised to discover that Nobel laureate Harry Markowitz called diversification one of the economic world's rare "free lunches." By diversifying, investors gain risk reduction without return diminution (or gain return enhancement without risk expansion).

Based on the experience of advisors who deal with individual investors, the most compelling reason for portfolio diversification is human nature: We seem to instinctively chase performance and overly concentrate our holdings in particular investments or asset classes. Institutional investors, however, do better. (See Figure 6.1.) They're only human, too, but institutional investors have several inherent, albeit subtle, advantages over individuals. First, they typically must follow a written investment plan that lays out a long-term strategy. Pension funds, in fact, are required as fiduciary investors governed by the Employee Retirement Income Security Act of 1974 (ERISA) to have written guidelines in place to govern investments. By contrast, the most recent Phoenix Wealth Survey of millionaire households indicates that fewer than one-third have a written investment or financial plan.

Legendary investor Warren Buffett, chairman of Berkshire Hathaway, may have summed up the individual investor's problem best in his

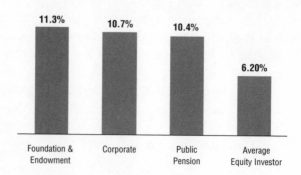

Ten-Year Average Annual Returns for Institutions

| 11.3% | 10.7% | 10.4% | 6.20% |
| Foundation & Endowment | Corporate | Public Pension | Average Equity Investor |

FIGURE 6.1 Follow the Leaders
Source: Mercer Investment Consulting (figures shown are median rank of funds in universe); "Average Equity Investor: Quantitative Analysis of Investor Behavior" Report, 2005 Update, Dalbar, Inc. As of 12/31/04.

quip, "Investing is simple, but it's not easy." By that he meant that diversification and long-term time horizons—simple concepts both—drive returns. But investing, even though simple in concept, is not easy because human emotion weakens and heightens the pressures presented by falling security prices and other disturbing macro issues. Many investors fall victim to the sins of impatience, performance chasing, short-termism, emotional rather than rational analysis, and a lack of risk management and rebalancing.

Conquering these sins requires a helping of old-fashioned institutional religion. And by that I mean the four-step institutional investment process. (See Figure 6.2.)

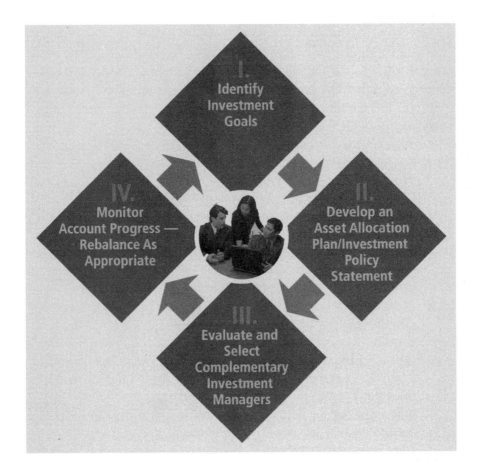

FIGURE 6.2   Institutional Investment Management Process

STEP 1: THE INVESTMENT GOAL—BEGIN WITH THE END IN MIND

The institutional investment process forces a long-term view by creating a framework for better investing. Part of the challenge of translating institutional concepts is that individuals are usually more reluctant to define their goals than is the board of a hospital endowment or a pension fund. Institutional clients have a clear responsibility for the stewardship of assets designated to benefit a specific group; individuals, by contrast, are tasked only by themselves and their individual sense of responsibility. Since individuals can be more elusive, developing a written investment goals and policy statement will tie them down and require them to think about their goals.

STEP 2: THE INVESTMENT POLICY STATEMENT—THE BLUEPRINT

An effective investment policy statement breaks out all the key issues necessary to guide the parties responsible for executing the investment solution. (See Appendix B for a sample investment policy statement.) These include:

- Income or total return goals.
- Time horizon, which is the length of time until future liquidity events such as retirement or college education are expected to occur. This is one of the most important determinants in asset allocation and risk tolerance profiling.
- *Risk tolerance.* Delineated in arithmetic form, typically as a percentage volatility tolerance, risk is really an absolute determination based on real-life requirements.
- *Asset allocation guidelines.* In addition to objective, numerical criteria, special considerations also are included, such as preferences for certain asset classes.
- *Social, environmental, and ethical issues.* Some investors, for example, may wish to avoid securities of companies that produce greenhouse gases or that supply arms.
- *Roles and responsibilities.* This is an outline of the duties of the investment advisor, investment managers, and custodian.
- *Investment manager selection criteria.*

■ *Control procedures*, specifically review criteria, timing, and rebalancing.

A good investment policy statement sets up the remainder of the four-step process, because it provides the rules of the road.

STEP 3: SELECTION OF COMPLEMENTARY INVESTMENTS

This is the section on diversification. My friend Ed Blodgett of Brandes Investment Management often reminds clients and advisors that true diversification is reached when "You're always upset about something!" Nick Murray offers another epigram: "Diversification is the conscious choice not to make a killing in exchange for the blessing of never getting killed."

A well-constructed portfolio can confound even the savviest investor because long-term success requires a level of diversification that can seem almost like overkill. Making a few big bets appears to be the nature of many investors, who have a hard time keeping track of many ideas that seem to have little in common. "Aren't we spreading ourselves too thin?" is a common query you may have heard.

But David Swensen says,

Diversification demands that each asset class receive a weighting large enough to matter, but small enough not to matter too much. Begin the portfolio structuring process by considering the issue of diversification, using the six core asset classes. The necessity that each asset class matter indicates a 5 or 10 percent allocation. The requirement that no asset class matter too much dictates a maximum of a 25 or 30 percent allocation. The basic math of diversification imposes structural parameters on the portfolio construction process.

A diversified portfolio based on a client's specific attributes outlined in an investment policy statement attempts to take away the guesswork and market timing that leads most investors down the wrong path and denies them their long-term goals. What would true diversification look like? Consider the allocation to domestic equity in all three pie charts in Figure 6.3. At the end of March 2005, public pension funds had a 45

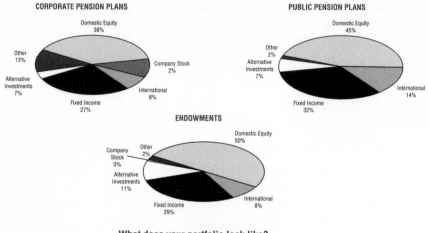

What does your portfolio look like?

Some of the investments shown above may involve higher risk. These include, but are not limited to, REITs and hedge funds. In addition, some of the investments may either not be available to the general public or require a very high initial investment for participation. As of 3/31/05.

FIGURE 6.3   Institutional Asset Allocation Return
Source: 2007 Standard & Poor's Money Market Directories, 37th Annual Edition.

percent exposure to domestic equity, while corporate pension funds allocated 38 percent to the class and endowments/foundations were at 50 percent. Contrast those numbers with the recommendations provided by many financial advisors, which, based on guidance from most large brokerage firms' research departments, are greater than 50 percent at this writing. (See Table 6.1.)

In addition to being less dominated by domestic equities, institutional portfolios are more exposed to international equities and alternative investments than are individual portfolios. (See Figure 6.4.) At Harvard and Yale, in fact, alternatives comprise nearly half the endowments' holdings. As we discuss in the next chapter, alternative investments differ substantially, encompassing real estate and timber in the case of Harvard and various hedge fund and absolute return strategies at Yale. Private equity, venture capital, portable alpha, and enhanced indexing are other alternatives that have grown to become mainstream

TABLE 6.1 Morningstar Asset Allocation Return

Last 30 Years

1976–2005	Number of Months	Geometric Mean (%)	Standard Deviation (%)
S&P 500 Total Return	360	12.72	16.92
U.S. long-term government TR	360	9.49	11.76
50% stocks, 50% bonds	360	11.46	11.35
75% stocks, 25% bonds	360	12.18	13.62
25% stocks, 75% bonds	360	10.56	10.62

Last 20 Years

1986–2005	Number of Months	Geometric Mean (%)	Standard Deviation (%)
S&P 500 Total Return	240	11.93	17.25
U.S. long-term government TR	240	9.74	10.4
50% stocks, 50% bonds	240	11.22	10.63
75% stocks, 25% bonds	240	11.67	13.47
25% stocks, 75% bonds	240	10.57	9.38

Last 10 Years

1996–2005	Number of Months	Geometric Mean (%)	Standard Deviation (%)
S&P 500 Total Return	120	9.08	17.23
U.S. long-term government TR	120	7.6	9.89
50% stocks, 50% bonds	120	9.02	9.19
75% stocks, 25% bonds	120	9.24	12.56
25% stocks, 75% bonds	120	8.48	8.15

Source: Ibbotson Associates, a Morningstar, Inc. subsidiary.

components of a fully diversified institutional solution. Slightly modified, they can be important additions to individual investor portfolios as well.

What is the benefit of having exposure to multiple asset classes, including equities, fixed-income securities, real estate investment trusts (REITs), international investments, and various alternative investments? Oddly enough, the answer is peace of mind. Modern portfolio theory posits that exposure to multiple asset classes whose correlations are

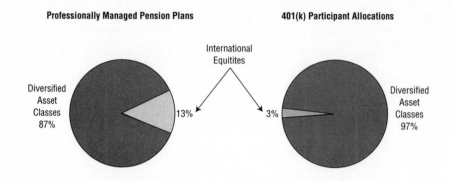

What's your international allocation?

FIGURE 6.4 Average 401(k) Investor versus Institutional Investors in International Equities

Source: Greenwich Associates, "Asset Allocation Strategies Target Incremental Alpha," February 2005; Profit Sharing/401(k) Council of America, as cited in "Case for International Investing," MFS, August 2004.

less than perfect or negative should in theory increase the return of a portfolio for a given level of risk or maintain the expected return level of a portfolio with less risk. Let's see how a $100,000 diversified portfolio for a client of moderate risk tolerance would fare against a less diversified holding. (See Table 6.2.)

To achieve an approximate 10 percent level of return, a typical 60 percent S&P 500/40 percent fixed-income portfolio has 19 percent more volatility as defined by standard deviation than the diversified portfolio and produces a lower annualized return. The diversified portfolio also outperforms an investment in 100 percent large-cap growth stocks by 110 basis points annually with half the volatility.

One of the Advisor for Life's guiding principles is to help clients avoid unnecessary risk, which we can define as more risk than required to achieve objectives. Since diversification mitigates risk, make sure your clients understand its benefits.

TABLE 6.2 Return Analysis

Portfolio	Annual Return	Cumulative 11-Year Return	Ending Value	Standard Deviation	Annual Return Divided by Standard Deviation	Sharpe Ratio
Diversified	10.3%	194.7%	$294,664	12.1%	85.20%	0.44
60% S&P, 40% Fixed	10.0%	185.7%	$285,676	14.4%	69.75%	0.35
40% S&P, 60% Fixed	9.2%	162.9%	$262,949	10.8%	85.17%	0.39
Fixed Income	7.2%	115.5%	$268,230	5.3%	135.78%	0.42
S&P	11.4%	229.1%	$329,126	20.2%	56.53%	0.32
Large Growth	9.2%	163.2%	$263,162	25.5%	36.10%	0.16
Large Value	13.2%	290.8%	$390,801	16.6%	79.38%	0.49
Mid Growth	11.3%	226.2%	$326,215	25.0%	45.39%	0.25
Mid Value	15.4%	385.3%	$485,280	15.8%	97.60%	0.66
Small Growth	6.8%	107.1%	$207,135	24.9%	27.46%	0.07
Small Value	14.2%	329.8%	$429,778	17.5%	81.14%	0.53
International	6.7%	103.1%	$203,116	19.1%	34.86%	0.09
REITs	14.6%	346.4%	$446,360	17.0%	85.55%	0.56

Assumes 5% risk-free rate
Sharpe Ratio = (Annual Return − Risk-Free Rate)/Portfolio Standard Deviation.

STEP 4: REBALANCING TO IMPROVE RISK-ADJUSTED RETURNS

Leadership changes present an opportunity for the Advisor for Life to add value through the rebalancing of client accounts. (See Figure 6.5.) There are two dimensions of this rebalancing, which should become central to your value proposition as an advisor and a key component of your practice's investment philosophy:

1. Strategic rebalancing, which returns the portfolio to the strategic allocation levels set in your initial solution and reduces risk.
2. Tactical rebalancing, which makes opportunistic, anticipatory bets on the relative value of asset classes and/or historical market patterns.

Consider the elements chart presented later in the chapter as a source of ideas for tactical rebalancing; you can see assets that have been in favor for extended periods and those long out of favor.

The value of rebalancing can be quantified. (See Table 6.3.) If we take the $100,000 diversified portfolio discussed in step 3 and add annual rebalancing, we find that we have lowered volatility by about 9 percent and increased the annualized return by 30 basis points—an increase of almost $9,000 compared to a diversified portfolio without annualized rebalancing. The effect of annual rebalancing has a similar

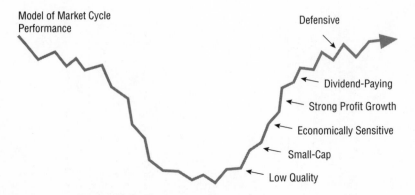

FIGURE 6.5   Investment Counsel Alpha: Rebalancing

TABLE 6.3 Return Analysis—Rebalanced

	Annual Return	Cumulative 11-Year Return	Ending Value	Standard Deviation	Annual Return Divided by Standard Deviation	Sharpe Ratio
Fully Diversified (Buy-and-Hold)	10.3%	194.7%	$294,664	12.1%	85.20%	0.44
Fully Diversified (Rebalance)	10.6%	203.6%	$303,562	11.0%	96.51%	0.51
60% S&P, 40% Fixed (Buy-and-Hold)	10.0%	185.7%	$285,676	14.4%	69.75%	0.35
60% S&P, 40% Fixed (Rebalance)	10.2%	192.0%	$292,037	12.3%	82.90%	0.42
40% S&P, 60% Fixed (Buy-and-Hold)	9.2%	162.9%	$262,949	10.8%	85.17%	0.39
40% S&P, 60% Fixed (Rebalance)	9.4%	168.2%	$262,949	8.7%	107.56%	0.50
Fixed Income	7.2%	115.5%	$268,230	5.3%	135.78%	0.42
S&P	11.4%	229.1%	$329,126	20.2%	56.53%	0.32
Large Growth	9.2%	163.2%	$263,162	25.5%	36.10%	0.16
Large Value	13.2%	290.8%	$390,801	16.6%	79.38%	0.49
Mid Growth	11.3%	226.2%	$326,215	25.0%	45.39%	0.25
Mid Value	15.4%	385.3%	$485,280	15.8%	97.60%	0.66
Small Growth	6.8%	107.1%	$207,135	24.9%	27.46%	0.07
Small Value	14.2%	329.8%	$429,778	17.5%	81.14%	0.53
International	6.7%	103.1%	$203,116	19.1%	34.86%	0.09
REITs	14.6%	346.4%	$446,360	17.0%	85.55%	0.56

Assumes 5% risk-free rate.
Sharpe Ratio = (Annual Return − Risk-Free Rate)/Portfolio Standard Deviation.

effect on the two balanced portfolios as well. And if you compare a diversified, rebalanced portfolio to a nonrebalanced large-cap growth portfolio, the impact is even greater: The diversified rebalanced portfolio outperformed the large-cap growth investor by 140 basis points annually with less than 43 percent of the volatility.

CASE STUDY: A Chance to Rebalance

The flat market in U.S. stocks in 2005 illustrated how the discipline of the investment management process benefited institutional investors. The –0.67 percent drop in the Dow Jones Industrial Average was the smallest annual change in that index since 1926, but investors seeking returns to fund their retirement plans were frustrated if they owned only those stocks.

Fortunately, bonds did better than the 30 Dow stocks. Smaller stocks, represented by the NASDAQ market index, were up more than 2 percent. Funds that invest in real estate securities were up an average of 11.75 percent, while international portfolios rose by more than 14 percent and Latin American–only mutual funds were up north of 50 percent.

Like institutional investors, individuals should have exposure to all of these asset classes in all years, rebalancing when the total gets too high. According to surveys, institutional investors had a commitment of 8 to 14 percent of their portfolios in foreign stocks. However, only 11 percent of the clients of a major national brokerage firm had any foreign equities in their accounts. If the ownership of international stocks is any guide, individuals have some catching up to do if they want to follow the path forged by institutional investors.

FOUR STRATEGIES FOR BETTER PORTFOLIOS

For advisors, the 2005 market represented an opportunity to rebalance client portfolios. I polled several top advisors early in 2006 and asked about the strategies they were bringing to the attention of top clients. One very successful advisor at a wirehouse office in New York City told me he was returning to every client who did not use his practice's asset allocation guidance, and comparing their year-end performance to that of asset classes such as real estate and emerging markets that performed well in 2005. I have included his three favorite ideas—alternative investments, international equities, and long-term growth equities—in the following discussion and added a category I call "quality." Note the simplicity of each idea. The ideas are presented as they were at the time.

Diversify with Alternative Investments

Stocks and bonds are only part of a total investment strategy. Other types of assets can enhance the long-term risk-adjusted return of a portfolio because they tend to perform at different times. For example, more than 10 percent of Harvard University's successful endowment fund is invested in real estate—much of it acquired while the stock market was going down. Specific strategies that have value as diversifiers include hedge funds, natural resources like gold and timber, as well as specialized areas of the markets, such as global utility stocks. Recent surveys indicate institutional investors typically allocate 12 percent to alternative investments. (See Figure 6.6.)

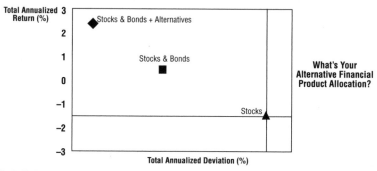

FIGURE 6.6 Diversify with Alternative Investments
Source: Phoenix Investment Partners.

Increase International Exposure

There is considerable potential in international stocks, and few long-term individual investors have allocated sufficient funds to the asset class. By comparison, institutional investors have much higher participation in foreign markets.

The growth of the global economy has fueled rising stock prices around the world—an opportunity for investors. Despite the tremendous bull market in U.S. stocks, during the 20-year period ending December 31, 2004, the U.S. equity markets lagged those of 13 other established countries, including the United Kingdom, Germany, France, and Italy. (See Figure 6.7.) The market capitalization of non-U.S. companies now exceeds that of U.S. companies.

Buy Growth Stocks

An important aspect of diversification is owning multiple investment styles, most commonly those of growth or value. Like other asset classes, investment manager styles rotate over time, moving in and out of favor.

A review of styles using the chart in Figure 6.8 depicting the recent

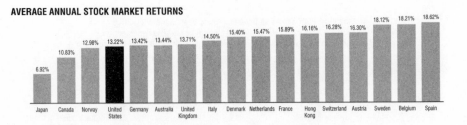

AVERAGE ANNUAL STOCK MARKET RETURNS

Historically, diversifying internationally has rewarded investors.

Average annual returns for 20 years ended 12/31/04. Returns are based on the countries' respective Morgan Stanley Capital International (MSCI) indexes that had a 20-year record. Market capitalization is the total dollar value of a company's outstanding shares.

FIGURE 6.7 Global Markets Return
Source: International Stock Investing MLIM; ZephyrStyle ADVISOR; Phoenix Investment Partners.

FIGURE 6.8 Elements of Diversification—Equity Markets

Source: Frank Russell Company.

The chart ranks asset-class performance for each year from best (top) to worst (bottom).

Year	Best	2nd	3rd	4th	5th	6th	7th	8th	9th	Worst
1989	Large Cap Growth 35.92%	Mid-Cap Growth 31.48%	S&P 500 31.43%	Large-Cap Value 25.19%	Mid-Cap Value 22.70%	Small-Cap Growth 20.17%	Fixed Income 14.53%	Small-Cap Value 12.43%	Int'l 10.80%	REITs 8.84%
1990	Fixed Income 8.96%	Large-Cap Growth -0.26%	S&P 500 -3.19%	Mid-Cap Growth -5.13%	Large-Cap Value -8.08%	REITs -15.34%	Mid-Cap Value -16.09%	Small-Cap Growth -17.41%	Small-Cap Value -21.77%	Int'l -23.21%
1991	Small-Cap Growth 51.19%	Mid-Cap Growth 47.03%	Small-Cap Value 41.70%	Large-Cap Growth 41.16%	Mid-Cap Value 37.92%	REITs 34.54%	S&P 500 30.54%	Large-Cap Value 24.61%	Fixed Income 16.00%	Int'l 12.50%
1992	Small-Cap Value 29.14%	Mid-Cap Value 21.68%	REITs 14.52%	Large-Cap Value 13.81%	Mid-Cap Growth 8.71%	Small-Cap Growth 7.77%	S&P 500 7.69%	Fixed Income 7.40%	Large-Cap Growth 5.00%	Int'l -11.85%
1993	Int'l 32.94%	Small-Cap Value 23.84%	REITs 19.67%	Large-Cap Value 18.12%	Mid-Cap Value 15.62%	Mid-Cap Growth 13.36%	Small-Cap Growth 11.19%	S&P 500 10.00%	Fixed Income 9.75%	Large-Cap Growth 2.90%
1994	Int'l 8.06%	REITs 3.17%	Large-Cap Growth 2.66%	S&P 500 1.32%	Small-Cap Growth -1.55%	Large-Cap Value -1.99%	Mid-Cap Value -2.13%	Mid-Cap Growth -2.17%	Small-Cap Value -2.43%	Fixed Income -2.92%
1995	Large-Cap Value 38.35%	S&P 500 37.51%	Large-Cap Growth 37.19%	Mid-Cap Growth 34.93%	Mid-Cap Value 33.98%	Small-Cap Growth 31.04%	Small-Cap Value 25.75%	Fixed Income 18.48%	REITs 15.25%	Int'l 11.55%
1996	REITs 35.25%	S&P 500 23.25%	Large-Cap Growth 23.12%	Large-Cap Value 21.64%	Mid-Cap Value 21.37%	Mid-Cap Growth 20.26%	Small-Cap Growth 17.48%	Small-Cap Value 11.26%	Int'l 6.36%	Fixed Income 3.63%
1997	Large-Cap Value 35.18%	Mid-Cap Value 34.37%	S&P 500 33.38%	Small-Cap Value 31.78%	Large-Cap Growth 30.49%	Mid-Cap Growth 22.54%	REITs 20.29%	Small-Cap Growth 12.95%	Fixed Income 9.65%	Int'l 2.06%
1998	Large-Cap Growth 38.71%	S&P 500 28.76%	Int'l 20.33%	Mid-Cap Growth 17.86%	Large-Cap Value 15.63%	Fixed Income 8.69%	Mid-Cap Value 5.08%	Small-Cap Growth 1.23%	Small-Cap Value -6.45%	REITs -17.50%
1999	Mid-Cap Growth 51.29%	Small-Cap Growth 43.09%	Large-Cap Growth 33.16%	Int'l 27.30%	S&P 500 21.14%	Large-Cap Value 7.35%	Mid-Cap Value -0.11%	Fixed Income -0.83%	Small-Cap Value -1.49%	REITs -4.62%
2000	REITs 26.36%	Small-Cap Value 22.83%	Mid-Cap Value 19.18%	Fixed Income 11.63%	Large-Cap Value 7.01%	S&P 500 -9.19%	Mid-Cap Growth -11.75%	Int'l -13.96%	Large-Cap Growth -22.42%	Small-Cap Growth -22.43%
2001	Small-Cap Value 14.02%	REITs 13.93%	Fixed Income 8.44%	Mid-Cap Value 2.33%	Large-Cap Value -5.59%	Small-Cap Growth -9.23%	S&P 500 -11.87%	Mid-Cap Growth -20.15%	Large-Cap Growth -20.42%	Int'l -21.21%
2002	Fixed Income 10.26%	REITs 3.81%	Mid-Cap Value -9.64%	Small-Cap Value -11.43%	Large-Cap Value -15.52%	Int'l -15.66%	S&P 500 -22.10%	Mid-Cap Growth -27.41%	Large-Cap Growth -27.88%	Small-Cap Growth -30.26%
2003	Small-Cap Growth 48.54%	Small-Cap Value 46.03%	Mid-Cap Growth 42.71%	Int'l 39.17%	Mid-Cap Value 38.07%	REITs 37.14%	Large-Cap Value 30.03%	Large-Cap Growth 29.75%	S&P 500 28.71%	Fixed Income 4.10%
2004	REITs 31.55%	Mid-Cap Value 23.71%	Small-Cap Value 22.25%	Int'l 20.70%	Large-Cap Value 16.49%	Mid-Cap Growth 15.48%	Small-Cap Growth 14.31%	S&P 500 10.86%	Large-Cap Growth 6.30%	Fixed Income 4.34%
2005	Int'l 14.02%	Mid-Cap Value 12.65%	REITs 12.17%	Mid-Cap Growth 12.10%	Large-Cap Value 7.05%	Small-Cap Growth 5.26%	S&P 500 4.93%	Small-Cap Value 4.71%	Large-Cap Growth 4.15%	Fixed Income 2.43%
2006	REITs 14.73%	Small-Cap Growth 14.36%	Small-Cap Value 13.51%	Int'l 9.47%	Mid-Cap Value 7.62%	Mid-Cap Growth 7.61%	Large-Cap Value 5.93%	S&P 4.19%	Large-Cap Growth 3.09%	Fixed Income -0.65%

◄ worst | performance | best ►

115

history of markets indicates that growth investing produced terrific gains in 1994–1999, but has underperformed value since that time. Is growth due for a rebound?

Upgrade Portfolio Quality

Another measure of investment value is quality. (See Figure 6.9.) Some companies are more successful than others, resulting in stronger growth and earnings over time. These companies are generally accorded greater value over the long term.

But in the short run, lesser-quality companies can attract the attention of aggressive speculators and outperform better-quality firms. Opportunities for investing in quality companies follow periods when high quality has underperformed. We are currently at the lowest point in the relative performance of high-quality securities versus low-quality stocks, and high-quality investing has been out of favor for three years. Is quality investing due for a comeback? There are early signs of improved performance in the quality sector.

3-Year Rolling Differential Returns of S&P High-Quality vs. S&P Low-Quality Ranking Stocks

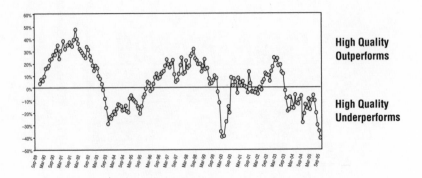

Higher-quality stocks in the S&P 500 index with an S&P quality rating of A– or higher.
Lower-quality stocks in the S&P 500 index with an S&P quality rating of B+ or less. As of 9/30/05.

FIGURE 6.9   Quality Cycle
Source: Fact Set S&P; Kayne Anderson Rudnick.

Bucking Bull Market

It's hard for even the most experienced investor to maintain composure and to focus on the long term when experiencing markets like the ones we've endured in just the past few years. Figure 6.10 depicts the performance of both the Standard & Poor's 500 index and the NASDAQ Composite beginning in 1995. There was a powerful bull market, the best in history, during the period ending in 1999, with an unprecedented 85 percent return on the NASDAQ. The following three years, 2000–2002, saw the markets collapse in the tech wreck—a traumatic and devastating decline that was the worst of all time (the 1930s market included a 28 percent deflation rate, making the 2000–2002 market the biggest decline on an adjusted basis). The real test for investors is the current period, in which there is no definite direction to guide decision making and strategy. This is the type of market in which investing guardrails are most valuable.

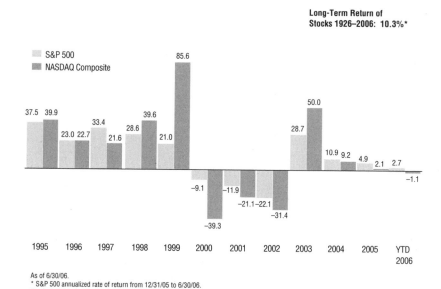

Long-Term Return of Stocks 1926–2006: 10.3%*

- ▨ S&P 500
- ▨ NASDAQ Composite

As of 6/30/06.
* S&P 500 annualized rate of return from 12/31/05 to 6/30/06.
The S&P 500 index is a free-float market capitalization–weighted index of 500 of the largest U.S. companies. The NASDAQ Composite index is a market capitalization–weighted index of all issues listed in the NASDAQ (National Association of Securities Dealers Automated Quotation System) Stock Market, except for closed-end funds, convertible debentures, exchange-traded funds, preferred stocks, rights, warrants, units, and other derivative securities. These indexes are calculated on a total return basis with dividends reinvested. Indexes are unmanaged and not available for direct investment.

FIGURE 6.10   A Picture of Volatility

Even otherwise sophisticated people underestimate the impact of market gyrations. The perspective afforded by the chart in Figure 6.10—that of an uninterrupted series of gains followed by a protracted decline—seems simple enough *in hindsight*. The bounce in 2003 seemed natural, but proved unsustainable. Most investors would not view the market from this perspective—11+ years rolled into a single picture. They instead tend to focus on individual years and discern trends based on the most recent period. You hear it in your daily conversations: "The market is doing better these days" or "The market has been slow for a long time." Note the average annual return over the 80-year history of the modern markets—10.3 percent. There are only two years on the chart in Figure 6.10 that almost match that return.

CHAPTER 7

Alternative Investments

- *Why are alternative investments natural for affluent households?*
- *How has the alternatives market grown in recent years?*
- *What are the most important categories of hedge funds—and where can your clients invest today?*

Investments outside an inner core of stocks, bonds, mutual funds, and separately managed accounts have come to be known as alternative investments. Here is a brief overview of these vehicles, with an in-depth look at the most popular of them all—hedge funds.

Item: Publisher John Hay Whitney purchases Pablo Picasso's *Garçon a la Pipe* (*Boy with a Pipe*) in 1950 for $30,000. The painting is sold at Sotheby's for a record-breaking $104,168,000 in 2004.

Item: George Steinbrenner purchases the New York Yankees from CBS in 1973 for $10 million. *Forbes* magazine estimates the Yankees are worth north of $1 billion in 2006.

These success stories have two things in common: The acquisitions were made by two wealthy Americans and they constituted investments in alternative assets that paid handsome rewards. So if great art and baseball teams are alternative investments, it's fair to ask what else falls under that umbrella. There is no regulatory or universally accepted definition of alternative investments, but many observers contend the broad investment class encompasses futures, options, and other derivatives; real estate; foreign currencies; precious metals;

private equity funds; and other sophisticated vehicles that include art, other collectibles, and, yes, sports teams. Broadly, they are assets whose performance, it is hoped, is not correlated to the variety of stocks, bonds, and mutual funds that U.S. investors have bought for years.

Why the seemingly sudden cachet of these alternatives? The meltdown in the equity markets at the turn of this century and the political-economic events that followed forced the Federal Reserve to cut the fed funds rate to historically low levels in order to stimulate growth. The low interest rates that soon prevailed contributed to a rebound in equities, but income-oriented investors were adversely affected as most fixed-income vehicles failed to provide the desired level of portfolio yield. The inclusion of international investments was intended to reduce the effect of a domestic downturn, but the increase in globalization and symbiotic relationships between the economies of the world have systematically increased the correlation between the performances of the world economies and markets. Increased volatility in U.S. markets in late 2000 spread to other markets around the world, and the inclusion of global allocations failed to reduce the overall portfolio volatility of most investors during the start of the new century. The search for investment alternatives that would not move in lockstep with U.S. equities and fixed-income markets began in earnest.

Alternative investments are not new to most investors; most have had an investment in real estate, for example, through their primary residence. The benefits of a real estate allocation and its low correlation to the equity markets became apparent when real estate prices in most of the United States exploded through 2005 as investors were able to earn double-digit and sometimes triple-digit returns on properties whose appreciation was fueled by a low interest rate environment that led to attractive mortgage rates and investors pulling money out of the stock market after the 2000 downturn.

REAL ESTATE

What is new to investors in real estate, at least, is the ability to allocate to the asset class at lower minimums and in a more cost-efficient manner. Investors can invest in publicly traded real estate investment trusts

(REITs), which were created by Congress in 1960, to gain exposure to real estate without being a direct investor in a property. REITs pool their investors' capital and invest in income-producing properties, including office buildings, shopping centers, apartment houses, and warehouses. Some REITs function as a funding source for real estate ventures. By law, in order to qualify as a pass-through entity that avoids taxation at the corporate level, a REIT must meet certain criteria, including distributing 90 percent of its taxable income in the form of dividends. At least 75 percent of a REIT's investment assets must be in real estate.

REITs pay dividends in the range of 6 percent to 10 percent due to the required 90 percent distribution of taxable income. For an investor seeking portfolio income, they provide an option other than the meager dividends typically paid by common stocks. REITs also allow investors to diversify their income-producing securities beyond corporate and municipal bonds, bond funds, and agency securities. Publicly traded REITs are much more liquid than a direct investment in real estate, and there are now more than 197 publicly traded REITs with combined assets of $330 billion that can be bought and sold daily on a number of exchanges. The asset class has grown tremendously in terms of number of publicly traded REITs and market capitalization. (See Table 7.1.)

In addition, there are number of mutual funds, closed-end funds,

TABLE 7.1 Growth of REITs

Year End	Number of REITs	Market Capitilization*
1971	34	$ 1,494
1981	76	2,439
1991	138	12,968
2001	182	154,899
2002	176	161,937
2003	171	224,212
2004	193	307,895
2005	197	330,691

*Millions of dollars.
Source: National Association of Real Estate Investment Trusts (NAREIT).

and exchange-traded funds (ETFs) that provide professional management of the asset class. These can offer broad exposure or a concentration on a segment of the REIT market like residential or commercial real estate. There are even funds that specialize in subsectors like movie theaters or medical buildings, as well as international REITs.

Including REITs in a diversified portfolio improves its risk/return trade-off and historically has provided greater portfolio returns with less volatility due to the low correlation of REITs to the equity and bond markets. Besides providing the opportunity for long-term capital appreciation and current income, REITs are an effective inflation hedge because they have the ability to increase rent payments, either contractually or by attracting new tenants.

When analyzing a REIT it is important to review not only the dividend paid but the underlying REIT company's fundamentals because the success of the business aspect of the REIT will allow it to sustain and grow its dividends over time. An investor should take a total return approach to REITs and calculate dividend yield as well as share price appreciation when investing. A drawback of REITs is that their relatively high dividends are considered "nonqualified" by the IRS and are taxed at the higher 35 percent rate. Also, in a rising interest rate environment, many REITs perform poorly because they employ floating rate debt in their capital structure.

COMMODITIES

Commodities are raw materials that are used as inputs in the production process to manufacture finished goods ultimately purchased by consumers and corporations. The commodity asset class consists of energy (oils and gases); industrial metals (aluminum, zinc, lead, nickel, and copper); precious metals (gold and silver); livestock (cattle and hogs); and agriculture (wheat, timber, soybeans, corn, sugar, coffee, and cocoa).

In a study entitled "Facts and Fantasies about Commodity Futures" that covered almost 50 years of commodities prices, K. Geert Rouwenhorst, a professor at the Yale School of Management, and Gary Gorton, a professor at the University of Pennsylvania's Wharton School, found:

> Fully collateralized commodity futures have historically offered the same return and Sharpe ratio as equities. While the risk premium on

commodity futures is essentially the same as on equities, commodity futures returns are negatively correlated with equity and bond returns. The negative correlation between commodity futures and the other asset classes is due, in significant part, to different behavior over the business cycle. In addition, commodity futures are positively correlated with inflation, unexpected inflation, and changes in expected inflation.

The groundbreaking paper further supported the benefits of including commodity investments in a portfolio in order to increase returns and lower portfolio volatility by means of the negative correlation with equities and the effective hedge against inflation.

There are a number of ways to add commodities to a portfolio. The original method was to actually purchase the underlying commodity such as a herd of cattle or bushels of wheat. This approach suffers from obvious drawbacks such as the need for physical storage and care of the asset. An investor also could purchase the publicly traded stock of a commodity producer, but there can be basis risk where the underlying commodity increases in value but the stock performs poorly because of mismanagement. Investors can trade commodities on the futures exchanges, but this can be logistically difficult due to complicated margin requirements and the variability of trader skills. Managed futures funds, which have been in existence for several decades, are funds managed by experienced Commodity Trading Advisors (CTAs) who manage money for institutions, pensions, and endowments. The capital is invested on a discretionary basis, and a managed futures fund is just as likely to be short commodities as it is to be long, which may add volatility to the asset class. If an investor is looking for long-only exposure, this may not be the ideal way to add the asset class to a diversified portfolio.

The simplest way for an investor to gain either broad commodity or subsector exposure is to purchase one of the many actively traded commodity mutual funds or ETFs. Commodity mutual funds may use commodity futures/swap contracts to gain their exposure. Newly created ETFs are a simple way to gain passive exposure to a commodity asset, and they trade the same way as other ETFs. Commodity mutual funds and ETFs have lowered the minimums required for investment in commodities and have eliminated the custody and transaction issues associated with other methods of acquiring commodity exposure. Also, investors do not have to contend with the issues of margin calls and rolling positions that coincide with purchasing and administering a futures position.

HEDGE FUNDS

The most dramatic development in alternative investments over the past five years has been the explosive growth of hedge funds. (See Figure 7.1.) Before we discuss the role hedge funds play in a diversified portfolio, it is important to understand how a hedge fund is structured and the minimum requirements an investor must meet to make a contribution.

A hedge fund is a private investment company that is created and operated under certain exemptions from registration under the Securities Act of 1933 and the Investment Company Act of 1940. Most hedge funds are structured as limited partnerships whose suppliers of capital are "accredited investors" or "qualified purchasers." Under Securities and Exchange Commission Rule 501 of Regulation D, an accredited investor may be someone who has individual net worth, or joint net worth with a spouse, that exceeds $1 million at the time of the purchase; someone with income exceeding $200,000 in each of the two

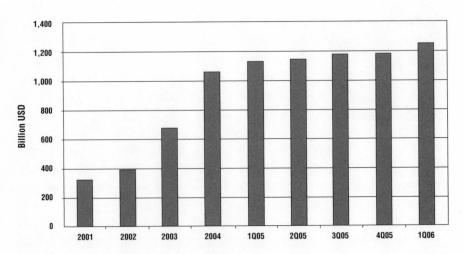

FIGURE 7.1 Hedge Fund Industry Assets under Management
Source: Barclays (www.barclaygrp.com).

most recent years or joint income with a spouse exceeding $300,000 and a reasonable expectation of the same income level in the current year; or a trust with assets in excess of $5 million that was not formed to acquire the securities offered whose purchases a sophisticated person makes.

A qualified purchaser must be a financially sophisticated investor not in need of the protection of state registration when securities are offered or sold. A qualified purchaser must own not less than $5 million in investments; those that own and invest on a discretionary basis for others must control not less than $25 million in investments. An investment in a hedge fund can be made only after an investor provides evidence of meeting the minimum requirements of an accredited investor or a qualified purchaser and has received and completed a Private Placement Memorandum (PPM).

In order to avoid registering under the Securities Act of 1933, a hedge fund must, among other requirements, make its offering available only to accredited investors and qualified purchasers; it is not permitted to market directly to the public as registered investment vehicles such as mutual funds and ETFs are allowed. Hedge fund managers must rely exclusively on referrals, word of mouth, and the reputation of the firm to attract new qualified prospective clients.

The capital supplied to a hedge fund by its limited partners—the qualified purchasers and accredited investors—is invested at the discretion of the hedge fund manager. The liability of a hedge fund investor is limited to the capital supplied, an important factor considering the use of leverage, or borrowing, in many hedge funds. Typically an investor can make a contribution to a hedge fund either in a "funds-based account," where all pooled investors have identical exposures, or a "managed account," where each investor's exposure can be tailored according to his or her appetite for risk.

A hedge fund's capital is managed by a portfolio manager (usually the general partner) or a team of financial experts. In order to limit their personal liability, most hedge fund managers create a corporation or limited liability company (LLC) to serve as the general partner. On behalf of investors, the portfolio managers design, implement, and monitor a particular investment thesis or strategy as defined in the fund's PPM. It is not uncommon for a hedge fund's portfolio manager also to be one of its largest capital providers.

Unlike mutual funds whose managers are restricted by federal law to abide by their fiduciary duty to their investors and by National Association of Securities Dealers (NASD) rules limiting sales charges and distribution fees, there is no limit on the fees that a hedge fund manager can charge. A hedge fund will charge an annual asset management fee and a performance fee based on a percentage of the fund's profits and income for the year. A typical hedge fund will charge the industry norm of 2/20, or a 2 percent asset management fee (most funds charge this quarterly, in advance) and 20 percent of the fund's profits and income (collected annually).

$$\text{(Beg Assets} \times \text{Asset Fee)} + [\text{(Portfolio Rtrn} \times \text{Beg Portfolio Value)} \\ \times \text{Perf Fee]} = \text{Total Compensation}$$

$$(\$100 \text{ million} \times 2\%) + [(10\% \times \$100 \text{ million}) \; 3 \times 20\%] = \$4 \text{ million}$$

A hedge fund can incorporate certain benchmarks known as hurdle rates or high-water marks to make the fund more attractive to prospective qualified investors.

A hurdle rate restricts a manager's ability to take a performance fee to periods when the fund's return is in excess of a benchmark index like the S&P 500. A hurdle rate rewards a manager only for the portfolio's alpha (the excess return above a benchmark or return derived from active management) and not for the portion of the portfolio's return attributed to beta (return attributed to market exposure or compensation an investor receives for exposure to the specific risks of an asset class).

$$\text{(Beg Assets} \times \text{Asset Fee)} + \{[\text{(Portfolio Rtrn} - \text{S\&P Rtrn)} \\ \times \text{Beg Portfolio Value]} \times \text{Perf Fee\}} = \text{Total Compensation}$$

$$(\$100 \text{ million} \times 2\%) + \{[(10\% - 5\%) \times \$100 \text{ million]} \times 20\%\} = \$3 \text{ million}$$

Hedge funds are expected to deliver absolute returns, and investors typically are unwilling to accept negative returns. A high-water mark requires a manager to recover any portfolio losses specific to each investor from previous periods before a performance fee can be charged to the investor during a period with a positive return. High-water marks must be tracked for each investor due to the fact that investors enter the fund at different times. Most hedge funds utilize a high-water mark.

Hedge fund managers often incorporate the use of leverage, borrowing against portfolio assets or buying securities on margin, in their portfolios. The use of leverage provides a portfolio manager with far greater purchasing power than the pooled capital provided by investors. Prime brokers, the broker-dealers who engage in the highly lucrative business of providing various services to hedge funds, have been more than willing to offer margin loans to hedge fund managers over the past few years, as historically low interest rates have made managers more willing to borrow and have increased the amount of leverage used by many funds. The degree to which leverage is used in a hedge fund can provide substantial outsized returns. But leverage also adds risk and can lead to the sudden loss of an investor's entire fund contribution. Suppose, for example, that investors put $10 into a fund, which then borrows $90 and invests the $100 total, as shown in Table 7.2. If the total investment grows by 10 percent to $110, investors would earn 100 percent on their initial $10. But let's say the $100 pool loses 10 percent and becomes worth only $90. In that case, the investors' original $10 investment would be wiped out. (For the sake of simplicity, the analysis in Table 7.2 ignores the impact of borrowing costs.)

Long-Term Capital Management, the hedge fund whose management team and board members included some of the brightest financial minds of the twentieth century, including Robert Merton and Myron Scholes, co-winners of the Nobel Prize in Economics in 1997, developed complex financial models to take advantage of the perceived fixed-income arbitrage available in the sovereign debt marketplace. The fund had a tremendous track record in its early years. For four years starting in 1994 and ending in 1997, its annual returns were

TABLE 7.2 Leverage Effects

Initial Investment	Loan Amount	Total Investment	Return	Ending Investment
$10	$90	$100	10%	$110
$10	$90	$100	−10%	$ 90

28 percent, 58 percent, 57 percent, and 21 percent, respectively. New and existing investors were making large contributions of capital into the fund, and eventually the fund stopped accepting new investors. At the beginning of 1998, the fund had $4.7 billion of equity, and its managers had leveraged the portfolio to north of $120 billion. When the Russian government unexpectedly defaulted on its bonds in September 1998, the portfolio sustained massive losses as loan providers demanded liquidation of the fund's positions. The ensuing downward spiral in the fund's value required the Federal Reserve to take action in order to avoid a disaster in the financial markets. The banking industry has taken steps with the major lending institutions to avoid a similar event in the future, but most hedge funds still incorporate some degree of leverage.

When investing in a hedge fund, an investor should review the lockup period, or the time during which investors may not remove their assets from the portfolio. Two-year lockups are common, and longer lockups are possible. Lockups enable portfolio managers to implement a strategy without fear of mass redemptions if the fund is down over the short run.

Investors can invest in a hedge fund directly, if they qualify, or through a fund of funds, structured notes, or hedgelike mutual funds. The tax implications of investing in each vehicle differ, so advisors are wise to suggest that an investor discuss alternatives with a tax expert before considering a hedge fund investment. Advisors making hedge fund recommendations should know something of the many strategies available. Here are a few of the most popular approaches. (Table 7.3 provides data.) As you will see, many are quite similar.

Equity Long/Short

This is the original hedge fund strategy created by Alfred Winslow Jones, an associate editor at *Forbes*, in 1949. Jones called his technique a "hedged strategy," giving rise to this asset class, which seeks absolute returns, often by taking advantage of arbitrage opportunities among different markets and investment vehicles.

The equity long/short approach is the one employed by the greatest number of managers and has the most assets under management. It relies on superior stock selection and usually uses little leverage. The

TABLE 7.3 Hedge Fund Industry Assets under Management by Sector

Sector	First Quarter 2006*	Fourth Quarter 2005*	Third Quarter 2005*	Second Quarter 2005*
Convertible Arbitrage	$ 33.6	$ 38.5	$ 38.5	$ 45.2
Distressed Securities	$ 78.1	$ 78.1	$ 80.7	$ 79.2
Emerging Markets	$169.9	$140.5	$130.6	$109.1
Equity Long Bias	$184.4	$170.1	$160.4	$143.7
Equity Long/Short	$201.7	$183.9	$179.0	$182.5
Equity Long-Only	$ 35.2	$ 29.6	$ 28.6	$ 19.6
Equity Market Neutral	$ 48.8	$ 47.3	$ 41.8	$ 43.2
Event Driven	$ 72.4	$ 93.2	$ 99.5	$101.3
Fixed Income	$123.1	$121.2	$129.9	$128.9
Macro	$ 59.8	$ 50.6	$ 54.4	$ 54.3
Merger Arbitrage	$ 19.2	$ 19.8	$ 19.9	$ 19.3
Multi-Strategy	$132.2	$125.2	$129.6	$136.7
Other[†]	$ 20.5	$ 18.2	$ 21.4	$ 15.5
Sector Specific**	$ 74.0	$ 68.4	$ 70.5	$ 67.1

*Industry-wide estimated in USD billions.
[†]Other: Includes funds categorized as Regulation D, Equity Short Bias, Option Strategies, Mutual Fund Timing, Statistical Arbitrage, Closed-End Funds, Balanced, Equity Dedicated Short, and without a category.
**Sector Specific: Includes sector funds categorized as Technology, Energy, Biotech, Finance, Real Estate, Metals and Mining, and Miscellaneous oriented.
Source: Barclays (www.barclaygrp.com).

portfolio manager buys (goes long) securities that are estimated to be undervalued and shorts (or purchases a put on) securities (or indexes) that are overvalued. The manager is free to select any security for both sides of the portfolio and can be long or short to any degree. Long/short is the ultimate stock picker's strategy and provides a superior manager the ideal strategy to add portfolio alpha. The strategy has a somewhat higher correlation to the overall market than a market neutral strategy, but still can provide absolute returns. The risks are in the many ways the portfolio manager may err in security selection or market timing, which can lead to large portfolio losses in short periods.

Equity Market Neutral

This is a variation of the equity long/short strategy. Here, portfolio managers attempt to use their superior security selection while neutralizing the effect of the macro environment on the portfolio. The manager selects a portfolio based on a method known as "pairs trading" in which the manager goes long a security and shorts an equal dollar amount of another security in the same sector, industry, market capitalization, or country. Stocks in the same sector tend to have returns that correlate with the performance of the overall sector, but superior companies should appreciate faster than weaker companies when the sector is advancing and decline more slowly than their peers during a sector downturn. The strategy derives most of its return from the manager's ability to select both the stocks that will outperform and those that will underperform. The biggest risk is that the manager will pick the wrong stocks for either or both legs of the strategy.

Relative Value Strategies

A perfect arbitrage is one in which a manager can buy a security and simultaneously sell it in another market at a profit without taking on any risk. Perfect arbitrages theoretically do not exist in an efficient market where securities are properly priced. In a relative value strategy, the portfolio manager attempts to lock in the price differences of two securities by purchasing an undervalued security and selling (short) an overvalued security while taking on some degree of risk. The manager attempts to reduce the position's market exposure through various hedging techniques (short sales, derivatives) and to take advantage of the perceived arbitrage opportunities in the market. These strategies usually require the use of leverage, as spreads are relatively small. The problem with relative value strategies is that a successful manager's trading strategy is usually copied, and as more managers implement the strategy the price inefficiencies can shrink or evaporate entirely. Also, the manager's long position can fall and the short position can move against him, resulting in investor losses on long and short positions simultaneously.

Opportunistic

Opportunistic hedge fund strategies seek out undervalued securities while actively looking to short securities that are overvalued. Unlike a relative value fund, the manager of an opportunistic fund does not try to hedge market exposure or attempt to attain excess returns on both long and short positions. An opportunistic fund can produce tremendous returns if the portfolio manager is able to select undervalued positions for the long positions and overvalued securities for the short positions. The risk is in making the wrong choices.

Convertible Arbitrage

Convertible arbitrage is a market neutral investment strategy that involves the simultaneous purchase of convertible securities and the short sale of the same issuer's common stock. The premise of the strategy is that psychology and illiquidity sometimes lead to pricing anomalies between convertibles and underlying common shares. In this strategy, the portfolio manager buys a convertible bond and shorts the issuer's common shares to hedge the long position and remove the effect of any stock-price movement through a process known as delta hedging. During times when there are only small movements in the stock price, the short position hedges those movements (making the position market neutral), and the investor collects the coupon payments. In addition, as a result of the short sale, is the investor earns a Treasury bill–like return from the short-sale rebate paid by the lender of the stock. If the stock price drops dramatically, however, the delta hedge breaks down and the short position will increase (when the short is covered, the manager must return the same number of shares that were borrowed, but profits if the stock price is lower) at a greater rate than the loss on the long bond position. In such cases, the investor captures the spread. If the stock price rises dramatically, the increase in the convertible bond will be greater than the loss on the short position in the stock because the convertible bond will trade at the greater of the straight bond value or its conversion value (when the stock rises, the conversion value increases as well). The risk of the strategy is that the two securities may move independently of each other and the stock price may increase as the bond's price decreases. Such a scenario was rumored to have happened in early 2006 to a large hedge fund that shorted General Motors stock and took a long position in GM bonds (although the bonds were not convertible). The bonds were downgraded during a rally in the stock's share price. Another risk is that a large number of managers may use the same strategy, so that a convertible bond's price may be bid up along with the underlying stock price and the spread that provides the return for the strategy may diminish or disappear.

Fixed-Income Arbitrage

Here, the fixed-income portfolio manager attempts to profit from pricing inefficiencies by going long and short various fixed-income instruments while limiting interest rate exposure caused by changes in the yield curve (remaining interest rate neutral). The manager will incorporate a high degree of leverage to magnify the results of the captured widening or narrowing spread between the two securities. The manager may try to exploit pricing inefficiencies between Treasuries and corporate bonds, various government fixed-income securities and municipal bonds through complex trading techniques and instruments (swaps, forwards, futures). The strategy has the ability to perform in all market environments, assuming the managers are correct in their security selections; the strategy also has a low correlation to the overall market. Risks? The strategy has been described as "picking up nickels in front of a steamroller" for its propensity to provide consistent non-stellar returns with periodic, full-blown meltdowns. It tends to perform best in low-volatility environments.

Event Driven

An event driven hedge fund strategy is predictive in nature. The portfolio manager purchases a security that seems to be undervalued due to an expected special situation or announcement. The returns are not dependent on the direction of the market, and the strategy has the ability to provide absolute returns in all environments.

There are many different event driven strategies. One is merger arbitrage, in which a portfolio manager typically takes a long position in a company that is the subject of a stock tender offer and shorts the company making the acquisition. The target company will normally trade at a discount to the offer price and the portfolio manager attempts to lock in the spread (or deal risk premium) between the offering price and the current market price of the target as the market price converges to offering price as the deal nears completion. The manager hedges exposure by shorting the acquirer and earns a short sale rebate on the proceeds. A manager also may use leverage to increase returns. The strategy requires a buoyant mergers and acquisitions (M&A) market, and the key risk involves the possibility a deal will fall apart.

Another event driven strategy involves distressed securities. Here, a hedge fund manager takes a long position in equity, bank debt, and the high-yield bonds of companies that are under duress, in default or bankruptcy, or near bankruptcy. These securities often trade at a large discount to their intrinsic value due to market sentiment, fear of the entity no longer functioning as a going concern, and the fact that many institutions are restricted from owning distressed securities. The fund manager is looking for a turnaround story that can lead to large trading profits if the manager is correct in this bet. If not, he can lose the entire investment.

Global Macro

The global macro portfolio hedge fund managers have fewer restrictions than other hedge fund managers. They can scour the globe to capture gains through leverage and the tactical use of derivatives when making investments in stocks, bonds, currencies, commodities, futures, real estate, and an endless list of other liquid and illiquid investments. These managers can market time the economy of any country or countries they choose and use fundamental or technical analysis to make decisions. One of the more famous global macro managers is George Soros, whose Quantum Group fund made $1 billion by betting against the British pound. Needless to say, this strategy, with its many moving parts and enormous information flows, is very risky, and most experienced successful global macro managers do not accept new investors.

Fund of Funds

For hedge fund investors who want to hedge their bets, a fund of hedge funds provides a diversified choice. Generally a limited partnership, a fund of funds pools investor capital and purchases a portfolio or basket of individual hedge funds. Here, the portfolio managers' value added is their expertise and ability to perform the necessary due diligence and their ability to select the best managers for inclusion in the fund of funds. Value also comes from tactically allocating the pooled capital into the various hedge fund strategies based on the fund of funds manager's perspective on the market environment. The ability to correctly time the investment into the next best-performing manager and remove a poor-performing hedge fund manager is what leads to long-term results. For the difficult and time-consuming process of analyzing the macro environment, studying the strategies of various hedge funds, and selecting 10 to 25 hedge fund managers from among more than 9,000 individual hedge fund managers, the fund of funds manager receives a fee—usually 1 percent on assets and a 10 percent performance fee.

For example, Ricardo L. Cortez, president of the Institutional and Private Client Group of Torrey Associates, LLC, a billion-dollar fund of funds in New York, points out that while there are some star managers who are able to attract enough money on their opening day so as to need no more clients, this is rare. "Most hedge funds," Cortez points out, "start out small and gather assets as they gain experience and establish a track record." Cortez says that one technique a fund of funds can employ for getting a capacity allocation with a hedge fund is to be an early stage investor. Being one of the hedge fund's first investors, when it really needs the assets, usually enables the fund of funds to get a capacity allocation so even if that manager closes to all new business, the fund of funds can still place money with that manager until the capacity allocation limit is reached.

Early stage investing also may allow the fund of funds to gain more transparency into the security holdings and strategies within the portfolio. In addition, a number of academic studies have shown that hedge funds often demonstrate better performance in the first few years of existence.

The main drawback to fund of funds investing is that extra fee layer on top of the already hefty fees charged by the hedge funds themselves. In addition, some of the top hedge funds do not permit fund of funds investments. What's more, the larger the amount of assets a fund of funds has under management, the more difficult it may be to enter and exit from investments in small and emerging hedge funds. Finally, investing in a fund of funds may unknowingly result in overexposure to certain securities held by the investor outside of the fund of funds.

Figure 7.2 shows the recent growth of funds of funds.

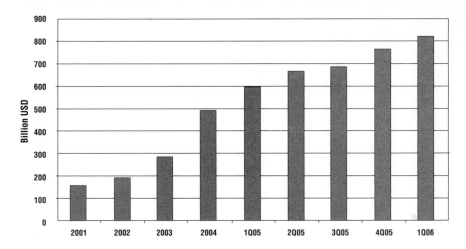

FIGURE 7.2   Fund of Funds Industry Assets under Management
Source: Barclays (www.barclaygrp.com).

Multistrategy Funds

Multistrategy funds can be thought of as a hybrid between a hedge fund and a fund of funds. An investment in a multistrategy fund is a direct investment by an investor that is managed by one investment team (similar to a hedge fund), but the pooled capital is invested in a variety of strategies (similar to a fund of funds). A multistrategy fund provides the diversification benefits of exposing a client to more than one strategy with the same level of investment that a direct investment in a single-strategy hedge fund would require. The biggest advantage a multistrategy fund has over a fund of funds approach is that the multistrategy approach eliminates the second layer of fees. And although multistrategy funds usually have lockup periods, portfolio managers have the flexibility to quickly reallocate the portfolio if a profitable opportunity can be exploited by one of the fund strategies.

The main drawback of a multistrategy fund is manager risk. Simply put, the manager can make investment decisions and/or timing choices that lead to inferior performance. A multistrategy approach also may have high asset management fees, with some approaching 4 percent and performance fees as high as 40 percent.

Other Ways to Gain Access to Hedge Fund–Like Strategies

Retail investors who are neither accredited investors nor qualified purchasers can gain exposure to hedge fund–type returns through mutual funds, investable indexes, and structured notes.

The first and probably most important advantage of the mutual fund approach is the low minimum investment. A number of the hedge-type mutual funds have investment minimums of $25,000; some are as low as $5,000. Mutual fund fees also are lower than hedge fund fees. Not allowed to charge a performance fee, hedge fund–like mutual funds often charge asset management fees slightly higher than those of a standard mutual fund to compensate for extra trading. Still, these are typically lower than the standard 2 percent rate charged by a hedge fund manager. Expenses for a mutual fund that shorts stocks may appear higher than the actual expense rate due to short dividends being considered part of the expense calculation.

Another advantage is that a mutual fund provides daily liquidity. And the daily pricing of mutual funds provides a greater level of transparency than that offered by hedge funds. Moreover, mutual funds are registered and provide lots of disclosure.

The drawbacks to the mutual fund approach are the limited strategies that are available. Most of the mutual funds that are offer hedge fund–type strategies are structured as long/short portfolios; few offer merger arbitrage, convertible arbitrage, covered call writing, distressed debt, and fixed-income arbitrage strategies. With the limited number of funds available, it may not be possible to create a diversified basket of hedge fund–type mutual funds.

Structured Notes

Structured notes are investments that pay a return linked to the performance of an underlying benchmark or index. These benchmarks or indexes can be based on any of a variety of asset classes, including equities, commodities, corporate credits, and foreign exchange. With hedge fund–linked notes, investors are paid a return linked to the performance of a portfolio of hedge funds. On the maturity date, the note pays the initial principal amount plus return, if any, based on the percentage change in the underlying hedge funds.

Since a structured note typically requires a minimum investment of $50,000, its barrier to entry is much lower than that of a fund of funds. The use of a structured note, because it is based on an index of many hedge funds, also greatly minimizes an investor's fund-specific risk. Most structured notes are continuously offered by a dealer, allowing the investor to purchase additional units at any time. Most have weekly liquidity (although there may be a redemption fee), and investors are not subject to lockup periods. Structured notes can be used in a core-satellite approach to hedge fund investing in which an investor makes a passive, low-cost investment in an S&P 500 ETF to capture market return while seeking alpha through a structured note.

A possible drawback to investing in a structured note whose return is linked to a hedge fund index or indexes is that some of the top-tier managers may not be included in the index database, whether by fund manager choice or because the manager fails to meet certain criteria to be included in the index, such as minimum asset levels, being open to new investors, and having a favorable portfolio track record. These restrictions may exclude top-performing funds that are closed to new investors and emerging fund managers that do not have the required track record or minimum asset levels.

PART III

Wealth Management Advice for Life

CHAPTER 8

Managing Dreams and Fears

A Total View of Wealth

- *How do affluent clients view their wealth?*
- *What concerns and fears can you help clients resolve?*
- *How do top advisors reconcile assets and liabilities into an overall view of wealth?*

U nreasonable expectations and unexamined fears are common barriers to the life most of your clients envision for their futures. An Advisor for Life must help clients synchronize their expectations with financial realities. At the same time, the advisor must fine-tune his or her risk-assessment radar in order to deliver the peace of mind that clients seek. In this chapter, we blend goals and risks into a single vision of the affluent household. How are they doing now—and how can you take advantage of their current position to help them succeed?

GREAT EXPECTATIONS

If the ultimate role for the Advisor for Life is to help clients prepare for and live the life of their dreams, then all but the most disciplined and wealthy clients will need assistance. Surveys tell us that most millionaires expect to receive about 80 percent or more of their working income in retirement, and that nearly half expect their assets to generate retirement income equivalent to their full current income. Unfortunately, the assets of most clients do not support such lofty assumptions. Consider that two-thirds of millionaire households report a net worth (exclusive of the primary home) of less than $2 million. Given that 31 percent of million-aires polled in the 2006 Phoenix Wealth Survey say their current income is $100,000 or less and that only half earn more than $125,000, the group's average assets are insufficient to generate expected levels of in-come for 30 or more years of retirement. The old saw in financial plan-ning was that retirees require about 70 percent of their working income once they stop working. But with retirements that stretch longer, encom-pass expensive leisure pursuits, and often include the care of an aged parent and/or subsidies to adult children—not to mention the wild card of skyrocketing medical expenses—the millionaire clients you work with today are most likely underfunded relative to the retirement they envi-sion. Few preretiree clients realistically consider the costs of retirement, and most—girls and guys alike—just want to have fun!

Your job is not to be a party pooper, but rather more of a party planner and coach. In fact, I was tempted to use "Coach" in the title of this book (although I'd probably end up on a bookstore shelf next to a biography of Vince Lombardi). History's best coaches have typically been stern taskmasters as well as inspirational leaders. The role of fi-nancial coach is often difficult—especially with specific client types—and it is clearly not a role relished by the horde of "financial advisors" (translation: salespeople) who prefer arm's-length transactions without all the entanglements.

Books about Coaches

You doubtless have your own favorite books about coaches, but some of mine include *Leading from the Heart* by Mike Krzyzewski, coach of Duke basketball and the 2006 U.S. National Team and the guy with more insight into building great teams than any other author or leader I've read, and *The Education of a Coach*, the story of Bill Belichick, coach of the New England Patriots, by David Halberstam, who has written some terrific chronicles of business, war, sports, and life (see the Introduction for a reference to *The Reckoning*, his book about the fall of Detroit's auto industry). And my favorite coaching movie is *Miracle*, the Disney version of Herb Brooks and the 1980 U.S. men's Olympic hockey team.

Whereas a salesperson gives prospects and customers what they want, an Advisor for Life guides clients to what they need. The advisory role is more complicated than the sales function and certainly more time-consuming. But it is the foundation of lengthy and profitable relationships. The role is not without risk, because it involves telling clients things they may not want to hear. For example, one advisor I know in Boca Raton, Florida, was telling prospective clients in 2005 and 2006 that he could prudently provide a current income of only about 4 percent per year on their assets; anything greater would endanger long-term inflation protection and jeopardize capital. He reports that at least half of his prospective clients were startled by the 4 percent figure and one in four bolted. But many returned to him after poor experiences with other advisors in the affluent Boca area who promised better (and less sustainable) returns.

The institutional version of the "bad news" story is also common. A top consultant in Kansas City, who has worked with many endowment and foundation boards to determine what they can afford, finds that expectations often are simply too high. Particularly with endowments, reality checks can be frustrating because the antidote to underfunding typically involves more fund-raising or reduced bequests.

Being the bearer of not-so-pleasant news, however, can have its rewards. Just as kids later thank their parents for setting limits, top clients frequently do the same, especially smart businesspeople who have achieved significant wealth because they know how to solicit and follow advice that helps them achieve their goals. Such clients are drawn to an Advisor for Life.

Risky Business

Imagine the wirehouse consultant in a small but affluent Florida city who had to report on losses sustained for the municipality by an aggressive growth manager. The exposure was so great that the fund lost millions—with the potential that the city might need to raise taxes as a result to make up the shortfall. How would you like to do business there in the aftermath?

GREATER CONCERNS

To become such an advisor, it is best to know what deeply motivates and worries affluent, successful individuals. A terrific survey conducted by my longtime friend and colleague Russ Alan Prince of Prince and Associates in connection with his recent book (with David Geracioti), *Cultivating the Middle Class Millionaire*, revealed that 88.6 percent of millionaires feared losing their wealth: not a little bit of their money—a lot or all of it. Interestingly, the more wealth held by the individuals, the more they feared its loss. Prince observed that these seemingly successful folks are "often only a few steps away from significant financial reversals." But are most advisors aware of this deep-seated fear? Hardly. Just 15 percent of advisors believed their clients are very concerned about losing their wealth. On perhaps this most basic wealth management issue, clients and advisors are not in sync.

Based on clients' biggest worry, Advisors for Life know that protection of wealth, not growth of wealth, should be their No. 1 priority. Concern No. 2 among millionaires is reducing the impact of taxes. More entry-level millionaires ($1 million to $3 million in net worth) are likely to be concerned about income taxes than those worth $3 million to $5 million (90 percent vs. 77 percent), while the latter group is quite understandably more concerned about estate taxes (22 percent vs. 82 percent). Similarly, by a two-to-one margin, the wealthiest families are likelier to be more concerned about capital gains taxes than families with more modest wealth.

One theme that runs through much of Prince's work is the disconnect between what advisors believe their clients worry about and what clients *really* worry about. That dissonance is certainly evident in the estate-tax area, where just 8.2 percent of advisors think their clients have concerns, as opposed to the 82 percent of top clients who care deeply about the impact of estate taxes.

Estate planning, therefore, remains an area of perennial opportunity for the Advisor for Life, although tackling it requires knowledge, persistence, and ingenuity. After all, as many as 75 percent of wealthy households do not have an estate plan that is less than five years old. Estate planning may be a big concern to your clients even if they have been unable to start the process. You may increase your value as an

Advisor for Life merely by initiating an estate-planning discussion that can start them on the road to achieving their objectives.

In addition to their attitudes toward taxes, Prince found that the modestly affluent differed from their wealthier cousins on other issues.

Households worth $1 million to $3 million, for example, were primarily concerned about having sufficient retirement assets. This was followed by concerns about adequate medical insurance, caring for heirs, and funding education for children and grandchildren. A sobering 48 percent feared losing their job or business, 38 percent were concerned with caring for aging parents, and 37 percent worried about a lawsuit. While also concerned about medical insurance and lawsuits, those with a net worth of $3 million to $10 million are most concerned about providing for their heirs. Lower down on their list of worries are concerns about having sufficient retirement assets, maintaining personal security, and being able to make meaningful gifts to charity.

With the lone exception of concerns about medical insurance, however, Prince found that most of the worries of both groups of wealthy clients did not even show up on the radar screens of most advisors. Fewer than 10 percent of advisors acknowledged their clients' concerns about lawsuits, personal security, aging parents, or job security. Only 1.8 percent noted charitable interests, just 28 percent were aware of educational needs, and barely half considered

Challenge for Life

A top advisor friend in Boston impressed me many years ago with his ability to bring top clients to the table of estate planning. With a managed accounts specialty, Steve was not by training an estate planner, nor did he wish to add another complex subject to his existing repertoire. Instead, he sought out a top estate specialist and created an alliance. Approaching prospects, Steve would not just ask about estate planning; he would directly challenge them: "What plans have you made to care for your family should something happen to you?" While not every prospect became a client—or even acknowledged an interest in estate planning—Steve found that some professionals would let him drive the process. Physicians and attorneys seemed to appreciate the middleman most of all.

retirement assets a potential problem. To be sure, the lenses used by most advisors to view their clients' worries yield a very distorted picture. Yet imagine how powerful the clear focus of an Advisor for Life can be!

WHAT TO DO

The profound disconnect between issues of concern to millionaires and the perceptions held by their advisors should encourage you to challenge all preparations clients have made to date. Do not assume the client has taken appropriate actions or that any previous advisor has raised or tackled important topics. In fact, don't even assume that a client's assurance that "everything is under control" is valid; clients' perceptions can be just as off-base as most advisors'. Prince, for example, found that nearly 70 percent of wealthy investors claimed to have an estate plan in place. When 101 successful private client attorneys surveyed by the team were asked to define a current estate plan, nearly 70 percent of the expert lawyers said that an estate plan that has not been updated in the past three years is "stale"—no longer current and effective. Contrast the answers given by the millionaire households who said they had estate plans: Nearly 90 percent of the plans of these wealthy investors had not been updated in three years, and more than half had not been touched in six years or longer.

Given wealthy investors' major worries and the likelihood these issues are unaddressed, an Advisor for Life must protect affluent clients from a variety of risks. Again, net worth tells more of a story—with a twist. Fully 97.5 percent of households with over $3 million in net worth had not updated their estate plans within the past three years, while their less affluent counterparts had by comparison been more diligent, with only 81.3 percent of clients failing to update their estate plans during the previous three years. Some 61 percent of $1 million to $3 million households claimed to have updated their estate plans in the past five years, compared to just 30 percent of the higher net worth families. Are the less well-to-do, those enjoying more recent successes and being more fluid, more concerned than those who have reached a higher level of affluence and don't perceive the need to further refine a plan already in place?

PROTECTING YOUR ASSETS

Lawsuit and litigation risk are often mentioned by affluent clients as concerns, yet the survey information just presented suggests that advisors are not in tune with this issue. The Prince/Geracioti data shows that more than half of financial advisors believe the majority of their affluent clients have adequate plans to protect themselves from risk of lawsuits or other confiscation. Yet the millionaire sample shows only 12.9 percent of the households have asset protection plans in place, and of those plans, more than half have not been updated in over five years. There is a lot of demand for your attention to details of opportunity when it comes to offering protection plans for affluent clients.

Asset Protection Has Many Faces

Consider the risks faced by the affluent—especially the ultra high net worth. People in positions of authority, power, and prestige are natural targets of nefarious profit-seekers. So many risks are presented to the wealthy people that they need to become attuned to their vulnerability. My grandparents on one side lived in a very small college town and because of their prominence (my grandfather was the college president), their home was always open and on display for countless visitors and guests. After his retirement from the college, their home was burglarized—the first such crime committed in that town in many years. The first man I worked for lived outside of Toronto and ran an international investment business. After a number of threats to his children, he built an imposing fence around his property and acquired a cadre of trained dogs to patrol the grounds. As a financial advisor, you are constantly at the mercy of unsophisticated clients, or their relatives and heirs, who may review your work and claim malfeasance—even fraud. You see risks every day.

Many significant risks appear during conversations with clients and prospects about their most important ventures. With such large percentages of affluent people concerned about serious financial reversals, what risks do *they* perceive in the businesses and the responsibilities they face? You may have to press for details and play the other side of their enthusiasm for a new idea. Remember the references to Ken Dychtwald's concept of a "cyclic" retirement? A great many early retirees may acquire more risk than they ever expected when diving into a new business or relationship. Exchanging one role for another may not be as easy as it sounds.

LIFESTYLE CAN BE A TRAP

We regularly hear about the free-spending boomers and how they are literally mortgaging their futures in a froth of excess. One of the greatest long-term risks to wealth is spending. Who will help the spenders bring their self-indulgence in check? Anecdotal evidence indicates that the boomers have become accustomed to car payments (did your parents ever "rent" an automobile?) and high mortgage costs. Born in the Great Depression, most of the boomers' parents were grounded in thrift and required years of economic prosperity to even consider taking on debt or buying expensive luxury items. Now such behavior is the norm.

One longtime colleague and top insurance advisor tells of his number-one contribution to his clients' wealth preservation—talking them out of discretionary major expenses. His concern is not about the vacation home or the second nice car; it's about the third home and the third car.

"In my experience, affluent people require rewards for their hard work and success," he says. "It's not my job—or my desire—to stand in their way. But I do step in when they begin talking about more. I need to help redirect them—and most of the time, they thank me for doing so."

Reality Bites

An advisor in Florida is not always so lucky. "I had a couple visit with me on referral from another client," he reports. "I gave them the budget I thought was supported by their current assets and prospective retirement income. The husband didn't say a word, but the wife responded indignantly that she just wanted 'to go out to dinner whenever I want.' Only later did I find out that the husband was shocked and embarrassed that his assets, the fruits of his longtime employment, were inadequate to support the lifestyle he had promised his wife (and himself). He was very angry with me!"

Anecdotes like these that I've gathered in this book may be helpful in guiding clients whose lifestyles are bigger than their wallets can fund. An interesting opportunity has developed during the writing of this book as the real estate markets have created windfalls for many clients. Prices have risen so far, so fast in many locales (according to Corcoran.com, in New York City the value of a three-bedroom condo has gone up 41 percent in one year!) that even relatively new owners have significant equity. A couple I know built a lavish beach home in a growing town on the fringes of the New York City metropolitan region. Newly—and early—retired from a corporate position, the couple planned to live out a very long retirement lifestyle right on the beach they had visited with their children for many years. Construction was completed about 2002. As the market for the limited inventory of beachfront homes soared, they did the unthinkable. They sold their home for a gain well in excess of $1 million after taxes and bought a much lower-priced, but very nice home on a beach street with no direct water views. One of their neighbors performed a similar trade with their long-term home near the water, selling it for over $1 million profit and buying a condominium for cash. "Now we have to walk to the beach instead of seeing it out the window," they both said. "But we've doubled our liquid assets." This unscientific sample of similarly aged folks highlights these two families as the exception rather than the rule.

ADVISOR ACTION PLAN

Don't be shy. Ask clients about the status of their estate plans. Ask about college planning, about medical insurance, and about aging parents. Ask about property insurance, too, even if such insurance isn't part of your practice. One advisor I know earned the trust of a wealthy client early in the relationship merely by suggesting that raw land the client owned be protected by insurance lest someone trespass, get hurt, and sue the landowner!

Armed with information, you should be talking to all of your top client households about their protection plans. For even the most diligent advisors, many of those plans should be updated. Consider how quickly time can pass. Life changes. Even your best work will go stale if you do not suggest a revision and note such suggestions and when they were made in client files. Just as we count on our mechanic to spot trouble with our car before it happens, your clients are counting on you to do the same.

Armed with a current view of wealth, let's now consider how wealth grows and how you can help your best clients grow along with it.

CHAPTER 9

You Can Help Clients Grow

- *What are the four phases of life advice?*
- *What is your role as a guide through a lifetime of financial issues?*
- *What is the client's responsibility?*
- *How can you help clients prepare?*

The financial planning road is a long one with many twists and turns. An Advisor for Life needs to be comfortable and confident navigating through potentially stormy seas and directing clients into a safe harbor. As you travel on your journey, consider answering the preceding questions. In Chapter 1 I introduced the concept of a financial life cycle as a clarifying perspective for both you and your clients. (The Advisor for Life Cycle is shown again in Figure 9.1.) Because most affluent people make their own money in their generation—they do not inherit it—your clients are in a constant growing and learning process about just what it means to be affluent. Without a legacy of family wealth and a ready-made group of advisors, today's well-to-do clients need to find their own paths. What an opportunity for the Advisor for Life!

The Life Cycle illustrates the financial life path of a typical high net worth household. The phases evolve from the initial savings and investment of Phase I, develop greater focus and a more specific plan in Phase II, and then move to the advanced stages of tax planning and intergenerational transfer. The upward trajectory connotes growth and development—the journey faced by the household as its financial success matures. With the perspective of an entire lifetime, it is easier for

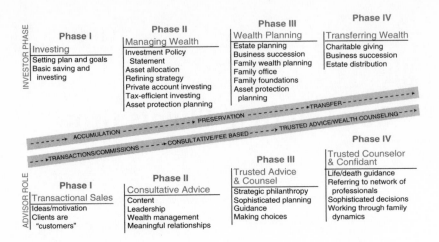

FIGURE 9.1 The Advisor for Life Cycle
Source: The Phoenix Companies, Inc.

clients to understand their current position relative to their future and to begin preparing for the next phase.

The second aspect provided by the Life Cycle is that of your role. I mentioned in Chapter 1 that the competitive bar has been raised for those advising baby boomers, as the development of investment management programs and defined contribution plans has given investors powerful asset allocation tools. Whereas advisors in the early days of the 1980s bull market were able to provide Phase II services as a competitive advantage, those are now entry-level requirements for any advisor hoping to attract millionaire clients. Just as it is important for clients to understand their journey into greater affluence and the need for increasingly complex planning, they must understand how your role grows as well. One of the perennial challenges for financial professionals is the ability to prove their value to clients so clients don't feel as though they've outgrown your ability to help them. This is truly the path of the Advisor for Life.

A third role for the life cycle is to position your competition. With so many different business models, competition is everywhere. Banks, insurance companies, brokerage firms, mutual fund companies, and direct providers can all sound the same—even to industry professionals.

The Quarterly Learning Session

A top advisor team I met many years ago in Toronto utilizes the life cycle chart to frame an educational path for its clients. Seizing the reality that most clients make their own money in their own generation, the team has dedicated itself to teaching clients how to be affluent.

The team meets quarterly with top clients. Embedded in each meeting is an educational session about a financial topic designed to advance the clients beyond the solutions currently provided to them. Clients who are Phase II investors with asset allocation and investment policies may receive specific information about estate plans or advance directives—Phase III issues. The team's approach, according to a senior partner, is to give clients the confidence that the team is always seeking far ahead on their behalf. The subtle message is: Our clients will never outgrow us.

How can clients be expected to differentiate your services? More on this issue in Chapters 12 and 13.

Just as clients need to know where you fit into their lives based on what services you offer, you need to position your competition as well. Some of the very best advisors take great care to distinguish their practices from those of competitors—and also to point out services of other popular firms that are complementary to their offerings.

Landscaper for Life

A friend who runs the landscaping division of a large nursery tells me all the time about people who buy plants and trees from "big box" home supply stores and then call him to plant the items in their yards. His prices for plants are exactly double those of the big box stores—they are better plants, of course, and the price includes planting, fertilizing, and a one-year guarantee of replacement in case they die. You get what you pay for, and you shouldn't pay for more than you need. The parallel to financial advice? The trick is to determine what the client really needs and know if such needs match your practice.

Would You Like to Try Door #2?

An advisor in Scottsdale, Arizona, has a very direct way of dealing with prospective clients. Situated for many years next to an office of a popular discount brokerage firm, he immediately asks walk-ins and referrals alike, "How can I help you? You can get a lot of services right next door for less!" Exposing early the issue of cost versus value provided has been a powerful icebreaker to start many of his best relationships.

I remember as a young advisor in the early 1980s when clients would bring in ads for budding no-load mutual funds and ask why they shouldn't buy them—essentially a not-so-veiled challenge to my practice and chosen investment options. The only appropriate answer was the one I quickly learned: "Of course you can buy those funds— why not? They are ideal for the do-it-yourselfer. Let me know how it works out!"

PROMOTING THE COMPETITION

Part of the challenge provided by working with the affluent is that they typically have some perception of your services before you've spoken a word. We'll return to this subject again in Chapter 12—differentiating yourself and your practice. For now, in the context of the Life Cycle chart, it is important to provide clients—and especially prospective clients and referral sources like CPAs—with a clear view of what you do for affluent families relative to other providers. And part of that comparative process involves highlighting what those providers do well.

Think about it. To simply say you are better than everyone else sounds implausible and arrogant. It might be true, but smart people with money need more substance. Determine what the competitor does well and immediately cede that ground. In the long run, there is plenty of room in the affluent market for a few good providers. It is the weak advisors who should fear competition.

An even more aggressive use of competitive analysis is used by another wirehouse team, which pioneered the use of case studies to help

Taking on the Trust Company

A wirehouse advisor team in Fort Lauderdale, Florida, has for many years learned how to coexist with its competitive nemesis, a well-known national trust bank. The team had lost several competitive proposals to the bank, which bundles its cost of money management with trust powers to create a single package for clients concerned about long-term protection and asset stewardship. The bundling masks the true costs of the bank's services, and linkage of trust powers and asset management discourages clear evaluation of each service. The bank's trust powers and institutional longevity give it a clear advantage over the advisor team from the affluent clients' perspective, because even though the team's firm also has a trust company, it is far smaller and barely known. Moreover, from the perspective of local attorneys—an important referral source for the team—the bank is also a potential source of new business.

Using the Advisor for Life Cycle, the team has been able to place in context the true added value of the trust bank, which is in Phase IV—the transfer of wealth. The team's primary goal is to acquire the most profitable component of the client relationship, which is the assets to be managed—Phase II. By positioning their expertise in Phase II, they allow the trust company to maintain its logical niche in Phase IV. The team goes as far as to say to clients that they support using the trust bank as the successor trustee eventually (when the clients die)—which can be very comforting for clients and their attorneys. The team promotes its value as investment manager, utilizing open architecture and multiple, unaffiliated investment managers as a process superior to that of the bank's, which has struggled to deliver a competitive offering. By ceding the trust role to the bank, the team acquires long-term assets to manage and gives up the next generation, which may be many years away.

clients understand complex services like the liquidation of concentrated stock positions. We'll revisit the case study concept in a dedicated chapter later on (Chapter 15), but for now consider the role in the case study of competition. The team and its leader, whom we'll call Sam, present different potential decisions within the case so clients can select the most appropriate path. Then the team provides a matrix of competitors, showing how other providers can address all or part of the same solutions. By not only introducing but also analyzing the role of potential competitors, Sam has found he can preempt many questions, saving clients valuable time. In my experience, most affluent professionals and business owners have neither the time nor the interest to evaluate five different referrals. They want your professional judgment about the best person for them and perhaps another referral for comparison. In all my years referring affluent families to top advisors I have found only one family who relished the process of interviewing five advisor teams in their search for a primary Advisor for Life, and this was a three-generation decamillionaire family that had outlived its previous advisor team after a 30+-year relationship.

The not-so-subtle message of Sam's approach to competition is that he is not afraid of it, nor has he often been defeated by it. Why show the competition to your prospective clients if they beat you? His team's case studies are predicated on the confidence that they won those competitions. When you deal from a position of strength, you can describe in detail every aspect of the process—and be confident as you do so.

THE ADVISORY BALLET—COMPETITION KEEPS YOU ON YOUR TOES

The reality is that the Advisor for Life has competitors for life. Get used to it, embrace it, and, more importantly, create a process for monitoring and evaluating your competition. Keep notes from every competitive situation, and review each lost and won proposal with your team. When you lose, follow up with the prospect and the prospect's advisors with questions. They should be impressed with your interest, and you may be surprised with a referral or even a second chance at a later date. But you must approach the process with sincerity and a commitment to learning how you can improve. A top advisor at a wirehouse branch in western New York State confided to a colleague of mine several years ago that he and his team, despite their apparent success, were typically "winging it" when they met with prospective clients. After losing a competition for a significant new relationship to an out-of-town competitor who had flown in to seek the account, the advisor said he "took a long look in the mirror and didn't like what I saw."

He and his team had become lazy about new business presentations because they had captured so many good clients during the bull market

> ### Decorate for Success
>
> David, a top advisor in Florida, competes so often with the local of-fice of a national trust bank that he has taken the unusual step of re-moving one more point of potential competitive advantage held by the bank. For many years, private banks and other advice firms have catered to an affluent clientele that enjoys the finer things in life. Many of these firms have created working environs that make their clients feel special. Mahogany paneling, plush carpets, fresh flowers, and china coffee cups resonate well with a portion of the affluent marketplace in David's area. Several years ago, David hired an inte-rior designer to visit several local trust companies and then to re-model his offices to resemble those of the private banks. He financed the cost from his own pocket, with the begrudging support of the branch manager. Now his office is elegantly furnished, replete with artwork and flat panel monitors in place of clunky cathode-ray tube (CRT) display devices. Nowhere to be seen is his collection of "top advisor" plaques or fund company paperweights and coffee mugs.

of the 1980s and 1990s. Heightened competition after the market crashed forced the team to an introspective mode of evaluating their abilities ver-sus those of new competitors. The loss of a multimillion-dollar prospect was a wake-up call to the team, and, true to their competitive spirit, they took up the challenge to create more focused and effective future positioning.

ASK YOUR CLIENTS

The most valuable tool for competitive analysis is an open and ongo-ing discussion with your best clients and their advisors. You want to know at all times who is prospecting in your marketplace and who provides interesting new ideas. CPA firms and attorneys are a rich re-ferrals source, and that reality makes them the constant targets of prod-uct providers who seek affluent households.

I visited a wirehouse office in Newport Beach, California, a few years ago. A top advisor there had formerly worked with affluent busi-ness owners in the local branch of a national consulting firm. He long ago realized that he could be very successful as a full-time financial advisor based at an investment firm, so he set up practice at the wirehouse. He was supplied with regular referrals from his former colleagues at the consulting firm, and built a substantial and successful practice. During my visit, though, he showed me a letter sent by the consulting firm to one of his clients whom it had referred. The firm was now touting its newly acquired financial advisory capability and wanted the client to return. Needless to say, the referral stream dried up at the same time.

The success of firms like Ernst & Young was the importance to its clients of creative tax solutions. As I noted in Chapter 8, taxes are an area of specific concern to affluent households, yet many advisors are not sensitive to those issues—especially if the taxes are related to a noninvestment issue, such as a business liquidation or transfer. Important wealth-related topics like business succession create huge opportunities for other advisors to supplant even longtime relationships. Loyalty becomes irrelevant if you don't offer the service most needed by the clients. Your job is also to make sure clients come back—staying relevant and in regular communication are two of the best ways to make sure they do.

THE MONTHLY COMPETITION BREAKFAST

You should regularly be meeting with top clients. So why not dedicate at least one meal per month to a discussion of competition? Seek out top clients who are mobile and well connected. Ask them about current issues specific to their needs and be open about your interest in maintaining a professional edge. What needs do you best fill for the client? If your team could improve in just one area, what would that be? What other firms provide a positive impression? If something happened to you, where would the client turn for advice? Next to you, who is the client's closest and most valued advisor? Why?

And don't forget online providers—has the client seen any direct appeals or ideas that are interesting and worthy of further evaluation? This open dialogue is an ongoing source of information to help you focus. It is also an invaluable forum for clients to share their observations and to better understand what you can do. If you are always asking how you can improve service and querying clients about competitors, they will be more comfortable sharing their concerns when those issues arise. Preempt your competition and tie your best clients closer to you.

THE STEALTH COMPETITOR IN THE HIGH NET WORTH MARKETPLACE

Examples abound of advice firms working their way into the books of accounting and law firms by providing complete advisory platforms that offer to shoulder the entire burden of investment management, from policy statements to asset allocation and reporting. Direct marketers have become a powerful force, with specialized software and other services to help these advisors better manage their clients. And because so many firms that directly provide services to your clients are now owned by companies in the financial-advice arena, you may find yourself forced out of long-term relationships by a competitor you thought was your ally—or at least was not in your business. Early success in this arena was achieved with accounting firms anxious to fatten their dwindling margins during the 1990s. The bear market crunch of 2000–2002 shook up many of those ventures and the less committed firms retreated back to accounting. Along the way, technology has improved to provide better solutions. It also has increasing competition. Technology is the true battlefield for service to the affluent market, and many top advisors underestimate its power until it's too late. Compounding the problem is that dependence on a small number of referral sources, especially accounting and law firms, can leave you vulnerable to changes in their business plans. If a technology platform offered to one of these firms is established that is similar to what you offer, you may find yourself battling for clients formerly referred by that same firm.

I recently addressed a group of top clients of a national clearing firm that offers far more than the simple trading and execution services of years ago. Outfitted today with a robust collection of banking services, fund management, and fee-based platforms, the firm has clients ranging from trust banks to investment advisors, small and large brokerage operations, and even accounting and law firms. These nontraditional players have the power of their client lists, and the clearing firm provides the infrastructure to harvest additional profits.

Look for linkages like those just described to be one of the most important battlefields as competition intensifies in the high net worth marketplace. Location is the key value driver in real estate, and it will have a vital role in the marketing of financial services. Consider the potential for a significant annuity or defined contribution player to extend its grip on a client after the rollover. Firms' identities will evolve to match the potential for extending the client life cycle. A firm that has captured a Phase I client for a simple transaction or new mutual fund purchase will be increasingly (if not already) capable of helping the client transition to Phase II. Software needed to track Phase I clients need not be sophisticated. Simply running a list of mutual fund shareholders above a certain asset level can prompt current direct marketers to send an appeal for life annuities or managed accounts—even referrals to affiliated financial advisors. That type of marketing is already in operation. Other more sophisticated offerings target Phase II clients in favor of charitable gift funds or trust services. To remain the Advisor for Life, you must be constantly alert to the competition for your services—beginning with your very best clients.

Bear in mind that technology can aid the small firm as easily as it can the large one. Technology is one area that regularly gets more cost-effective, meaning a small firm does not need to be shut out of the technology revolution. In fact, it's advisable for smaller firms to stay on the lookout for ways in which new technologies can help them in all areas, from marketing to reporting, and be at the forefront of change instead of trying to catch up to it.

Who is the technology chief in your office? It should be a formal responsibility and not something casually looked after by a low-level employee. A firm can save itself significant time and money by doing its technology homework well in advance. Attend trade shows and seminars. Peruse technology trade publications, and always be on the lookout for ways in which you can better put technology to work for your firm. Clients generally admire this. Better yet, it can make competitors nervous.

Advisor Questions

- How do you talk about the future with your clients? How will you work together? How will you adjust to their future needs? In other words, how will your role evolve and how will you respond to this change? How do you evaluate your competition today?
- Who is your toughest competitor—and why?
- How have you adjusted to take on and defeat your toughest competitor?

- What one or two competitors do you fear the most in the future of your practice—and why?
- What can advisors do to head off that competition?
- How do you bring up new areas of service to clients—how do you "climb the life cycle"?
- How do you identify and employ technological advances that can give you a more efficient office? Do you wait for a competitor to do so first, or do you proactively pursue such areas?

CHAPTER 10

All in the Family and Keeping It That Way

- *What roles can you play in working with an affluent family?*
- *How can you create effective family meetings to improve communications?*
- *How should you tackle key issues like college funding, estate planning, and long-term care?*
- *How are family offices addressing the needs of wealthy families?*

M ost affluent families want to preserve their wealth and pass it on to heirs responsibly. You can help them do that—if you are able to sort through the emotions that often entangle spouses, adult children, and aging parents. Let's examine those issues, as well as estate planning, advance directives, long-term care, education funding, and intergenerational responsibilities.

POSTCARD FROM A CAMPFIRE REVIEW

A number of years ago, in 1991, as head of marketing for an investment manager, I was invited to my first family retreat. The consultant to a prominent family was organizing a review of its investments and I was invited to represent my firm. The site was a bit unusual—deep in the Adirondack Mountains at the family's compound. I drove for hours to reach the "cabin," which was the largest home I had ever been in up to that time. It was a real log house, but the scale was enormous, with a fireplace that could have easily swallowed my car. The enclave held several similar but smaller homes, each dedicated to a different nuclear branch of the larger family.

The family's wealth was created many years ago; four generations would be represented at the meeting. When I arrived, the family was taking a break from the proceedings, which involved reviews of other managers. A tall, elegant lady greeted me warmly and invited me to take a seat at the table. The rest of the crowd slowly reassembled—a wide variety of characters ranging in age from early 20s to over 60 and dressed in a hodgepodge of styles—a typical $50 million family.

The investment-management consultant, Brad, distributed booklets I had brought and introduced me with an excellent short version of our story and why he included our firm at the meeting. He also added something I've come to appreciate over the years, a few very specific notes about when we would do well and when we would be expected to underperform. These guideposts were led by the words "We will expect that this manager does well when the market is . . ." and "Conversely, we will expect this manager to lag our others and the market when the market is . . ." He looked around the room for nods of understanding.

After I reviewed the portfolio performance of the previous year, I encouraged questions: "Which of these companies benefited from the Gulf War?" asked one of the younger men. "How do you define free cash flow from operations?" asked a 40ish woman. "Does this manager have a performance fee available?" asked another. "Do we utilize Steve's firm in the education trusts as well?" It went like this for two hours.

Clearly, this family knew how to handle their wealth. But since 80 percent of millionaire households arrive at their status through their own efforts, there is no embedded culture of affluence in their world; they have to "learn" to be millionaires. The Advisor for Life can be that wealth educator. Often, that means assuming a mix of roles:

The Consigliore

In the *Godfather* film trilogy, actor Robert Duvall plays advisor to Marlon Brando and the successor generation, headed by Al Pacino. Duvall's consigliore (pronounced: con-sill-yore-ay) is the antithesis of his clients in every way—a cool-headed businessman who quietly carries out important assignments behind the scenes and without bloodshed. At times he rivals Brando's three sons in intimacy to the patriarch.

Duvall's character illustrates the powerful bond possible when an advisor works with a complex family. Simply having the trust of multiple family members creates a nearly impenetrable wall to potential competitors—there is too much history and intimacy to warrant a change. Once you've earned an entire family's trust, you have achieved the pinnacle of advisory value. You have precluded competition, consolidated assets, and made yourself the center of advisory activity.

The Interpreter

Most families have intergenerational communication issues. Younger members often develop their own views, as their needs and interests differ from those of their parents. They often collide on a host of topics, so why should money be any different? The advisory challenge is—at minimum—to help each generation understand the other so that resources and time are not squandered. You may add value simply because you are not party to the angst and can restate each side's position to the other clearly and without emotion.

At the family gathering in the Adirondacks, a couple of younger members expressed concerns about investments benefiting from military contracts and others involved in chemical and pesticide production. Accommodating their values without unduly hampering the investment manager could have become a point of real contention between the older and younger generations, but the advisor coolly provided comfort to both sides. Because he had taken time before the meeting to query each key family member about their individual concerns, he had in effect "learned their language," and was prepared.

The Peacekeeper

Money issues can challenge even the closest of families. Money can consciously or unconsciously be used as a tool of control between generations or spouses to affect behavior or enforce preferences, such as when a parent withholds funds of support from a child who wants to attend the "wrong" college or who prefers living at home as an adult instead of financing their own apartment. Rebelling against that control is a natural response, and you may find yourself one of the few in the family galaxy able to remain objective. One of the peacekeeper's most valuable functions is to maintain communication during a crisis, so when the situation cools a forum for discussion remains.

The Facilitator

Maintaining open communication to various family members is a key role. The logical progression is to become a facilitator, helping to bring the parties together. Creating an open-exchange venue can by itself become the added value you provide. Family meetings need not be elaborate; they can be simple opportunities for different members to be updated on financial topics, ask questions, and acquire a sense of participation.

The Chief of Staff

Successful executives and business owners know that having a chief of staff or senior aide can dramatically improve effectiveness. Seldom is one individual able to plot strategy *and* execute tactics. The chief of staff frees the executive to think the bigger thoughts, negotiate important agreements, and remain clear of productivity-sucking minutiae.

A major complaint about both the medical profession and the financial advice industry is the lack of a quarterback or central guide to pull together the various specialists needed to help the patient or client. As obvious and important a role as this can be to a family, and especially to its primary decision maker, I'm continually surprised by how often even top advisors fail to include key specialists outside the obvious professions of accounting and law. As a consultant to the international division of a global private bank, I was once dumbfounded to hear from the chairman that his financial advisor had never suggested to him the potential benefits of a protective collar on his substantial holdings of company stock. When the equity markets dropped in 2000–2002, the chairman's family lost millions, in contrast to other executives who had applied valuable hedges. The advisor was eventually replaced, but what was he thinking?

The Master Liquidator

One of the most important capabilities for any top advisory practice is to aid in the primary liquidity event that funds a family's living expenses. Whether it's the sale of a business, processing of a retirement plan's proceeds, or distribution of an estate, your practice must swiftly assemble a team to take control of the situation and see it through to completion. I am always amazed to hear how a long-term advisory relationship evaporated because the client did not have confidence that the advisor could handle the complexity of these important transactions. Situations like the protective collar example in the preceding paragraph are common, and the area of concentrated stock ownership creates a once-in-a-lifetime opportunity for the

Providing Motivation

Scott Finlay: "The advisor's role is to motivate the client. Motivate your clients and let them know you are there to understand their fears and needs and you have hit a home run. I am an interpreter and a facilitator. For example, take clients with children. My job is to extract everyone's goals and objectives and interpret them in a way that will satisfy the needs of the entire family. Then I facilitate to create a cooperative game plan. This creates a mind-set where your client *wants* to keep you. For my older clients, I go to their homes to conduct meetings. They feel comfortable in their own environment and it makes the process flow better. For most clients, the number of meetings is determined by them, but it is usually quarterly and it is done by phone. One important point is the content of these calls: For us, this 20-minute call is 15 minutes of life and 5 minutes of business. This is how I stay on top of important family issues that can have tremendous impact on how we manage the client relationship."

client and for a potential competitor to you. Even clients who have valued your services for a lifetime will not compromise their most significant wealth transaction out of loyalty. I have watched too many times as advisors assumed they would inherit a transaction but did not because they failed to proactively present their game plan and key players.

Major liquidity events involve complex tax issues—beyond the scope of most advisors' expertise. Even a simple pension buyout can have complex structuring issues. You may have the expertise, but if you have not opened early dialogue on the topic, you may learn the hard way that they don't know that you know. And when the biggest check in their lives is hanging in the balance, they will not take chances.

MAKING FAMILY MEETINGS WORK

Whatever role the Advisor for Life adopts to educate his or her clients about family wealth matters, there will come a time when a group meeting is appropriate.

Family meetings need not be elaborate affairs in private compounds. Most families probably hold some version of the meeting to discuss issues such as vacations or weekend plans. A meeting to discuss finances is more formal and requires a good facilitator. Several top advisors attempt to create structure and guidance for their clients through family meetings.

Structuring the family part of the day requires advance planning. Most advisors I know discuss the family members with the decision maker prior to a family meeting and note any recent changes in the life of each, such as a new job, pending college application, sports team accomplishment—even a new pet. They also probe for primary concerns, like a lost job, new car expenses, upcoming engagement, or medical issues. The advisors must be able to make efficient use of their time with the family, since they will have this formal face-to-face encounter only once a year. Whenever I tell the family meeting story to advisor audiences, they typically recoil at the prospect of committing so much time to even their top households, yet when I mention this to

An Alternative Meeting Strategy: Forget Structure Altogether!

As we've seen, a successful family meeting requires advance planning and thoughtful structuring. Or does it? George, a top-level advisor in the Midwest, has discovered that allowing clients to take the lead and structure—or not structure—a meeting as they see fit often works best. "I'm the typical type A advisor, and it's my natural inclination to rush in and offer a solution or give advice almost immediately," he says. "But I've discovered that if I just keep my mouth shut, listen and not rush, clients will tell me far more about their dreams, wishes, and goals than I ever could learn by asking them. And this is not just about uncovering the assets they have with other advisors, which invariably comes out anyway. It's about helping to do a much better job for them."

George plans a full-day meeting once a year with each of his best clients during which he does whatever the client wants to do. George often hangs around a client's office or company headquarters. Sometimes he sits in on a meeting, while other times he wanders the business premises and talks to key people, such as the controller and legal counsel. He meets friends and business associates. While both family and business colleagues expressed surprise initially at George's presence, they quickly warmed to the idea. They often asked him questions about the market and investing. In addition to learning more about the clients and the potential for additional services, George immediately differentiated his level of service from that of any competitor.

"No one else was offering to spend a whole day with my clients," he said. This didn't go unnoticed by clients' friends and colleagues. Within the first few months of his full-day meetings, George had three multimillion-dollar clients by referral. He is convinced his physical presence made these referrals possible. Today, all this prospecting is done as a by-product of his one-day meetings.

"Sometime during the meeting, I ask my clients just two or three questions. First, I ask if they are happy with my service. If they say they are, I ask whether they think it would behoove me to prospect more people in their industry. Usually they say it would. Then I ask the following question and shut up: 'If you were in my shoes, and knowing what you know about me and my business, how would you go about prospecting in your industry?' I let them think about it and come up with a response."

clients, they are disappointed that such meetings take place only once a year.

Consider the following outline for planning and conducting your client family gatherings:

1. *Premeeting with decision maker.* Structure the agenda of key items by first discussing each family member. What is different about each person's situation since the last meeting or the past year? What new challenges or opportunities do they face?

2. *Create an agenda.* Since the meeting takes place just once per year, you'll want to use the time wisely. An agenda communicates the structure of the day and sets expectations for all parties.

3. *Send the agenda in advance to each family member.* Note that you are looking forward to seeing them and hearing directly how you can help.

4. *Determine the other professional attendees.* Are there issues requiring the advice of the family accountant or attorney, or both? As an advisor, I would hold annual family meetings and request at least a report from each of three distinct advisors—accountant, attorney, and life insurance advisor. For a typical half-day annual session, have the advisors attend (and bill accordingly) for only their report and discussion time, not the entire meeting. This approach reinforces your role as the facilitator.

5. *Meet at the home or a setting comfortable for all members.* Suggest that telephones be turned off and all interruptions minimized for the benefit of your time together.

6. *Hold one-on-one sessions, however brief, in advance of the group gathering.* This connection attempts to preempt the concern that you are simply executing an agenda created by the decision maker. Make sure you refer to any specific concerns or conflicts revealed in these sessions—in an appropriate way. That may be during the general family meeting or alone with the decision maker.

7. *Remain objective and relatively silent.* Ask questions, but do not make editorial comments or attempt to solve problems.

Your job is to facilitate discussion and unearth feelings. There will be plenty of time for processing the implications of what you've heard. Give everyone the chance to speak, and encourage those more reticent to share.

8. *Keep to the schedule, unless the group is clearly moving in a different direction.* The agenda is a guide, not a straitjacket. If a topic is dragging on or if one person dominates an issue, use the agenda to guide the group to more productive areas, making sure to note key concerns.

9. *Keep notes.* Make it clear that you are writing down important points so you can return to those notes when formulating recommendations. Distribute a bullet-point summary of your notes to the meeting attendees and ask for corrections and contributions. Recirculate the updated version prior to making recommendations.

10. *Determine next steps during the meeting and summarize your observations.* Ask for confirmation and prioritization of the issues tabled during the meeting. Discuss a realistic timetable to produce recommendations, and query which family members should be involved in next steps. This is an ideal opportunity for the decision maker to pass the torch and include children or disengaged spouse.

11. *Ask for comments about the meeting's value.* Ask each member what he/she learned. What was the single most important issue to that person? Were any concerns not covered? When should we meet again?

With not much more than an investment of time, a family meeting can have a lasting impact on your practice. Just think of the barrier that your strong relationships with family members would pose to another advisor. Who could scale that wall? And what about the referral value? When family members explain to friends and colleagues that they were spending a day with their financial advisor, what a boost your reputation earns! Advisor George reports that meeting days are now his number-one referral source as a result of prospective clients inquiring about the experience.

The Family Meeting

Trisha Stewart: "One of the main issues for clients is educating their children about their wealth and the responsibilities and aspirations for it. Likewise, for advisors, finding a way to build a relationship with the clients' children and to connect with both the client and their children as people is important. One way we have addressed these issues is through various seminars held throughout the year for clients' adult children. For the senior generation, these programs provide useful education that they are often unable to provide to their children themselves. For the junior generations, they not only gain new information and perspectives on their wealth and family, they also have the opportunity to meet and connect with peers—people of similar age, similar wealth, and with similar issues—in a closed and private setting. Most forums and public seminars do not provide that. It is important to be clear about the topics and level of sophistication assumed for each program. For college-age children and young adults, a program that introduces them to financial and investment concepts might be appropriate. For more mature and experienced adult children (between the ages of 25 and 45), who are beginning to think about having an active role in the leadership of the family, we hold a weeklong seminar on sustaining the family enterprise. During this week, we address topics such as family organization, creating a family governance, how to prepare yourself to take on this role, and so on. To the extent you don't have the resources to create your own educational programs or you have a client that doesn't want to be indebted to you, there are also academic programs on family business and investments available nationally and locally.

"Another way to broaden your advisory relationship with a family is in the context of a family meeting. Often, you can help the client frame the agenda, thinking through what topics to address and in what order. A simple example is a client who wants to retire and plans to hold a family meeting to decide on who in the next generation will take over the management and oversight of the family wealth. In one such instance, in talking with the client about the family and prior family meetings, it became clear that before any decision could be made about a switch, he needed to give the rest of his family a deeper understanding about what they had, how they got there, and what his goals were, and they, as a family, needed to discuss

what their vision is for the future—what they want to achieve with
their wealth and with their lives—before they decide who is going to
take over. The client decided to completely change the agenda for
the family meeting; we came in to address investment strategy and he
hired a professional facilitator to lead the family discussion of goals
and challenges. He postponed to a later date the family discussion
and decision about who fills what roles."

A WORD ABOUT FAMILY OFFICES

While we're on the subject of families, consider the operation of family
offices. The family office concept—in which a small group of professionals handles every money-related function for a wealthy family—is
as old as the money it serves. The Rockefellers and other prominent
families who made their fortunes in the nineteenth century created
family offices, many of which expanded to serve other extremely
wealthy families and grew into today's private banks and trust companies. According to high net worth experts Russ Alan Prince and Hannah Shaw Grove, authors of *Inside the Family Office*, an advisor
offering the four core services of a family office—investment management, administrative support, advance planning, and lifestyle—can
generate four times the revenue of the same services separately provided by different advisors. Thus the two dimensions of family advice—intergenerational relationships and multiple services—combine
to offer the highest profitability to the family wealth-management advisor. By maintaining intergenerational relationships, you can create
greater longevity for your clientele, and by providing multiple prod-
ucts/services you leverage the relationship's profitability while further
ensuring greater tenure.

By offering core services, your practice effectively becomes a mul-
tifamily office (MFO). Prince and Grove surveyed 234 MFOs and
found that all provided administrative services and record keeping,
which entail a host of duties most financial advisors take for granted
but that are highly prized by affluent families. These include investment record keeping, which all the MFOs provided; tax services or tax
return assistance, offered by three-quarters of the offices surveyed;

data aggregation, offered by 30 percent of the firms; and personal bookkeeping and bill paying, provided by about one-quarter of firms.

Prince and Grove also learned that coordinating external providers is a key added value of family offices. Some 84 percent of MFOs coordinate the selection and monitoring of external investment managers, and 82 percent have contact with hedge funds. Almost three-fourths of MFOs provide advance planning—legal strategies and planning tactics to reduce taxes, protect assets, enhance wealth, and facilitate charitable giving. Within this category is estate planning, which Prince and Grove report is continuing to increase in importance. Rounding out the list of top family office services are what Prince and Grove call lifestyle choices. These include providing formal family education programs; business and personal/family security; concierge services, including travel and event planning; assistance in developing and managing collections; luxury acquisition services; managing residences; managing aircraft and marine vessels; helping to find and retain chefs, nannies, trainers, and personal secretaries; and arranging for health-care services, including trust administration and emergency assistance.

Security is an interesting and evolving topic. While it calls to mind hulking bodyguards and bulletproof limousines, a closer look reveals that the four major security concerns of the wealthy are much like anyone else's: worries about the physical safety of family members, the confidentiality of personal information and data, protection of wealth from theft and fraud, and protection of property and other material assets.

Personal-safety recommendations can include kidnap/ransom insurance, especially if a family member travels to exotic locations or has a high-profile position in a sensitive area. Hiring security agents/bodyguards, private investigators, and drivers trained in defensive/evasive techniques has become more common. Even if an advisor does not routinely handle security matters, running background checks on prospective domestic workers, a relatively simple service that includes checking immigration and credit records, can pay dividends. Prince and Grove report that about 30 percent of the MFOs in their survey are currently providing family security services and that within three years that percentage will double.

CONCENTRATING ON THE CORE

But let's go back to the day-to-day reality for most advisors—who, fortunately, do not have to scout out armored limousines on a regular basis. The vast majority of the affluent families they serve are not so wealthy that they can write a one-time check for four years of college without a lifestyle hiccup or fund a decade in a nursing home for a parent with Alzheimer's. These wealthy families still require help in planning and funding life's major events, which entail educational expenses, intergenerational wealth transfer, and long-term care (LTC). Let's look at each and how an Advisor for Life can make a contribution.

Education Expenses

Even affluent households are concerned about the cost of higher education. According to The College Board, an independent education group, the average annual cost of a four-year private college during the 2005 school year was $21,235—up nearly 6 percent from 2004. Millionaires have high standards and greater expectations than ordinary families, and are willing to pay. But with college costs rising by up to 8 percent annually, all but the most wealthy will have to plan. An advisor with funding ideas can help a family pare down the extraordinary expense of college. Even for families whose children have entered their teens, it's almost never too late to start a college-funding strategy.

But costs are only part of the college headache; admission is a major worry. Help clients with the process by starting a college discussion when their children become teenagers. Let them know about local college fairs or share with them others' experiences. Encourage an early meeting with their child's guidance counselor to help them become aware of the many choices available early in the game.

Long-term funding for college could begin with a 529 college savings plan. This is often a sensible, flexible, and tax-advantaged way to save for qualified higher-education expenses such as tuition, fees, room and board, books, equipment, and supplies at any accredited college, university, professional school, or technical school anywhere in the nation, as well as at some foreign schools. Vocational schools also may qualify. Every dollar in a 529 college savings plan account grows tax-deferred until the money is withdrawn. Upon withdrawal, earnings are taxed at the child's rate. Eligibility to contribute to an account is not limited by income. Contributions in some plans may be as low as $50 per month and can be increased or terminated at the discretion of the account owner, who may realize estate-planning benefits.

More complex college funding strategies include shifting income from the parent to the student, especially when aid is not an issue. If the family owns a business, it can pay wages to the student rather than directly pay tuition with income. The student then takes advantage of the standard deduction and being in a lower tax bracket. Similarly, a child can receive a gift of stock with the intention of selling it at a lower capital gains rate and using the proceeds for college. Another choice is a 127 plan, in which a student 21 years of age or older can become an employee of a family business and receive up to $5,250 annually for higher education costs. The student's benefit is tax-free, and the business earns a tax deduction.

Each of these ideas is relatively simple, but requires time to explain fully to a client.

Estate Planning and Advance Directives

By now you've realized that my intent is to frame the various components of life advice for your practice, much as a builder might frame a house. Similarly, my treatment of estate planning is merely a framework. I am not an attorney, and I would be out of my league if I attempted to describe the nuances and legal details of a comprehensive estate plan. But estate planning is critically important for your clients, and it's essential that an Advisor for Life understands estate planning basics so that she can confidently initiate a discussion and remain central to the solution process.

The key issue in estate planning concerns how the client wants to be remembered. Lawyers, accountants, and financial experts can make sure a client's wishes are carried out most effectively and efficiently, but clients may need assistance clarifying what their wishes are. Your discussions with clients about their legacies may lead to the topic of trusts, one of the legal structures used to carry out legacy wishes, often with the purpose of minimizing the tax consequences of bequests. Many types of trusts are available, but they can be complicated and expensive to create and maintain. Only by carefully studying an individual's estate planning issues can the proper trust strategy be devised.

Trusts generally are either revocable or irrevocable. A revocable trust can be changed or canceled anytime after it is established. The federal government considers the assets in a revocable trust to be under the grantor's control, so income taxes must be paid on any revenue the assets generate. Estate taxes may be due on remaining assets at death.

An irrevocable trust cannot be altered or canceled once created. Assets placed into an irrevocable trust are permanently removed from one's estate. As this trust is considered a separate entity, any appreciation of its assets is not considered part of an estate, thereby eliminating estate tax liability.

Become familiar with the estate planning resources your firm or vendors may offer. At the same time, establish relationships with leading estate attorneys in your area. Big changes in the tax laws seem to be an annual event, and major estate tax changes are scheduled for 2010. Prepare yourself.

While estate plans are critically important to affluent families, a recent Phoenix Wealth Survey found that only 32 percent of millionaire households have an estate plan created within the past five years. If legacy issues are not enough to overcome client inertia in this area, here's a hot button that is likely to trigger action: advance directives, or the legally binding documents executed by currently competent individuals to establish the medical treatments they would want should they become incompetent. Do your clients have a living will or a health care proxy, the two primary advance directives? The Patient Self-Determination Act of 1991 encourages patient involvement in life-sustaining treatment decisions by providing patients with the right to refuse any and all medical interventions—even life-sustaining ones—if the proper documentation is in place. A living will usually permits a terminally ill patient to have life-sustaining treatments withheld or withdrawn if the patient is unable to so instruct the physician. Health care providers are also typically provided legal immunity when they execute the living will. A health care proxy, or durable power of attorney for health care, allows another person to act on behalf of the patient if the patient is unable to act or speak on his or her own. Unlike a traditional power of attorney, the health care proxy is not invalidated if/when the individual becomes incompetent. The proxy is designated by the patient with the assumption that the named proxy will make decisions consistent with the patient's values.

An Advisor for Life can segue from a discussion of living wills to broader long-term health care issues. Inquire of every key client household if they have a current plan, including directives, and if not, whether they would like assistance to execute one. Bill, a wirehouse advisor in Connecticut, says advance directives are especially important during the recovery period from a serious event like a stroke. He recommends long-term care (LTC) policies to help cover in-home or nursing home care after the assigned waiting period of the policy, which typically runs 20 to 120 days.

Only 27 percent of millionaire households say they have LTC insurance. After stocks, bonds, and mutual funds, both living trusts and LTC insurance were ranked highest among millionaires as the products they are most interested in obtaining in the next three years. No wonder. By 2020, the number of Americans over 65 who will need long-term care is expected to rise to 12 million. A U.S. Department of Health and Human Services study notes that people who reach age 65 have a 40 percent chance of entering a nursing home at some point in the future, and about 10 percent of those who do will stay there five years or more. Medicare generally doesn't pay for custodial care, and Medicaid payment requires that most of the patient's personal financial resources first be exhausted.

Knowledgeable financial advisors need to help clients estimate their specific risks—including those posed by people for whom the client is financially responsible, such as parents, grandparents, handicapped children, and possibly siblings. This includes determining how long-term care would be financed if necessary and arranging assets so adequate funds will be available if needed. Ken Dychtwald, author of *Age Wave*, estimates that 70 percent of boomer households have not held a detailed financial discussion with their parents. If boomers are to become financially responsible for their parents, the sooner that information is shared, the better. Caring for one's parents has substantial financial and emotional costs, but one way to mitigate the burden is to start talking and planning early.

The Advisor for Life can make a huge contribution here by getting this conversation started in a meaningful way. Advisors should encourage the adult children of aging parents to know the location and contents of their parents' wills, the name of their attorney, the executor of their estate, and whether there are any provisions for power of attorney in the event of disability. They should also know the location of their parents' banking, insurance, and investment relationships, and know their parents' estate attorney, CPA, and investment advisors. Adult children also should have access to their parents' most recent tax return. Have they spoken to their parents about long-term care, assisted living, or who would provide daily care in the event of a stroke or other debilitating attack?

These are all important issues in which an Advisor for Life can play a critical role.

By now, of course, some of you may be thinking: "But I don't get paid for any of this."

I hope never to hear that line again. Given the recent performance of the financial markets, we've been overpaid for investment advice. I suggest a new definition for the business of financial advising: Get paid for those services clients value enough to pay for—those that have evolved from achieving competitive investment returns to helping ensure a family's financial success. Absent the bull's return, families will require more hands-on management of their issues. And we have the most to gain from their success.

TOP ADVISORS TALK ABOUT FAMILY ISSUES

Bill King

You would be shocked at how many people lack a rudimentary estate plan. I have a friend who is a Harvard graduate of the class of 1942. At a recent class gathering the group (now in their 80s) was asked, "How many of you have a will?" The answer? Less than 50 percent. And these Harvard folks are *not* an anomaly. In so many cases, there is a gaping hole with estate plans—no executors, no health care proxies, and no wills. There is a huge opportunity and responsibility in this profession. It is to uncover this issue. You may not make much money from it at the outset, but you have to be a professional nudge. We will refer to outside legal counsel to help the client as needed and make it all fit. Through our firm's trust company, we provide executor and trustee services. We have the tools to run numbers for charitable remainder trusts. We have to add value to succeed, and this is one way we do it. We will work to provide what makes the most sense for the client and her family, now and for future generations.

Mary Beth Emson

[*Mary Beth considers the family practice of The Kelly Group at Smith Barney a true generational wealth practice with father Brian Kelly Sr. and brother Brian Kelly Jr.*]

Our practice parallels our clients' lives in that we have generations in our business as they do in theirs. The natural progression for us is to focus on three generations: founders, spouses, and family (children). We view the client and his family from an asset-liability-legacy planning perspective. Our real strength emanates from our ability to identify client vulnerabilities—health, parents, children, fear of failure, will I no longer be able to retire when I planned to?

We home in on *life* events with clients. How will their lives be affected when their wealth picture changes for the good or the bad? Some of our top client concerns are: How many homes do I *really* need? How will I pay the monthly bills and keep the lifestyle I have? What happens if one of my children is a failure and needs to come back home? What will the fallout be if the legal documents I have (trusts, wills, etc.) don't protect the family? What will I do with myself if I can't retire? These are the types of vulnerabilities we try to get the client to think about. In some cases the vulnerabilities are unknown and we have to confront them when they happen. One life event will frame the others that follow—losing a parent, experiencing divorce, having a debilitating accident. Any of these can change the financial equation that you set up with the client. Getting to the unknown vulnerabilities or the what-ifs is a hard sell in an advisory practice. These are the things that the client can't or simply won't confront, and cracking this code can take time. In some cases you just can't do it.

We sometimes have to play hardball and simply say, "What will happen to your family if you die tomorrow?" We ask, "What are your long-term care vulnerabilities?" (This is not an issue for the very wealthy client, who will use assets in lieu of an LTC policy.) "When you die, what do you want to convey philanthropically? How do you think you can gift to your children and grandchildren without killing the family initiative? How does money really enhance the next generation and the generation after that? Do you ever think that it doesn't or just can't?" In our practice, our generational approach and real-life pointed analysis help to break down the communication barriers that impede the family planning process. In a funny way, we are our own guinea pigs because we have a multigenerational practice. We understand family dysfunction and view the client from a true human standpoint, not just a numbers standpoint. We pride ourselves in knowing our clients better than anyone else—sometimes we know their issues better than they do. We even know the names of their dogs.

LONG-TERM CARE INSURANCE: DIFFERENT OPINIONS

Steve Grillo

Long-term care is an extremely important part of the investment planning process. We explain how likely it is that at some point in their lives adults need some form of care beyond what relatives can or will provide. The need for some assisted living is a concept most people don't want to face—no one likes to think they are fallible. We usually suggest that clients use the income from their investments to fund the LTC policy. We might suggest that a client take a 1 percent solution from their $600,000 portfolio to fund an LTC policy, but it is not an easy sell. We do about six to eight policies per year, which does not seem like much, but go out and try to get a late 50- or early 60-year-old to buy it. They struggle with getting their arms around this product. One scenario I use is to ask, "How would you feel or what impact would it have on your spouse if $70,000 per year was drained from your portfolio?" And that is a conservative estimate—multiply that by some number if you live in a high-rent city.

John Rafal

Long-term care can be the big scare sale of the century. In come cases long-term care [insurance] makes sense and in others it does not. We had a client who was spending so much in long-term care premiums he could have bought a small nursing home. The product is important, but it is complex and is not necessarily the right choice for all clients.

CHAPTER 11

Money for Life

- *How do your clients view retirement?*
- *How are the baby boomers planning to spend their retirement years?*
- *How will your clients make key life choices in retirement?*
- *How will your clients be remembered?*
- *What are the choices for lifetime income benefits?*

You have helped clients accumulate assets for their retirement. An Advisor for Life also must be able to help clients enjoy their savings while acknowledging and defining their goals. Here's how to help clients visualize and fund their future, as well as understand that it's okay to enjoy it.

> *"You know you have achieved the role of being the true trusted advisor when your clients look to you for permission to spend their own money."*
>
> —John Rafal

Earlier, we discussed goal setting and orienting your clients (and you) to the process of developing more definitive goals. We discovered that very few people look ahead with enough specificity. They plan for retirement in the way they might embark on a trip without bothering to obtain directions. Sure, they might reach their destination—or maybe not. And if they are men, they may wander around even longer because they won't stop and ask for help. A June 2006 survey of baby boomers aged 50 to 59 with an average net worth of $1.7 million revealed that nearly two-thirds did not have a written financial plan for retirement; 27 percent of the same sample, gathered by Phoenix Marketing International and reported in *Boomer Market Advisor*, had never discussed retirement with a financial advisor. As a demographic reminder, the boomers are fast becoming half of the affluent households in the United States, so this *is* the marketplace for your services; and they need training—fast.

Let's delve deeper into the goal-setting process. Having discussed goals in a broad sense, followed by a summary of risks and then strategies and tactics to manage goals and risks, we can now take a deeper dive into the "foundation" discussions—particularly those involving life goals. It is this arena in which the most profound changes are taking place.

BLESSINGS AND CHALLENGES OF LONGEVITY

One of the essential facts of life for baby boomers approaching retirement is that they probably will live longer, on average, than any group in history. You doubtless have become familiar with the literature on our nation's disintegrating social safety net, especially the stories about how when Social Security was established, the eligibility age was practically the same as average life expectancy. Life sure has changed since the 1930s. Ken Dychtwald, the most insightful and articulate observer of the aging trend, notes in his *Age Wave* that increased longevity is a "bonus" earned by recent generations as medical care has improved and healthier lifestyles have evolved. If you knew you would likely live only to your mid-60s, there would be no reason to plan for much of a retirement—there would be none! But as we reviewed earlier, today's 65-year-old has a 1 in 10 chance of living to age 100. What should your clients do with all that time?

Ken Dychtwald likens retirement to a surprise bout of freedom. In his talks around the country, he often asks that you imagine your spouse and you get a call from a trusted member of your extended family who unexpectedly offers to pick up your children for a weekend visit. Right after she drives away with the kids, the two of you look at each other with the realization that you are free. That feeling, says Dychtwald, is what retirement should feel like.

Of course not all of your clients will embrace that freedom—some will actually have a difficult time adjusting, particularly those with highly structured careers with lots of perks and ego satisfaction. But don't be surprised if the baby boom generation achieves a new level of growth in its retirement years. Unlike the boomers' parents, for whom longevity was a surprise, the boomers know now that they are likely to reach a ripe old age. As Dychtwald notes in *The Power Years*, his first book for the general public, "Our generation is coming to realize that we will have numerous decades to live past the age commonly thought to be the time to stop working. What we do with that time will set us apart from all previous generations."

The Advisor for Life must go beyond aiding clients to save and invest for a terminal point called "retirement." Instead, the most critical role is to help finance an extended lifestyle of unknown duration. The single most significant development in financial services during our lifetimes is the conversion from an asset accumulation model to an asset disbursement and retirement income model that is driven by the demographics of aging. The sheer complexity of retirees' interests— and the likelihood of multiple changes during retirement—will make a competent advisor the true facilitator of a successful life.

To help clients achieve the retirement of their dreams, you must offer assistance in four key areas: helping decide where to live; what to do in terms of work, education, and leisure; how they will be remembered, which encompasses legacy issues; and how they'll pay for it all. Let's discuss each area.

WHERE TO LIVE

An acquaintance in New York City, whom I'll call Roger, is a very successful trial attorney who has represented some of the world's largest corporations. His retirement is approaching, and he recently took his first big step in establishing his retirement lifestyle—buying a house in Colorado.

"My wife and I had frequented Aspen, and we thought it would be a great place to have a retirement home," he says. "The house was completed this spring and I flew out to spend a few days in June. The first time I walked in, I was thrilled. Then I looked around again and suddenly felt a wave of panic. What had we done? Was this house our retirement?! What were we going to *do*—just sit in it and be retired?"

Clearly, Roger had not thought through day-to-day living in retirement. But others have. Many early wave boomers, because of common interests in skiing or golf, have created communities organized around their favorite activities. These "senior neighborhoods" are identical in concept to the communes founded by many of the same folks when they were free spirits in the 1960s and 1970s. Gated communities with bylaws governing conduct and property ownership are springing up all over the country. They are aimed at seniors who want control over a most basic need—their homes.

The view of "home" is changing as the boomers transform the retirement landscape. As recently as 1999, fewer than one-third of retirees planned to move after retiring. Limited by a perception of mortality, previous generations didn't make elaborate plans for retirement living—who knew it might last so long? Now the number of retirees seeking a move has nearly doubled, according to study conducted by home builder Del Webb cited by Dychtwald. What are your clients' plans for retirement living? Do you know if the plans involve a move?

They may, in fact, involve several moves. My grandmother retired in 1972 and lived in four distinct locations and circumstances as she aged over the subsequent 34 years. At first, she mirrored the plans of 41 percent of current retirees—she didn't move anywhere, preferring to enjoy a more leisurely pace in the college town where she and my grandfather lived for many years. Two months a year, they would travel to a golfing community in Florida they had frequented for much of their working lives. After a few years of active, work-dominated retirement, they moved to North Carolina and an upscale assisted-living community with a country club. They maintained an active social calendar, continuing to travel and serve charitable interests. My grandfather even wrote a couple of books. They considered their new home a geographic and lifestyle compromise that was simpler than maintaining a full-time home and having an extended vacation spot.

As my grandparents aged and their mobility decreased, they demanded more support from the assisted living facility. They began using the dining room for all of their meals instead of preparing them in the kitchen of their condominium. They played golf less but still went to the club for dinner once each week. They traveled less, and had taxis take them to the airport instead of driving their own car. When my grandfather's health began to fail, medical facilities nearby were invaluable and were supplemented by the caregivers at the assisted living center's own nursing home. When he passed away in 1994, my grandmother remained in the company of close friends for some time before her own health began to wane and she moved back north to be closer to family. Still fairly independent into her late 90s, my grandmother chose an assisted living facility in Pennsylvania, and lived out her years in that location, moving eventually to the nursing home side of the development.

My other grandparents, by contrast, chose to move immediately upon retirement to a new home in Florida where they could enjoy full-time their passions of boating, fishing, and gardening. They reveled in maintaining their home and gardens and were active in political, professional, and charitable causes. They traveled only to visit family—and not often at that. They lived in that single location until my grandmother passed away and my grandfather became unable to care for the home by himself.

Just from these two examples, you can see that where one lives in retirement varies widely depending on personal taste, circumstances, and the propensity of the individual to think ahead. While not a requirement for planning retirement, a discussion about housing for the various stages of retirement can be important to have with any preretiree or the newly retired, if only because choices made early in retirement can help soften the blow—and cost—of later requirements. My Florida grandparents, for instance, envisioned and lived a very active home life, and to make that practicable for as long as possible they chose a home that afforded them single-floor living space. My own parents have used similar vision in establishing their retirement house; it is easily convertible into a dwelling that can accommodate in-home care and an escalator.

An increasingly popular retirement living option for affluent seniors is the continuing care retirement community (CCRC), also known as life care, which offers an expensive but complete solution to virtually all the possible living problems of advancing years, especially unexpected ill health issues or the disability of the individual client or spouse (and sometimes both). No other choice of senior living arrangements provides the degree of comfort, security, and peace of mind offered by a CCRC.

In general, this is how it works: The older individual (or couple) applies to the CCRC of choice, usually in a familiar area, and a screening process ensues. This involves assessment of current health and finances. If both of these are deemed acceptable, the specific living arrangements are chosen. These typically include apartments and freestanding homes of various sizes. Standard amenities include restaurant-style meals, a garage, and all living unit maintenance and repairs. In addition, most CCRCs provide attractive social and recreational facilities such as libraries, hobby workshops, and swimming pools, as well as transportation to special events. Most important, however, is that once an individual or couple is accepted and moves in, there is a guarantee of seamless transfer to assisted living or nursing home care within the facility should a move become necessary. A CCRC resident is truly set for life, no matter what the future holds.

As pointed out in the AARP web site (www.aarp.org), "Some CCRCs are affiliated with a specific ethnic, religious, or fraternal order and membership may be a requirement." Also, some CCRCs require residents to have both Medicare Part A and B.

My father, a retired physician, observes that in terms of security, comfort, and enjoyable living, "the CCRC option is clearly the best." He says that many of his friends and colleagues who developed unexpected health problems, particularly Alzheimer's disease, are incredibly lucky to have made this move before symptoms appeared. Since the only real drawback to CCRC living is the expense (AARP estimates that entrance fees range from $20,000 to $400,000 and monthly payments from $200 to $2,500), these costs should not be a problem for the affluent client. It is certainly worthwhile for seniors to investigate this option carefully—and early. Once health problems become manifest, it is too late to expect acceptance by a CCRC. All affluent seniors and their financial advisors should become informed about the advantages offered by CCRCs.

RETIRE TO . . . WORK?

Most millionaire boomers say work will play a role in retirement, less for the money and more because they enjoy what they are doing or what they envision themselves doing. But I expect that economic need will become far more powerful a driver of working in retirement as boomers move into their 50s and 60s and begin making the calculations reviewed earlier. Simply put, they will need more income than their current assets can generate. That's why you should be helping to guide your boomer clients' dreams into reality and challenge them to develop concrete plans for their hazily visualized futures. For example, the overachieving boomer professional may see a teaching career after years in the corporate pressure cooker. Does she know what she'll have to do in order to earn such a spot on the roster of a local college? Teaching certification and an advanced degree in education or her chosen topic are typical entry-level requirements. Does she have those in place, or a plan to get them? A professor at my college was a very successful real estate executive and "retired" to pursue a lifelong interest in higher education. He was ultimately successful in achieving a professorship, but he had dramatically underestimated the amount of time needed to acquire the master's degree required by the school.

What kind of work do boomers want in retirement? Ken Dychtwald surveyed boomers and discovered that their plans coalesced into five groups:

Cycling between Periods of Work, Education, and Leisure—40 Percent

The characteristics of this lifestyle have freedom and independence written all over them. Not wanting to be bound by any single vocation or activity, this largest group of boomers will seek variety supported by their newfound freedom. How they manage the cyclicity will become a job unto itself, and many will relish the ability to experiment and explore.

Part-Time Work—19 Percent

Consulting, job sharing, and telecommuting are already mainstream in most service industries today. As many of your clients near retirement, their best bet for a challenging retirement job may be a reduced version of the one they have today. There is also a possibility that the current employer will maintain benefits—an important consideration for retirees. Finally, the part-time job allows a newly retired professional to test the waters of retirement without having to take the deep dive. The self-esteem and self-actualization provided by a successful career can be difficult to relinquish and—for most people—nearly impossible to replace. Continuing on at some level is a great option for professors, teachers, lawyers, physicians, veterinarians—even financial advisors.

One often overlooked aspect of the boomer retirement wave is that a relative worker shortage will result as their demographic cohort departs the full-time job scene. Skilled older workers will be in demand to fill in gaps of experience, knowledge, work ethic, and maturity. Smart companies will take advantage of these employees, using them as mentors and counselors to the next generation. The Society of Human Resource Management reports that 41 percent of its corporate members are now utilizing former employees as consultants.

Another dimension of part-time work is, of course, the possibility of obtaining a job in a new or unrelated field. What hobbies or other interests might permit one of your clients to work for another industry if there is less of a need to earn a high income? A colleague of mine nearing retirement has been working part-time as a golf teacher, and plans to continue as his passion develops into a full-time pursuit after his formal retirement. I recently became acquainted with a retired airline pilot who now works part-time at the garden center I frequent on the Connecticut shoreline. He admits to spending most of his income on additional plants for his home and those of his friends. "The discount is terrific!" he enthuses. My mother has taken her lifelong interest in gardening and nature and works part-time at the national wildlife refuge near her home in Florida. A nearly retired friend of mine is an accomplished and wealthy sales professional who is pursuing his Certified Financial Planner (CFP) designation with the confidence that he will at least learn information that will help him manage his own finances. What would you do if you didn't care about how much you earned?

Start Own Business—10 Percent

A passion, hobby, or interest may stimulate more entrepreneurial energy than can be satisfied with a part-time job. A hard-charging executive may relish a new challenge—the only difference among your clients may be the scale of these ventures. A top advisory practice I know in New York City has been working with the CEO of a public company that was recently acquired. The buyout's terms require the executive to remain with the company as it transitions to the new owners over the next two years. After that time, the advisors know, their client will want to get back into the game. "It's in his DNA," observes the practice's principal, who is busy looking for potential partners to help his client raise capital.

Full-Time Work—5 Percent

"Why change?" ask these survey respondents. You doubtless know a few of these folks, many of whom suffer from a lopsided life devoted to work. But don't underestimate the value of the status quo to some people. They may have achieved a perfect balance with work, leisure, and family life and may not see a reason to alter their current life—including a full-time job. I have met many financial advisors who fit this description. One sage professional in the Philadelphia area was well into his 80s when I met him in 1989, and still commuting by train from the Main Line to Center City. Another great father/son team, the Merrimans, became an institution in Providence, Rhode Island, providing services to clients when the elder Merriman was past 90!

Not Work for Pay Again—19 Percent

This is the group that wants to hang up its spurs for good. Noting that the study's sample is across income levels, Dychtwald observes that these folks tend to have lower education levels and have been toiling at less-fulfilling or lower-paying jobs. The affluent boomer retirees that are your target market are not often found in this category.

"Other" retirement-life plans were held by 6 percent of boomers.

Because most of the baby boom generation is currently under-funded relative to projected retirement income needs, the discussion of employment should be central to any retirement planning efforts. The possibility of being forced back to work is a very real risk and best considered earlier in retirement. An interesting way to illustrate the importance of earned income relative to investment (unearned) income is to simply compare the two. Suppose your client earns $25,000 (after taxes) from a part-time job. To generate that kind of annual income, at this writing your client would need nearly $600,000 in capital, assuming a return of 4 percent on a double-tax-free municipal bond. A little extra earned income goes a long way!

ENJOYING LEISURE

Leisure can involve travel for fun, a hobby, a sport—and probably all three. While it's unlikely that much of the boomer generation will simply plunk down in a lawn chair and grab a fishing rod, there is a powerful tonic of freedom and independence that will support renewed interest in dormant pastimes or the opportunity to take up new interests.

Leisure time is also social time. Organized forms of leisure activity will dominate the scene, such as bicycle and motorcycle clubs, birding and travel groups, and classes for cooking and gardening. These activities provide social interaction, highly valued by retirees seeking camaraderie as well as a way to explore these hobbies.

Your contribution to clients' enjoyment of their leisure time may not be obvious or even necessary. But consider that high-income professionals and entrepreneurs may have suppressed their "leisure genes" during years of hard work and might benefit from a little boost from you. A wirehouse branch office I know in Pittsburgh partnered with a local travel agency to hold a workshop for affluent clients interested in a partial or full world tour. Well-to-do clients like the concept of tailored services instead of joining a charter junket, so there was significant interest in building trips customized to the families—especially to specific countries and sights. We review more strategies for driving referrals in Chapter 15, but remember that helping clients with fulfilling leisure-time activities can be a strategy for promoting your practice.

One leisure activity, adult education, continues to grow in popularity. In 1970, about 5 percent of college students were 35 years old or older. Today that number exceeds 22 percent—more than one in five students nationwide. Retirees are filling up college courses as well as teaching at the college level and at extension schools. My father was recruited to teach a course for an extension university in Florida on the topic of taking charge of your own health care—a course for seniors taught by one of their own!

What programs are available in your area at local universities, colleges, and community colleges? I was surprised to learn that my university had a very active local extension program and that both faculty and local alumni participated broadly. Do you have a relationship with schools that you can leverage with clients—if only to help clients see the potential for educational experiences? You might consider providing a course yourself, as do many advisors, on some aspect of financial advice or capital market theory.

HOW THEY'LL BE REMEMBERED

My father and fellow columnist, retired physician Dr. Glen Gresham, offers the following anecdote: A patient fidgeted in his chair in a doctor's waiting room. Impatient as always, he was torn between complaining about being kept waiting and a creeping anxiety about what the doctor might tell him. Approaching 60, he had always been healthy, hard-charging, and successful. His marriage was still solid, his kids were launched on promising careers, he still excelled at tennis, and he had no financial worries. There were, however, clouds gathering on his horizon.

For several months, he hadn't felt quite up to par. He was frequently tired, was sometimes edgy, and had "gut problems." His initial hope that this would all just go away was fading and, when his urine turned dark, he caved in and called the doctor.

He was in the doctor's office well over the anticipated 15 minutes. When he emerged he felt dazed and, for the first time, deeply afraid. He automatically took his sheaf of test orders and referrals, nodded reflexively when told to "have a nice day," and felt his perfect world collapsing around him. Within a week, he had been through what seemed like an endless battery of tests and was hospitalized for exploratory abdominal surgery. The verdict was totally ominous: He had cancer of the pancreas; it had started to spread and he would probably be dead in a matter of months.

What to do now? Go to bed and stay there? Commit suicide? Have a last big fling? Pray for a miracle? Go to Mexico for some radical treatment? He could see no way out. He would have to accept his fate. As his family and associates watched, he rallied and turned his attention to two goals: making every day count and doing all he could to make sure that his life had counted for something. After a few days in deep thought, he picked up the telephone and called his trusted financial advisor to help him carry out his wishes.

WHEN THE END IS NEAR

Unlike someone in his or her late 80s or 90s, people stricken with a terminal illness in their prime seem to have been dealt a terribly unfair and tragic sentence. Yet, after the shock begins to wear off, most patients acquire a sense of purpose and an almost resigned serenity about their situation, says my father. Psychologists and gerontologists suggest that it is the definitive nature of their condition that provides the calm. After a lifetime of planning and worrying about unknown liabilities and risks, terminally ill patients know for sure what will happen. That certainty helps them frame their remaining days with clarity and purpose.

At no other time of life does the work of a financial advisor have the potential to do so much good. By first supporting the goals and desires of your client—or the relative or friend of the patient—you can become a partner in shaping the patient's legacy. You can provide financial leverage for heirs and charitable interests, as well as emotional participation that will bring even greater meaning and purpose to your work with other households. Some of the specific tasks you can perform are:

- *Beneficiary checkup.* Determine who needs providing for and see that the necessary support is in place. Remember that only about one in four millionaire households has a current estate plan, so revisions not only are likely, but may also be substantial. Beneficiaries should be updated and trusts created with parameters matching the patient's concerns and desires.

■ *End-of-life financial planning.* The trauma of losing a parent—especially in the prime of life—is often accompanied by the discovery of multiple loose ends. Business obligations, tax issues, disorganized or missing account statements, forgotten safe-deposit boxes and insurance policies all complicate a family's ability to grieve and move on. Accountants, lawyers, advisors, and bankers should all be informed immediately and asked to analyze the situation and provide recommendations. All documents and account statements should be centralized. Safe-deposit boxes should be emptied to avoid a probate seal. Personal effects should be listed and assigned to heirs to avoid the inevitable squabbles about who deserves what precious family heirlooms. To reduce infighting in the patient's final days, the executor should be provided with all of the information and heirs should be told that decisions have been made and they will be informed at the appropriate time. Hospice, home care, or assisted living should be arranged in advance, including the delivery of any necessary medical equipment, like an electric bed, stairway elevator, or wheelchair ramp. Decisions about who will supervise home care, who will provide transportation to medical treatments, and whether relocation for end-of-life care at a facility is required should be made.

■ *Helping clients leave a legacy.* The amount of financial support left behind pales in comparison to the impact of personal statements, letters, and speeches. Never can a person have more impact than when all around them can see what that person has chosen to share in his or her final days.

My grandfather, Perry Gresham, was an eloquent philosopher and gerontologist who became a champion for the elderly in his 70s. His last project was a book about one of our ancestors—a project he had contemplated for many years. Despite the ravages of cancer, his book project helped maintain his physical and mental energy. And he knew that the book would be the final entry on his personal history, as well as a gift to his family.

By definition, affluent people have achieved a measure of success in their lives; that success could and should be shared with others. There is typically some measure of ego as well. You can help clients channel their energy and emotion by facilitating a lasting impact of the clients' life. Beginning with the simple question, "How do you want to be remembered?," you will unlock feelings that have likely been festering below the surface but lacked an outlet. Turn the abstract into reality by narrowing the target of the question. Ask: "How do you want to be remembered, and by whom?" Most affluent people live amid a complex web of relationships. They may want to be remembered in different ways by family, friends, business colleagues, clients and customers, their neighbors, the community at large, their industry, and their college or university. Ask them.

There are hundreds of ways to have an impact—and even more variety when you consider the scale of impact. Your wealthiest clients may want to establish a family foundation to facilitate charitable giving during the client's lifetime, but also to drive a sense of purpose and continuity of that charity through to the next generation and beyond. Encouraging charitable gifts continues to rank high among surveys of affluent households. But because the tax benefits and costs associated with foundations make their use optimal only for your largest clients, consider the alternatives:

- *Donor advised funds (DAFs)*. These low-expense vehicles provide an immediate tax deduction and facilitate multiple donations. Typical minimum investments average just $10,000, and often allow the funding gift of appreciated stock or other assets. DAFs are increasingly popular with financial services firms, many of which have created their own funds for clients.
- *Charitable remainder and lead trusts*. These top the list of traditional "split interest" vehicles that serve your clients' charitable goals while also providing retirement income.
- *Family foundations*. Creating a foundation can be a fantastic experience with lasting generational impact, although many advisors suggest that their continuity depends on early involvement by the succeeding generation. Advisors also suggest that the cash deployed to create a foundation should be substantial

enough to avoid leaving a legacy of complicated record keeping on top of a marginal asset base.

Charitable vehicles of all kinds provide some of the most powerful and longest-tenured assets for your practice. Having a proficiency in the details of these vehicles is not critical, but having an immediate referral to an expert—or access to a preferred donor advised fund—should be a staple of the Advisor for Life practice.

There are, of course, less complex financial ways of being remembered. For example, New York's Central Park is home to thousands of benches bearing the names of donors—living and not. These benches are used and enjoyed by millions of people, not just the families and friends of the donor. Colleges and universities are becoming more flexible and creative in providing sustainable recognition for alumni gifts. Asking your best clients about their current efforts will doubtless lead you to ideas to be shared with others—and help you develop this most personal of bonds with your clients. Can you imagine a competing advisor successfully insinuating himself between you and a client for whom you have helped facilitate a lasting memory among family and colleagues?

Consider the efforts of a wirehouse advisor team on the Florida Gulf Coast that has become known in the community for its highly successful charitable fund-raising efforts. Every year, the team changes the beneficiary of its campaign, which aims to raise a sum well into six figures. Because of the scale, the effort receives significant community support and media attention. But the crowning touch is the ability to name a chairman of the effort—and it is always a client of the team's practice. What a benefit!

HOW THEY'LL PAY FOR IT

In many ways, this entire book is about funding retirement—mentally, spiritually, and financially—as a means for creating a lasting impact as the Advisor for Life. But savings and investments will not be adequate to support the retirement income needs of most baby boomer households. That's true for even the affluent families, given their current spending habits and lifestyles. Supplemental income and funding vehicles will become more prominent, and your practice may already be utilizing some of these products.

Income for Life—A Solution by Any Other Name than "Annuity"

My colleague, Walter Zultowski, PhD, has long studied affluent households in search of better solutions to their challenges. He recently assembled focus groups of high net worth consumers and queried the group about the features they desired in a retirement income plan. The answers included commonsense items like guaranteed income, some level of market participation, inflation protection, and death benefits—in short, all the trappings of annuities. Yet the millionaires reacted negatively to the product label "annuity." Many top advisors are including annuities and living benefits in their client wealth solutions. Walt and Eric Sondergeld of LIMRA International offer the following overview of annuity offerings. (See Figures 11.1 and 11.2.)

Using Annuities to Provide Guaranteed Income Later

- Fixed deferred annuity.
- Equity indexed annuity.
- Combination of fixed and variable deferred annuities.
- VA Guaranteed Minimum Account Benefit (GMAB).
- VA Guaranteed Minimum Income Benefit (GMIB).

Using Annuities to Provide Guaranteed Income Now

- Immediate annuity/annuitization:
    - Immediate fixed annuity.
    - Immediate variable annuity with floor.
    - Single premium immediate annuity (SPIA) with immediate variable annuity (IVA).
- Variable annuity with Guaranteed Minimum Withdrawal Benefit (GMWB):
    - Standard (e.g., 7 percent for 14 years).
    - For life.

I believe that annuities will become a core product for serving the retirement income needs of baby boomers. There will be needed changes in the pricing and accessibility of annuities and annuity-like products, but the essential benefits of annuities are highly desired by clients of all income levels.

Using Annuities to Provide Guaranteed Income Later

	Pros	Cons
Fixed Annuities	• Guaranteed growth	• Limited upside potential • Income later not always part of the sale
Equity Indexed Annuities	• Principal protection with upside growth • Comes in a variety of flavors	• Limited upside potential • Income later not always part of the sale • May not be able to annuitize during index period
FA & VA combo	• Locking in minimum value at some future date that can be annuitized • Annuitization doesn't have to occur in same contract	• Upside limited by fixed exposure • Income later not always part of the sale
VA GMAB	• Highest growth potential with principal guarantee • Annuitization doesn't have to occur in same contract	• Income later not always part of the sale • Annual fee for guarantee
VA GMIB	• Can provide highest guaranteed income	• Annuitization required to get guarantee • May use different payout rates • Annual fee for guarantee

FIGURE 11.1   Using Annuities to Provide Guaranteed Income Later
Source: LIMRA International.

(Continued)

Using Annuities to Provide Guaranteed Income Now

	Pros	Cons
Immediate Fixed	• Guaranteed payout for the period selected	• Most do not offer COLA • No/limited access to money
IVA with floor	• Guaranteed payout for the period selected • Possibility for payments to increase	• No/limited access to money • Annual fee for guarantee
SPIA with IVA	• Guaranteed payout for the period selected • IVA allows for additional income and upside growth potential	• No/limited access to money
VA GMWB	• Immediate access to money • Do not need to annuitize	• Annual fee for guarantee • Lower payout rate than immediate fixed • Not guaranteed for life • Payments need to be initiated by client
VA GMWB for life	• Immediate access to money • Do not need to annuitize	• Guarantee can be lost if w/d too much • Annual fee for guarantee • Lower payout rate than immediate fixed • Guarantee can be lost if w/d too much

FIGURE 11.2   Using Annuities to Provide Guaranteed Income Now
Source: LIMRA International.

What Is Your Number—and Can You Reach It?

The Number: A Completely Different Way to Think about the Rest of Your Life by Lee Eisenberg, former editor-in-chief of *Esquire* magazine, says that most people have a difficult time with the realities of financial planning—especially in the latter stages of life. The "number" is of course the dollar amount estimated by each of us to be the total needed to fund a lifetime and lifestyle. Far from being a simple indictment of boomer largesse, *The Number* suggests that a closer look at our lives might result in the ability to reduce the amount required, thereby increasing the chances of a comfortable retirement. "Boomers aren't only notable for being self-indulgent and profligate," author Eisenberg tells *Financial Advisor* (April 2006), "but also for being fairly ingenious about redefining the culture for their own purposes. I think those that are forced to confront a different lifestyle will do it somewhat cleverly, by adopting and propagating values that will make it seem easier. For example, we may see a re-emergence of the 'small is beautiful' theme that we heard in the 60s."

Advisors who say they don't yet see signs of a significant demand for more specific retirement products are about to receive a wake-up call. The oldest of the boomers are now reaching 60, the age when clients become more attuned to lifetime income. As one independent advisor observes, "Clients with even $3 million of accumulated assets won't be able to live on the interest and earnings alone."

PART IV

Building Your
"Advisor for Life" Practice

CHAPTER 12

What Is Your Value?

- *Who are you?*
- *What do you do?*
- *What makes you different?*
- *Why should clients do business with you?*

Do you truly understand and can you coherently describe your value to clients? Let's climb the Value Ladder with its creator, Leo Pusateri, and find out how to do it.

No amount of product or wealth management training, no certifications or accreditations can take the place of an advisor's ability to articulate clearly and powerfully her value to clients.

Why? Selecting a financial advisor is inherently emotionally charged. Prospective clients are choosing someone to prevent them being blindsided by risks, as well as to help them avoid making big mistakes, understand their options, confront realities about their financial situation, overcome emotion, and know when and how much they can spend. Financial advisors rank among the few counselors—medical, legal, and tax—who can materially affect a person's or family's current and future comfort and security.

Further, given the cacophony of competing messages, the financial services business is confusing. As Tiburon Strategic Advisors noted in September 2006, the "competitive playing field is crowded with over 400,000 financial advisors." And the landscape is changing. Independent reps now outnumber wirehouse brokers, and independent registered investment advisors are attracting assets faster than large broker-dealers. All of this amounts to what my friend Leo Pusateri and his firm, Pusateri Consulting and Training, call the client dilemma—baby boomers requiring financial advice more than ever, but so confused by investment options and the differences among advisors that they often are paralyzed by indecision.

Overcoming the client dilemma, Leo maintains, requires that advisors develop black-belt answers to seven simple yet critical questions of distinction:

Who are you?

What do you do?

Why do you do what you do?

How do you do what you do?

Who have you done it for?

What makes you different?

Why should I do business with you?

These seven questions compose the Value Ladder, a framework Pusateri Consulting and Training developed in 1997. (See Figure 12.1.)

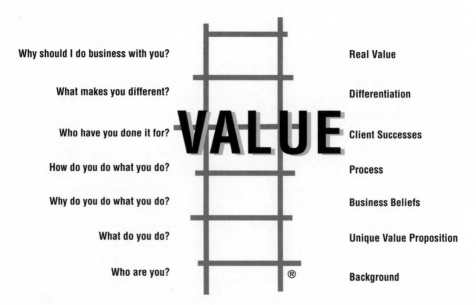

Why should I do business with you?		Real Value
What makes you different?		Differentiation
Who have you done it for?		Client Successes
How do you do what you do?		Process
Why do you do what you do?		Business Beliefs
What do you do?		Unique Value Proposition
Who are you?	®	Background

FIGURE 12.1   Value Ladder
Source: Pusateri Consulting and Training.

Pusateri has trained and coached thousands of top-producing advisors and advisor teams through this process. Some of its client firms—whether in Singapore, the United States, or Canada—have made answering these questions a requirement on a par with knowing sophisticated financial products and solutions.

Leo believes it is not only a prudent investment of an advisor's time, but an act of respect for clients or those considering you. By answering these questions, you are essentially conveying that you understand how difficult it is for prospects to make the right partnering decisions, and that they deserve to get a comprehensive sense of who you are, what makes you different, and what real value you would provide them with throughout a long-term relationship. Not only is it important to know your answers, but it also is critical to deliver them with confidence, passion, and speed. But first things first. Let's have Leo lead us through the Value Ladder in a process to discover your unique value.

VALUE LADDER STEP 1: WHO ARE YOU?

The question "Who are you?" or, as you are more likely to hear it, "Tell me a little about yourself," can seem like a no-brainer. What could be easier than talking about yourself and your background? But very few advisors take the time and effort to develop an adequate answer to this very common question. In failing to do so, they miss an opportunity to establish credibility, show that they respect the client enough to take the time to explain who they are, differentiate themselves at the very outset of a conversation, and position themselves—and not their products or solutions—at the center of the relationship.

It is worth lingering on two of these points before jumping into how best to answer this question for yourself. The first is credibility: Most advisors have spent inordinate amounts of time and money getting accredited to provide advice, yet few clients understand what the designations mean, let alone how to distinguish one from another. The second is discussing your background, which need not feel like bragging if you look at it from the client's perspective. They typically feel that presenting a full picture of your background is a sign of respect.

If you are the most important consideration for a client, then it stands to reason that it's critical for you to present yourself strongly at the outset of a relationship. The cliché is true—you get only one chance to make a great first impression. A well-considered, organized answer to the passing question "Who are you?" will set you apart immediately in a conversation.

Why start on such a basic question? Because most financial executives wing their answer, giving short shrift to who they are. In so doing, they miss a chance to convey a sense of professionalism and credibility. They forgo an opportunity to put themselves, and not their products or solutions, at the forefront of the conversation. Further, they fritter away perhaps the only appropriate time to highlight what differentiates their background. The 20-year veteran wirehouse advisor who says, "I'm a financial consultant at XYZ" has done nothing to differentiate herself from a discount advisor three years into the industry, working for a little-known firm.

Some advisors worry that the conversation should revolve immediately around the client, not the advisor. We believe the interchange should be balanced. Yes, it is critical to listen appropriately to a client. However, clients want to know with whom they are dealing. They don't want to discuss financial matters or life issues with just anyone. It's thus a mistake for an advisor to jump immediately into a questioning session.

How to Do It

Here's an example of an advisor who has done his homework and is prepared.

> I'm Jason Rodriguez, a financial advisor with my own advisory firm, Stanton and Rodriguez. I head our financial planning and investment management team that specializes in wealth solutions and life-cycle planning for affluent medical doctors and research scientists. Our firm is headquartered in the sunny paradise of San Diego, California, and has a combined 60 years of industry experience among our four principals.

Notice that Jason uses the terms *specializes*, *solutions*, and *sunny paradise*. Be precise in your word selection and make memorable statements. Leo and members of his firm tell people that they are from "beautiful Buffalo."

As a result of how Jason gave his answer, a prospect might then ask Jason more about his background, his experience, and how he focuses on research and medical clients.

As you describe your professional and personal background, your intuition will tell you how much to reveal or whether it is even appropriate to get into personal matters. But the point is to be ready to describe your professional and personal background succinctly, smoothly, and memorably. Here are guidelines to follow to develop your answer:

- Explain who you are in a fresh way, but start with the basics: your name, title, and firm you work for.
- Describe your organization: history, size, and strategic focus.
- If you work for a group within a larger firm, memorably describe the group—and make sure your entire team delivers the same message.
- Describe your role. If you are part of a multidisciplinary team, articulate your particular area of expertise.
- Stick to just the facts, and don't jump into explaining details of what you actually do.
- Interpret titles and avoid jargon. Assume that few people know what CFP, CFA, CIMA, or RIA mean, let alone how they differ. Consider explaining your accreditations in laymen's terms.
- Find the themes that run throughout your background, both personal and professional, and don't neglect the personal. Not all situations are appropriate to the sharing of personal information, but as most people are interested in what makes you tick, revealing aspects of yourself can provide connection points. Sharing your personal background also builds trust, because it requires a degree of candor.

Strategic Questions to Consider

- How well do I position myself now?
- What is my typical response to this question?
- In what ways does my response begin to differentiate my team and me?
- In what ways does it prompt further dialogue, or build trust and rapport?
- Is my team able to answer this question at a world-class level?

- If my entire team answers this question at a world-class level, what impact will this have on our sales process?
- Conversely, what impression will it make if my sales organization fails to answer this at a world-class level?

Don't take the simple question "Who are you?" for granted. It's like blocking and tackling in football. Adherence to discipline and mastery will set you apart. A good answer will naturally lead to the second Value Ladder question, "What do you do?"

VALUE LADDER STEP 2: WHAT DO YOU DO?

No question is more common than "What do you do?" Your answer should be anything but common.

Consider the following situation, which is fraught with peril and opportunity. A friend of yours hurries across your reception area with someone in tow whom you immediately recognize as the CEO of a successful local business that was recently in the news for having been sold. Beaming, your friend says, "Stephanie, I have wanted to introduce you to my good friend, Ted Capuano, for over a year. You both share a strong interest in red wine." After a few moments of chatting about wine, your vivacious friend leans in and says, "Stephanie, you have to tell Ted what exactly you do by day. I only see you in social settings."

The question seems innocuous, but the answer is an opportunity. Top advisors say their biggest clients picked them because of the rapport felt on both sides. Rapport—or chemistry—is established almost instantaneously. Affluent people take many different roads to achieving their wealth, but nearly all of them know how to evaluate people.

So, to your answer. You could say the obvious: "I am a financial advisor with XYZ Financial Services" and quickly divert attention back to Ted. Or you could say: "I steward wealthy families through the complexities of financial success through a five-part Life Planning process." The latter explanation, if properly delivered, might intrigue the prospect enough to inquire more: "What sort of wealthy families do you typically work with?" "What is your Life Planning process?"

Developing Your Unique Value Proposition

The second answer is obviously better because it contains your unique value proposition (UVP), which is a short statement that clearly and concisely captures the essence of what differentiates you from the competition. A compelling UVP can convert the passing "What do you do?" into a serious opportunity to sell your value. Do you have a UVP? Does it reflect your business?

A UVP is neither a tagline nor a mission statement. A tagline reinforces a brand, but does not explicitly discuss the value you provide. A mission statement attends to four constituents: clients, employees, shareholders, and the community, and thus usually is much broader than a UVP. Further, a unique value proposition goes beyond a value proposition, which does not need to sound different or one-of-a-kind.

In considering your UVP, ask yourself: What service do you provide that is most valued by your best clients? Is it your investment advice, or do you help with their total wealth picture? What type of clients are your best clients? Do you serve business owners or retirees? Can you say you know one group better than any other? Since clients look for advisors who understand their situation, how narrowly do you wish to define your clients?

What do your best clients like most about you? A survey of affluent investors asked the question of what they most valued about their advisor. None mentioned performance or products. All mentioned "service," "accessibility," "knows me and my business." To find out what clients think of the value they receive, the Pusateri firm offers a Real Value Audit, which is a process of surveying current clients so as not to assume what clients truly value.

Employing Your Unique Value Proposition

Tim Pagliara is the managing partner of Capital Trust Wealth Management, one of the top financial services firms in central Tennessee, which he founded with two partners in 2000, after transitioning from a successful regional practice. Tim has built a half-billion-dollar book of business around a singular focus, which he summarizes in a 16-word UVP: "We build wealth management solutions to meet the challenges that investors face in an uncertain world."

Tim can speak to every key word or phrase in his UVP. With degrees in law and business, he builds sophisticated wealth management solutions for individuals and families that few other advisors can credibly claim to offer. Tim also can speak very convincingly about his success in helping investors face an "uncertain world," having achieved positive portfolio growth rates from 2000 to 2006 by avoiding the technology stock bubble in 1999, but picking those same stocks at exceptionally low valuations in 2002. Tim's client successes validate his proposition, whether it is building a modest-earning school principal's wealth to over $1 million or helping a multimillion-dollar family estate recover millions mishandled by a trustee. It is no surprise that Tim is engaged as an expert witness in financial service negligence cases. Tim also uses his UVP to judge whether to take on a client. "I have turned away a $10 million account from someone who wanted me simply to do investment management. I am only interested at this stage in building relationships and being a true advisor," Tim notes.

He supports his UVP with his business beliefs. To meet the complex challenges of wealthy families, Tim coordinates closely with accountants and attorneys, and believes that "success comes not from control but from collaboration," which allays concerns of wealthy clients worried about miscommunication and power struggles among their trusted counselors.

Strategic Questions to Consider

- Is my unique value proposition truly unique? Would my clients instantly recognize it as mine?
- Do I use it in client dialogues? Do I have a "smile in my stomach" when I articulate it?
- How many words are in my UVP? Every word counts. Can I speak to each key word or phrase should a client want to challenge me or drill down?
- Does my team know and share my UVP?
- Do I need to revisit my UVP as I reconsider the value I offer? Have I revisited my UVP with current clients? Do they really understand what I offer?

Developing a UVP is rarely easy or quick, so do not be discouraged if you cannot compose one right away. Try out your UVP in client dialogues. Are you leaning forward in your chair when you say it? Is it provoking the client response you intend?

VALUE LADDER STEP 3: WHY DO YOU DO WHAT YOU DO?

The third rung of the Value Ladder challenges advisors to look at the essence of what makes them tick and the beliefs that drive their approach to investing, handling, and protecting wealth. Clients fundamentally want to know the drivers of your advice. Is it your personal convictions? Are these convictions—or business beliefs—aligned with their views on wealth or investing? Amazingly, few advisors actually put pen to paper and list their business beliefs.

Why are business beliefs so powerful? Here are five reasons:

1. They take a stand, convey an opinion, and place a stake in the ground.
2. Good beliefs start a conversation.
3. Beliefs reveal your passion and deeply held convictions.
4. They reveal personality in a sometimes faceless marketplace.
5. They are a litmus test, attracting people of the same mind and averting relationships where things as fundamental as beliefs are not aligned.

Do you have beliefs that can similarly galvanize a client's reaction to you? Your business beliefs can be derived from what your industry experience has taught you, what your clients have taught you, what you have learned from your mistakes and those of others, where you believe financial services are heading, and where you want to redirect your business. Your business beliefs should reflect your UVP. If your UVP speaks to comprehensive wealth management, then your beliefs should support why. If your UVP names a targeted market niche, perhaps your beliefs should, too. Do your beliefs reflect the needs of baby boomers and preretirees in particular, or investors at any stage in their lives?

Good business beliefs serve as a litmus test for compatibility. Your beliefs should be strong and provocative enough to attract clients who share your vision, but powerful enough to repel those who take an entirely different view of wealth. They should reveal your passion and conviction, as well as prompt conversation. They should challenge clients to consider whether they agree, and if so, whether they have acted in response. Moreover, your beliefs should be communicated briefly, roll off your tongue, sound punchy, and flow naturally, one from the next. Two ideas should typically be two separate beliefs.

Plodding or Powerful?

When asked about their beliefs, many advisors fall back on bromides. Sure, asset allocation and diversification are important, but as the basis of a belief system they induce yawns. Heard any of these lately? "I believe in asset allocation and diversification." "I believe in asset allocation in order to control risk." "I believe asset allocation is key to maximizing returns while minimizing risk." Say something like those and you'll be indistinguishable from the pack.

Now consider these belief statements: "I believe educated investors are more disciplined; disciplined investors earn more consistent returns; most investors are intimidated by the investment process; becoming financially independent requires committing 10 percent to 15 percent of income to savings; more risk does not necessarily net higher rewards."

These pass the "springboard test," which is the ability to prompt engaged dialogue. A client might ask:

- Am I an educated investor? Who is? How do you educate your clients?
- What is a disciplined investor? Am I one? If not, what would I need to change?
- How do you help investors not be intimidated by the investment process?
- How do you define financial independence? How would you help me to gauge my financial independence?
- Wait, I thought you needed more risk for higher returns. Is there a free lunch to be had in financial services?
- Why do you believe so strongly in the power of compound interest?

Strategic Questions to Consider

- What are my core business beliefs?
- Have I written them down?
- Do they sound uniquely like me?
- Do my clients know them?
- Does my team know them?
- Do I use the beliefs in sales and marketing materials?
- Would they resonate with my target market? Appeal to the affluent? Ring true to baby boomers?

Last, consider asking your clients what their beliefs on wealth and investing are. Rarely will you not produce an engaged discussion.

VALUE LADDER STEP 4: HOW DO YOU DO WHAT YOU DO?

It is hard to overstate the value of a unique, branded, differentiated process that allows a prospect to see how you would lead a relationship to make good on your unique value proposition. Consider a choice of doctors. Surgeon One has come highly recommended. You meet with him and ask what to expect if he were to do the operation. He gives you an avuncular tap on the knee and says: "We do these operations three times a week. We will sedate you and you won't feel a thing. We will open you up. Three hours later you will wake up with a nasty pain the chest, but all fixed up."

Surgeon Two, also of good reputation and equally highly recommended, answers the question very differently: "We have a six-step low-invasiveness process that we developed here at the hospital. We begin with step one, a full coronary work-through, two weeks before the operation. Step two is a stress test. In step three, my staff and I meet with you for a 30-minute review of our procedure. Step four is the operation. Let me tell you exactly what we do at this stage." The discussion proceeds with some detail.

In whose hands do you feel more confident? Surgeon Two in all likelihood, and not because of a better reputation, but because she sets out the clearer process. The real value of having a branded, unique, comprehensive process is that a process reduces uncertainty. Investing is inherently uncertain. The biggest taboo in financial services is, of course, guaranteeing performance. A process can be a counterweight to the inherent uncertainty of wealth management and investing. A process, although not an actual guarantee, acts as a firm commitment to how you will work with a client.

Merits of a Process

A process also can be a large differentiator. It can bring to light the various other types of alpha—or incremental value—you provide. A process also clarifies service expectations between a client and an advisor. Strict adherence to a process reduces compliance and legal risks. Importantly, a process also increases an advisor's referability.

Ken Gordon, a Vancouver-based financial advisor and chairman club member of CIBC Wood Gundy, developed the firm's five-step Tomorrow Never Lies process. (See Figure 12.2.) The process takes its name from the title of Ken's first book, which explains that life is about the choices we make as individuals. Life today, says Ken, is about choices made yesterday. Life tomorrow is about choices made today. "We will be instrumental in helping you choose carefully," Ken says in a brochure describing his process, "because tomorrow never lies." Ken completed the Pusateri Discovering Your Value process in 2000, and

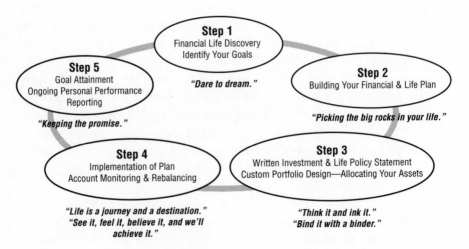

FIGURE 12.2 Ken Gordon's "Tomorrow Never Lies" Process
Source: Ken Gordon, The Gordon Group.

has been refining his Value Ladder answers continuously. He has continued with his commitment to help advisors, investors, and people in need by writing a second book, *Winning with Integrity.* Profits from his books go to his foundation, which gives to needy causes.

Ken's process, which he continues to polish, meets the seven Pusateri process criteria:

1. *It is named.* Ken's process is: Tomorrow Never Lies. He is currently reworking his thoughts to include additional fresh concepts from his new book.
2. *Uses unique language.* "Financial life discovery" is an example. Ken's unique approach comes alive with quotes. They prompt questions. Questions allow you to acknowledge, clarify, and confirm. Emotional connections result.
3. *Reduces uncertainty.* What uncertainty can come from Ken's steps? None. His process conveys a vivid sense of what you will do, and why it's important.
4. *Uses natural metaphors and analogies.* Ken chose not to use a metaphor, but uses his lexicon instead to infuse personality. To Ken these words are as natural a part of his personality as "beautiful Buffalo" is to Leo.
5. *Links back to your UVP and business beliefs.* Ken's UVP does that: "We deliver a proactive planned approach [five steps] to helping our clients achieve their financial objectives [achieve your life and financial goals] through integrity [keeping the promise], passion [which is apparent when you hear Ken articulate this], and a relentless commitment [wow!] to goal attainment."
6. *Shows real value to the client.* Can't you feel it through these words?
7. *Delivers real value at each stage of the process.* Clients walk away with value throughout the process, not just at the end.

Strategic Questions to Consider

- Have I made sure my process reflects my personality and that of my team?
- Does it convey a sense of real value to the client?
- Does it tie into my business beliefs or unique value proposition?

VALUE LADDER STEP 5: WHO HAVE YOU DONE IT FOR?

No matter how compelling your unique value proposition, business beliefs, or process are, affluent clients want to know how you have provided real value to others like them. Have you delivered against your UVP? Have you put your business beliefs into practice? Has your process led to success? Developing a polished, considered answer to "Who have you done it for?" is critical to building a powerful Value Ladder.

I agree with Leo that real value is delivered only when your solutions respond to a client's key emotional issues. But what are those issues? Leo Pusateri focuses on seven:

1. *Challenges*—things that inhibit the client from achieving goals. Example: "Market volatility is challenging our ability to meet our long-term portfolio needs."
2. *Circumstances*—a situation that accompanies an event. Example: "My wife's father is seriously ill and in need of personal in-home care."
3. *Concerns*—issues of interest or importance. Example: "She may have to quit her job."
4. *Frustrations*—issues causing the client to feel disappointed or unfulfilled. Example: "We just never seem to get ahead. There is always something holding us back."
5. *Needs*—what the client wants or requires. Example: "Our children will be entering college over the next two years. We need funds for tuition and maybe for Dad's care."
6. *Opportunities*—situations favorable to the attainment of a goal. Example: "We may be inheriting money from an estate sooner than expected."
7. *Problems*—questions raised out of concern or doubt. Example: "Will I lose my money on the stock I bought two years ago?"

After you analyze emotions, consider your solutions. What did you do or provide in response to the client's key emotional issues? Think here beyond the financial products you may have put into place to the service that you provided. If your UVP positions you as a wealth manager, develop client successes that speak to how you have provided

TABLE 12.1   Capturing Real Value

Client	Key Emotional Issues	Solutions	Real Value to the Client
1.			
2.			
3.			

value in not just building, but protecting or distributing wealth. Your client successes should prove the truth of your UVP.

Next and last, consider the real value you provided. Real value comprises both the qualitative (emotional, subjective) and the quantitative (logical, left-brained, measurable) benefits you provide. Most advisors shortchange this last step by not really considering the qualitative value they provide. The further you consider your real value, the more powerful the client success story is. Remember, you can never assume that a prospective client can understand how you have helped others unless you can clearly and concisely articulate real value you provided.

To help in this task, fill out Table 12.1.

Strategic Questions to Consider

- Do I find my client successes occur mainly for one type of client—for example, small business owners?
- Do I keep my current clients abreast of my client successes? Would they be curious to know? Would doing so reinforce or enhance my reputational value?
- Do my client successes validate my unique value proposition?
- Have I asked my clients how they perceive my real value to them?
- Have I shared my successes with referral sources?

VALUE LADDER STEP 6: WHAT MAKES YOU DIFFERENT?

If a client is not asking the question, surely he is thinking it: "What makes you different from the others who are managing my wealth or seek to manage my wealth? How are you truly different from other options I have to build or preserve my family's wealth?"

The advisor who helps prospective and current clients understand what differentiates him from others not only is providing a very valuable service, but is setting himself apart in the process. Advisors must differentiate themselves on three levels. Leo Pusateri and company use the metaphor of an Umbrella of Distinction. The top of the umbrella represents your company, the spokes your solutions, and the handle you, what holds up the umbrella.

As the canopy, you must distinguish your company against the competition. What is unique to your organization? Why did you choose it? What unique value does it provide to the client?

Next, what are your spokes, or how broadly are you defining your solutions? Consider not just financial solutions, but the planning and services you provide. Once you define your solutions, look at how they compare to those of the competition.

Last, picture yourself as the handle that holds up this umbrella. You are the ultimate and most important point of distinction to a client. How do you distinguish yourself?

Five Competitive Differentiation Concepts

As you examine your company and solutions differentiation, look at them through the lens of five concepts.

1. *Uniqueness.* What do you do that your competitors do not?
2. *Competitive advantage.* You do it. Your competitors do it. You feel you do it better than any competitor.
3. *Parity.* You all offer this, with none of you having a competitive advantage here.
4. *Competitors' advantage.* You all do it, but you feel your competitors frankly do it better than you.
5. *Competitors' uniqueness.* Is there something your competitors do that you do not do?

Write down three of your top competitors in your marketplace. Consider who your best clients would consider a viable alternative to you. On a company, solutions, and individual level, consider where your uniqueness and competitive advantages lie.

What Do You Stand For?

Business is first a meeting of the hearts. Only then does it become a meeting of the minds. If the most important thing you have to distinguish is *you,* and the most important way to distinguish yourself is by speaking from the heart and connecting with someone else relative to your standards, code of ethics, and core values, it is imperative you have this stuff down pat.

What do you stand for? What are your values? If I called your top clients, could they list you or your team as advisors who provide Ritz-Carlton-type service? Integrity and honesty are two important concepts, but they are so commonly used as to have lost meaning. Are your core values differentiated?

Strategic Questions to Consider

- Who are my true competitors? How well do I really know them?
- How well can I differentiate my company, solutions, and self?
- Do my team members know my core values?
- Do my clients know my core values?
- How would my clients differentiate me from other professionals in their lives? If I asked my clients what they think sets me apart, would I be surprised that what they stress is far from what I assume?

VALUE LADDER STEP 7: WHY SHOULD I DO BUSINESS WITH YOU?

A client's decision to partner with you boils down to the responses to these questions: "Why should I choose you and not another advisor competing for my business? What is the real value I would achieve in working with you? How would your unique value proposition translate into real value for my family and me?"

Clients need help in answering this question for themselves. Many advisors simply leave it to clients to determine what real value they should expect. Leo Pusateri contends that this is a big mistake. Advisors, they argue, need to have a black-belt answer to the question "Why should I partner with you?" and not put the burden back onto the client to figure out the answer to this difficult question.

The concept of real value as opposed to proposed value is important to grasp. In your unique value proposition you propose the unique value you would provide to clients. In your real value statement, you speak to how your unique value would become real to the specific client with whom you are speaking. Your real value is thus how your unique value, differentiation, background, beliefs, successes, and process all translate into value in responding to the needs your client has raised.

Real value is thus the benefit your unique value could provide to the prospect with whom you are talking. Ask yourself these questions:

- What key emotional issues (challenges, circumstances, concerns, frustrations, needs, opportunities, or problems) have they discussed with me?
- What is the real value they are seeking?
- What is it about my unique value proposition—and the rest of my Value Ladder answers—that caught their attention? How can I relate who I am, what I do, my beliefs and process, my client successes, and what makes me different to their needs?

Quantitative versus Qualitative Real Value

One of Leo Pusateri's strong convictions, as mentioned before, is that business is first a meeting of the hearts, which is followed by a meeting of the minds. Advisors should be able to articulate their real value in both qualitative and quantitative terms. Qualitative real value refers to the emotional value of a relationship, the elements that are difficult to measure but that result from hard work: confidence in your abilities, comfort that risks are covered, reassurance that you are scrutinizing their estate plans, and quality of life resulting from your having coordinated all aspects of their financial lives.

Quantitative real value refers to the measurable results that you produce, the logical benefits of your relationship. Look beyond the simple investment measures and consider how much money you have saved clients, not just made for clients. One of Pusateri's clients stresses that the value of avoiding mistakes and uncovering invisible costs is greater than the value of creating investment gains. This advisor can back this claim up with many client successes in which he and his team uncovered $500,000 in estate structure mistakes. Can you quantify your value to your clients?

Bill Nicklin, a veteran broker at Brown Advisors in Fishkill, New York, is not your typical advisor. He has stuck strictly to investing, and actively embraces the title "stockbroker." The way Bill, a Pusateri graduate and co-founder of the advisor resource Horsesmouth, clearly and confidently articulates his real value can serve as a good example for any type of advisor. If asked why someone should entrust their investments to him, he would say:

"My investment philosophy assesses risk and opportunity comprehensively. My methodology revolves around the fundamental factors affecting the value of business and other assets. For 30 years, by sitting on the boards of multiple manufacturing and distribution companies and running several technology-driven start-ups, I have made a close study or how businesses create wealth. In combination with three decades of investing experience, this expertise allows me to build and maintain portfolios positioned to address customer needs in almost every conceivable market environment. I am committed to mastering every component of my customers' portfolios and working toward every customer's distinct investment goals. Given my experience, knowledge, and methods, my customers and I have more than a fighting chance of getting the performance we expect."

Talk about confidence and passion! You would not go to Bill Nicklin for holistic wealth planning, but you certainly might consider him if you were looking at investment managers.

Three Strategies to Answer This Question

Here are three strategies for articulating your real value:

1. Walk up the first six steps in your Value Ladder answers, pointing out as you go the real value of your background, unique value proposition, business beliefs, process, client successes, and differentiation.
2. Pick client success stories (Value Ladder step 5) that would resonate with your client or prospect.

3. Tell the client that it is too early to answer why she should do business with you, and request a meeting to conduct a consultative dialogue. Not only does this approach convey confidence, it also prevents misdiagnosing the client's financial problems.

Conducting a Real Value Audit

Consider conducting real value audits with your clients. Leo Pusateri defines a real value audit as an annual or more frequent meeting between an advisor and a client to discuss nothing more than how real value was exchanged in the relationship. A real value audit can replace or supplement an annual review. Pusateri believes that the traditional annual review is helpful, but falls well short of truly uncovering how clients perceive real value in the relationship.

A real value audit is built around two questions to be answered by the advisor—What real value did I provide my client with this year? What real value did my client provide me with (successful referrals, for instance)?—and one question for the client—What real value did the advisor provide this year?

The results of such conversations can be remarkably revealing for the advisor. Clients invariably focus on aspects of real value that the advisor could have overlooked or misstated. Remember, the more complicated your offering, the more you need to help your clients to understand in simple terms that appeal to both left-brain and right-brain thinkers what real value they can expect in picking you to handle their financial futures.

Strategic Questions to Consider

- How do I usually respond to the seventh Value Ladder question, "Why should I do business with you?"
- How does my partner or team respond to this same question?
- How do I define the real value I provide to my clients?
- Have I ever asked what my real value has been to them?
- How would my clients define the real value I provide to them?
- Do I consistently ask my clients how they will measure my success?
- Am I currently measuring the real value I offer?
- Am I documenting the real value, and if so how?

THE MISSING PIECE

One key client question not addressed in the Value Ladder involves cost. The next chapter challenges you to examine your value against your price. Your Value Ladder answers can give ample fodder for substantiating your price. Leo Pusateri reports that the value inventory the Value Ladder's Discovering Your Value process requires has prompted advisors to adjust their fees with confidence.

CHAPTER 13

How to Quantify
Your Unique Value

- *How can you quantify your added value to affluent households?*
- *Which three categories of advice represent your greatest value?*
- *How can you more effectively present your added value in client reviews?*
- *How can you use financial advisor alpha to drive referrals?*

What value have you provided in various investment and wealth management areas? Don't let the markets define your added value against a benchmark—create your own. Then review these achievements with clients in a way they'll appreciate—and tell their friends about.

THE VALUE TEST

How do clients assess your value? I believe that clients arrive at an assessment based on an individual combination of reason and emotion. Here are two investors' stories that illustrate how value judgments are reached. The first conversation took place in early 2006 in the office of Phil, a certified public accountant, who was reviewing the personal tax return of long-term client Robert, a business owner, prior to filing.

> *Phil:* Let's go to Schedule D.
>
> *Robert:* Nothing much to look at there—another crummy year.
>
> *Phil:* Well, you are in good company of late. The market's been flat since the rally in 2003–2004. I haven't seen too many robust Schedule Ds around here in the past few years.
>
> *Robert:* Misery loves company, but seriously, my retirement plan is still just below the $2 million mark. I've essentially made no money in nearly five years! I'm not getting any younger, and my retirement is being pushed farther away. Shouldn't I do something?
>
> *Phil:* Well, be careful about making any sudden moves—you might end up with a different version of the same story. But I do suggest you talk with Mary Anne, your financial advisor, about the one thing that would soften the blow of these investment results.
>
> *Robert:* What's that?
>
> *Phil:* The fees for managing your retirement account—the managed account—were over $25,000 last year.
>
> *Robert: What?!* But I made no money! Is that a one-time fee? I hadn't focused on it—glad I copy you on the statements!
>
> *Phil:* It's an asset-based fee—the fee is a percentage of account value. It's very common, and many of my clients have the same arrangement.
>
> *Robert:* But come on, Phil, what did I get for my $25,000 last year? Nothing! In my business, if you don't provide any value, you lose the client—you certainly don't get paid, anyway!

My own experience is similar. Speaking to a large group of well-heeled investors in Fort Worth, Texas, not too long ago, my topic was the current investment market and strategies for investing. In the audience was a nice woman who was the client of an advisor who had helped arranged the seminar. She expressed the same frustration to me as Robert did to Phil: Her $1.5 million account had been charged more than $100,000 in fees over the past five years, during which time the value of her account had fallen. Recently, its value had increased—

about to where it was when she opened the account in 2000. "Am I crazy to stay put?" she asked me. "Or should I be glad I got my money back and move on? Most of my friends pulled the plug already."

Like it or not, these investors are onto something. After all, would you pay for services not rendered? Imagine paying a building contractor $100,000 over several months to add a room to your house—and then never getting the room done. You'd call a lawyer, right? In the securities industry, pricing traditionally has been tied to either transactions or performance. Currently, we are facing a sustained test of a pricing system developed during the historic bull market of the 1980s and 1990s. When retail separately managed accounts featuring comprehensive or wrap fees were introduced in 1987, they sported 3 percent annual fees. Competition and lower market returns have eroded the average fee to just over 2 percent, and discounts for larger accounts have always prevailed. But consider Robert's $2 million account, which paid $25,000 in fees to his advisor. Is that tenable? Shouldn't his fees have bought him something more than exposure to the capital markets?

Investors now have many cheaper alternatives to gain that same exposure, such as index funds and exchange-traded funds. The nation's largest investors—pension funds and ultra high net worth families—often negotiate performance-based fees from their advisors to minimize the impact of poor performance relative to a benchmark. I expect that performance-based pricing will become more commonplace at the market's lower end, perhaps in the softer form of return guarantees. The bear market of 2000–2002 strained the patience of even the most sophisticated investors, who have been actively seeking absolute return strategies to offset the decline of the listed markets. But back to the main point—what is the value of the advisory relationship? It must be beyond that of performance or transactions, if only to neutralize the impact of market behavior, which is out of your control.

If we were to shift away from performance-based pricing, here's how the conversation in Phil's office might sound:

> *Phil:* I can understand your frustration—many of my other clients are in the same place. The market is the market and there isn't anything you can do about it—not much Mary Anne can do about it. You are pretty well diversified—I have a lot of clients who are still way down because they bet too heavily on technology.

Robert: Good point—but it's still a lot of money.

Phil: Don't forget the other ideas Mary Anne had this past year. Remember that refinancing of your house—that was a big deal and helped you qualify for that other loan she helped arrange for your office building. You saved a bundle there and you're now paying yourself rent!

Robert: That's true.

Phil: And I don't think your wife will ever forget how Mary Anne saved the day with that long-term care policy she practically forced on you for your father-in-law. If you add it all up, I think you'll find that those couple of services saved you a lot more money than you realize—certainly a lot more than the fees on your managed account.

Robert: You're right, Mary Anne has really been a great advisor—I had forgotten the big picture.

Your Financial Advisor Alpha

To step away from performance, consider building your own advisory alpha.

A key yardstick of successful investment management, alpha measures a manager's added value, which is the portion of his or her performance that is not attributable to the risk of a particular asset class (that risk is known as the beta). While investment alpha is easily quantified, advisor alpha measurement is less clear-cut. But consider these components:

Investment Advice Alpha The investment process has four components: setting the client's investment goal, creating an investment policy statement with asset allocation, selecting complementary investments, and monitoring and rebalancing investments. Each component represents an opportunity to add value. For example, most advisors won't challenge clients' often wildly optimistic investment goals, which clients presume will cover future health care costs. But most people underestimate those costs and how long they will live—a combination that can be hazardous to their wealth. An advisor who helps a client prepare better for these events has added alpha.

Similarly, few clients have a written investment policy statement of any kind. Advisors able to bring clients to the planning process add alpha, as do those who select complementary investments, such as bonds during the tech bubble or alternative investments today. Finally, monitoring and rebalancing add value. Taking advantage of market shifts earns the respect of clients and creates terrific referral opportunities. Tactical rebalancing also answers the question of what you are doing for your fee. A client whose 60/40 equity/fixed-income mix in 1999 had morphed into a 40/60 mix by 2002 would have recognized your alpha, had you rebalanced along the way.

Wealth Management Alpha Earn it in several ways. Since wealth is not all about investments and assets, look across the balance sheet at liabilities for opportunities to help your clients. The simplest form of liability management is restructuring the mortgage debt of affluent households. Providing business lines of credit has been another door opener to high net worth households. How about this line from an advisor in Connecticut: "Your portfolio may be down because of the bear market, but we helped you save $30,000 in financing costs this year." That's alpha.

So is managing risk. Challenge clients to seek protection from life and business risks through disability, long-term care, and key-man insurance. These solutions very seldom sell themselves because most clients underestimate risk. Helping them appreciate those risks and taking steps to protect them is real alpha.

Relationship Alpha Millionaire households consistently rank "trust" tops among reasons they work with their current advisors. So what services can you provide to your best clients that would impress them (and lead to their trusting you)? What moves a client to refer another person to you? The best opportunity to establish relationship alpha is by focusing on the client's family. Specifically, help with dicey topics that families have trouble discussing on their own. Helping different generations discuss financial issues is a huge added value to the family's overall wealth and is a service frequently cited by clients as a key reason for loyalty to the advisor.

Now, calculate your alpha. Pick three top client household relationships and review each from the aspects just discussed. Make a list of the services you provided in the past year. Can you assign dollar values to any of those items? What other "added value" statements can you make about your work for each client—how would you character-ize the results if you had to make a report to the household? When fin-ished, you will have a better way to determine precisely what you have done for a client; you'll have your alpha.

Presenting Your Added Value: The Client Review

Providing advisor alpha is one thing; ensuring that your clients are aware of its delivery is another. Here are some suggestions about trans-mitting your value message in each of the three alpha areas.

Investment Advice Alpha Because it is measured by performance, which will tie you to the vagaries of the markets, investing is a slippery slope on which to prove your worth. Don't get trapped by investment report-ing that pigeonholes your short-term efforts. Instead, focus on more important, long-term issues such as creating an investment goal. Your value here results from challenging the client's assumptions and prob-ing for any life changes that would impact the investment plan. You might say, "Last quarter we revised your time frame in light of your business reversals and the difficulty of making a full retirement plan contribution this year; perhaps in subsequent years we could. . . ."

By having created an investment policy statement and asset alloca-tion plan, your added value comes from your suggestions and innova-tions educating the client about new strategies. You may tell the client, "We decided to add exposure to alternative investments, specifically market neutral strategies and real estate, to reduce volatility." By creat-ing a process of investment evaluation and selection, you might say, "We uncovered a new short-term fixed-income manager not well known to most advisors." And as a result of having performed account monitoring and rebalancing, you might say, "We reduced the duration of our fixed-income portfolio, which captured over $20,000 in profits and reduced our exposure should rates rise."

Wealth Management Alpha Easier to demonstrate than investment coun-sel alpha, wealth management alpha is derived from reducing costs and risks. You can perform liability management by reducing known or voluntary household and business expenses. For example, you might refinance a mortgage and demonstrate how much you've saved your clients. In risk management, your alpha comes from your proactive assessment of risk and your ability to reduce or eliminate the threat. You can protect assets, for example, by examining a client's employee retirement plan and determining what would happen if the markets fell.

Relationship Alpha This is central to attracting new clients as well as additional assets from existing clients and is perhaps the most valuable type of alpha from the client's perspective. Its two primary aspects are family dynamics and entertainment. Family dynamics are actions made possible by your relationship with the family and their trust in your advice. For example, when you are close to your clients, you can discuss the importance of long-term care insurance or the benefits of assisted living arrangements.

Entertainment is about helping clients enjoy their wealth. You can wish them well on their New York pied-à-terre because you obtained such good financing terms. Or you can congratulate a client with oil industry experience for the great call he made on the rise in energy prices—and the profits you engineered through futures contracts.

Pricing Your Added Value

Regardless of your efforts to create added value, you will always be challenged to price your services fairly. Inherent to every profession is the dynamic tension of value provided versus value perceived. Your best bet is always to maintain a few simple rules about your pricing and share them openly and actively with clients and prospects. If you are truly adding value, the transparency of your pricing will serve as a guide to you about the fairness of your fees. Earlier, I suggested that the marketplace for investment advice tends to produce prices that approximate 10 percent of gross returns. If a balanced portfolio were to earn an 8 percent return in a given year, therefore, a fair price for advice traditionally would be about 0.8 percent or 80 basis points. But the 10 percent equilibrium is unlikely to remain viable going forward as competition for market share intensifies among fewer providers. Lower costs will be forced on much of the market, although the very best managers (at successful hedge funds, for instance) will continue to extract above-market fees if they can sustain their performance.

The best way to earn a superior return on client assets, of course, is to deliver more for the clients' money. PepsiCo was stymied for years by the soft drink industry leader, Coca-Cola, until the day Pepsi surprised Coke by offering a 12-ounce bottle in competition with Coke's unique six-and-a-half-ounce green glass bottle. "Twice as much for a nickel too" was a refrain that eventually drew nearly 15 percent of the U.S. market to Pepsi at Coke's expense. Index funds and exchange-traded funds (ETFs) have the potential to unseat a lot of active managers in client solutions. You will have an increasing selection of investment options with aggressive pricing to help you deliver added value to your clients.

Helping a client appreciate your services sometimes requires creativity. Don't assume clients understand your value when you provide investment products that may seem average, commodity-like, or even boring. Provide them with a framework to showcase your efforts, and maintain that format in every quarterly review meeting.

Advisors Speak Out on Pricing

Wirehouse Advisor (Greg): "We educate clients about alpha and beta and then renegotiate fees each year based on the alpha. If it didn't exceed the benchmark then we only deserve a basic fee. We compute the alpha net of fees, the risk-adjusted excess net return. The client's fee is negotiated based on 'success experienced.' We also define success with a client as avoiding unnecessary risk, expense, and taxes."

Independent Advisor: "On the issue of fees, we believe that full disclosure is terrific, like a unified managed account (UMA) on steroids, and let the client choose between fees and commissions. We think the fee approach puts the advisor on the side of clients, and 70 percent of the time our clients accept the fee structure."

Wirehouse Advisor: "Fees are rarely a meaningful determinant in capturing clients, but we prefer to overdisclose to best align our interests with the clients' whether they pay a fee or commissions. Fees are usually not negotiated down, and the client decides if it is fees or commissions or a combination of both."

Another View of the Value Perception

Jeff Marsden, a founder and executive with PriceMetrix, a Toronto, Canada–based consulting group that helps investment firms and their financial advisors improve their productivity, has worked with many advisors on the issues of value and pricing. What he finds intriguing is the wide range of value that is realized (or achieved) by advisors and their firms.

After looking at the practices of several senior advisors—those with more than 10 years in the business and a majority of clients having more than $500,000 in assets invested in several products—Marsden found that their return on assets ranged from 0.2 percent to 1.2 percent. In other words, some were making only $200 on every $100,000 in their book of business, while others earned $1,200. Certainly, he wondered, the advisors' value to clients did not vary by a factor of six. There was a gap, as PriceMetrix came to realize, between the value clients perceive or understand as coming from the advisor and the value that is actually being realized. Productivity is improved by narrowing the gap between high "value perception" and high "value penetration."

PriceMetrix finds that clients generally value their advisors at a level far greater than the value realized by these advisors. For the most part, clients who seek or need Advisors for Life are willing to pay fully for a true full-service proposition—much like their willingness to spend $5 at Starbucks for superior coffee and the café experience. If investors know, understand, and believe in the value they are receiving, they will typically pay more than they are being asked to pay. In addition, their loyalty increases the more they understand the value they are receiving.

The problem, of course, is that clients don't always understand the value an Advisor for Life provides as a combination relationship manager, wealth manager, investment manager, team leader, coach, and CFO. How do you overcome the perception gap and increase your "value penetration"? Marsden offers four suggestions:

1. *Offer a clear, unique, well-communicated value proposition.* The goal here is to ensure that the clients have absolute confidence in your value as an advisor *and* that it aligns with the client's understanding of his or her needs. Make a review of your value proposition part of your regular client process.

(Continued)

Another View of the Value Perception *(Continued)*

2. *Embrace and familiarize yourself with a wide range of products and services.* Be prepared to discuss credit and liquidity issues as well as equities, and be a sounding board on small-business strategy if your clients are entrepreneurs.

3. *Focus on a defined market segment that will understand and appreciate your value.* As Marsden wisely points out, it is impossible to convince someone of your value to them if your work, values, and approach do not align with what they believe they need.

4. *Develop and implement a consistent pricing strategy.* Such a strategy will align with value delivered and maximize value penetration. Successful advisors appreciate the importance of not being random or undisciplined in their pricing.

CHAPTER 14

The Client Experience

- *How can you create a powerful first impression with prospective clients?*
- *What is it like to be a new client of a top advisory practice?*
- *How can you hold more effective client meetings to earn additional assets and drive referrals?*
- *How can you benefit from establishing a personal advisory board?*

A successful relationship does take two—both to start the partnership and to keep it going. You know what you want from your clients, but what do they want and expect from you? Here's a way to think about the complete experience, from first meeting to annual review.

Many advisors are so busy delivering the substance of their service they sometimes forget about its feel and perception among potential and current clients. So let's break down the client experience into its most important components and consider how an Advisor for Life might want to deliver those service elements.

THE FIRST CONTACT

A prospect calls for an appointment. Like many potential clients, this one comes to you from a colleague or an attorney or accountant you know, perhaps because the professional making the referral believes you can solve a particular problem.

Who answers the phone? Are you certain that the newcomer's very first contact with your firm is a friendly, courteous, and intelligent-sounding voice? Does the person answering the phone, or someone else, follow an established process to set up a first meeting? In fact, is there a procedure for such a call to stay with the receptionist or go to an assistant or an advisor? Is the first meeting held in person or over the phone? Is the prospect asked to bring information such as tax returns or brokerage statements to the first meeting? Does the first meeting cost money?

There are lots of questions. But they illustrate the importance of analyzing the intake process of your practice in thorough detail and systematizing it so that a professional and consistent level of service is delivered. An advisor we'll call Elaine, a financial planner in affluent Fairfield County, Connecticut, employs one distinguishing service element: She won't meet with prospective clients unless they agree to spend $500 for the first meeting. This fee is applied to their first-year charges if they become clients; if not, Elaine keeps the $500 to cover the cost of her time. In addition, she requires they bring a full financial inventory to the meeting, including tax returns for the previous three years. (Some advisors may feel that demanding so much information up front is presumptuous, but why not ask for it at the start? A client who balks may not really be willing to acknowledge your expertise and follow your recommendations.) One advisor in the metropolitan Washington, D.C., area says he "warns" referrals to expect a session of at least two hours to discuss their situation. He believes that since he is willing to invest his time in meeting a good referral, the referral also must make an investment of time. As much as 80 percent of his initial meetings are devoted to interviewing the prospect, not on presenting himself.

After you think about the people and process of the initial get-together, consider the setting. The meeting's location and its furnishings communicate information about your practice in subtle ways. David in South Florida has an office created by a decorator who was influenced by visits to the meeting rooms of local private banks. David's furnishings are rich and comfortable, and his flat-panel monitors communicate professional skill. In Houston, one of the nation's largest advisory teams set up a new office a few years ago in a very upscale residential community. The reception area featured a four-foot plasma-screen television—still a novelty at that time. An advisor practice I visited recently in suburban Detroit went high-tech with glass walls, modular furniture, and big plasma screens in every room. At the same time, it furnished a few private conference rooms traditionally to appeal to more sedate clients. One practice in Boston lines the walls of one of its conference rooms with black binders—one for each client household. This allows the firm to communicate not so subtly that it has many clients.

Having office decor that reflects the type of client you seek obviously helps your marketing efforts. But what if you don't yet have a fancy conference room or corner office to show off your stature? After all, those corner-office folks didn't start there. A good friend in New York City was a successful psychologist before making a midlife career switch to financial advisor. He joined a wirehouse branch near his new home on Long Island and was given a desk in the bullpen—quite a comedown for a guy used to a hefty income and a big office suite. Since his new "office" was unimpressive, and since his target market was business owners, he generally met prospects at their places of business. Based on his counseling experience, he was convinced that prospects would be more willing to meet him if they could do so in a place where *they* felt most comfortable. He also recognized that visiting them was essentially a way to show respect for the income, power, and confidence the businesses created. By showing that interest, he was going beyond what advisors typically did. In my friend's case, not having an office helped him acquire nearly $15 million in new assets in his first year, blowing away the other rookies.

Other out-of-office strategies are equally effective. A five-star hotel in New York City is one of my clients' favorite places to have tea—which is why it's now the only place we meet when we get together, three or four times a year. An attorney friend uses his club to greet regular clients. They enjoy meeting in one of the club's rooms reserved for such an event, followed by lunch or cocktails. When he travels to other cities, he uses his club's generous list of reciprocal clubs in locations where his firm does not have an office. An advisor team I know in Long Island makes frequent use of its firm's private dining facilities in midtown Manhattan, taking a room for a full day to meet with clients over breakfast and lunch.

THE RIGHT STARTERS

Whether you meet on your turf, the client's, or someplace else, the next threshold is starting your meeting. Here's one icebreaker I find intriguing: "What brings you to my door and not the next one?" asks Mike in Arizona, whose office at a wirehouse branch is located alongside that of a popular discount brokerage firm. A question that direct usually gets a response from the prospect, which often begins a conversation. Icebreakers are important because they convey your confidence and experience. One advisor I met many years ago tries to get prospective clients talking as quickly as possible about the things they feel good about before moving on to areas of concern, which they might be reluctant to discuss immediately. The advisor's favorite opening line: "Ms. Davis, I am very pleased to meet you! I understand that Ron Jones from Sterling and Shuster thought we should get together. Please tell me more about yourself." Simple stuff, but appropriately commanding and comfortable. You should be in charge the whole way. Opening up a person of wealth can be very difficult, especially if the prospect has been burned or denies having the problem that requires your help—both common situations. "Appeal to their success," says Richard in New York City. "Acknowledge, even admire, their accomplishments right up front. Ask about their rise to affluence and how they did it. That will get them off and running!"

Because I travel a great deal and meet many affluent people—and usually am in a hurry—I have a tendency to get right to the point. I'll typically ask someone I've just met, "How did you achieve your financial success?" As soon as I get their story in focus, I shift to "What is your next challenge?" That open-ended question typically stops the discussion as the person contemplates an answer. Sometimes I ask the question another way: "What do you want to do with your wealth?" The key here is to ask questions that may never have been asked before by any other person. Since most clients say they value advisors who challenge them, you set the stage relative to other, less skilled advisors by challenging your clients when you sit down with them—not in a critical way or as a peer or business colleague might challenge them, but as a loyal, longtime advisor who wants to help your client succeed.

No matter how good they are as conversation starters, however, one or two questions do not a process make. And the most important aspect of the information-gathering process is that it is, indeed, a process. It should be consistent, repeatable, effective, and *intriguing*. In fact, the initial interview process is one of the most often overlooked opportunities for new client referrals. Here's why: Meeting a new financial advisor is not a common occurrence in the life of an affluent person. It stands out. Chances are the person has spoken with many people in her quest to locate you, and will speak with those folks again after your first meeting. Let's listen in on the lunch conversation that Bill Jamieson, a publishing company principal, is having with Rachael Davis, who runs a small printing business used by Bill's company:

Rachael: Bill, I'm so sorry I'm late—did you order?

Bill: I sure did—I'm starving! What's up? You're *always* on time!

Rachael: I just came from a very interesting meeting.

Bill: I didn't know there was such a thing—not at my company, anyway!

Rachael: Really, this was different. I just met with a financial advisor who was referred to me by Ron Jones, our accountant. You know Ron.

Bill: Sure, he's terrific. But what about this advisor?

Rachael: I went there because I needed to redo our company's pension plan. We've grown and Ron told me it was time to reevaluate its structure.

Bill: Sounds thrilling. So again, why are you so jazzed about the meeting?

Rachael: Because this guy didn't ask about the pension plan right away. He said he had researched our company prior to the meeting and was interested in learning more about our plans to grow. He said it appeared from our success we were tracking for a bright future and he wanted to make sure we didn't have to revamp the plan again. He must have quizzed me for nearly an hour before we discussed the plan itself.

Bill: Interesting. My financial advisor doesn't know anything about our business—and she's never asked. I guess that's one of the reasons we keep our pension plan at the bank. But even they are hard to work with—especially with financing. No one seems to understand how cyclical our business is.

Rachael: Well, that's why I'm so pleased—this guy gets it.

Bill: Give me his name and number.

Do you make the effort to know about your clients before you sit down to your first meeting? A fairly new advisor I know at a wirehouse branch in Hartford, Connecticut, became one of the stars of his training class by personally visiting the offices of small businesses in his area and talking entirely and exclusively about each business's need for supplemental financing. Using business lines of credit, he established an impressive book of clients in less than six months. He attributes his success to his personal touch of arriving at the companies and his willingness to work alongside each business's current lenders and advisors.

Information is the key to converting a prospect to a client. If the client has shared sufficient information for you to have an opinion, you can use the rendering of that opinion to establish the formal account relationship. Most top advisors I know lay out the process of becoming a client of their practice toward the end of the first meeting. Our advisor friend Elaine, who charges $500 for a first meeting, collects a considerable amount of information at those gatherings, including tax returns. She then meets with the prospect again, for an average of two hours, to review the information. Because her information requests are so specific and her requirement for an initial meeting fee is so clear, she reports that those conditions weed out unsuitable potential clients. "By the time of our first meeting," she reports, "I've got a pretty serious prospective client."

Most top advisors seem to agree that signing a client typically involves a three-meeting process. The first meeting focuses on establishing rapport and asking the client to provide specific information. The second is dedicated to reviewing the information and discussing the prospect's most significant concerns or objectives in more depth. At the third meeting, the advisor presents recommendations and secures a financial commitment from the client to act on those recommendations. Explaining that process to prospective clients is an important part of educating them about how you work; most clients will not know and may not ask how you do what you do.

THE PROSPECT'S A CLIENT; NOW WHAT?

The bridge has been crossed and your prospect is now a client. So how often should you contact clients? The truth is, client contact remains the primary driver of client satisfaction, according to countless surveys of affluent investors. Prince and Associates, in work conducted for *Institutional Investor*, found that affluent investors who say they are "highly satisfied" with their primary financial advisor have an average of 14 contacts with that advisor over six months. Contact can be a telephone call, a personal meeting, or even a personalized letter or e-mail.

A mountain of research continues to indicate that affluent clients expect a monthly proactive communication from their primary financial advisor. Fit within the context of an annual contact plan, this contact is typically a telephone call from you, interspersed with face-to-face meetings an average of three times per year. For a survey I did a few years ago, 76 percent of advisors whose annual net income exceeded $300,000 reported that they had three or more in-person, in-depth review meetings with their top 50 clients each year. Another dimension of client meetings is that the expectation for reviews seems to rise with clients' net worth. A survey by Advisor Impact, reported in the July 2006 issue of *Financial Advisor* magazine, revealed that 59 percent of clients with over $500,000 in annual income expected at least three in-person reviews each year, and 43 percent wanted four or more. By comparison, clients whose annual income was less than $500,000 had more modest expectations—65 percent were looking for two or fewer reviews.

In my earlier book, *Attract and Retain the Affluent Investor: Winning Tactics for Today's Financial Advisors*, I told the story of George, a top-level advisor in the Midwest. George started as a broker in 1990 after other jobs in financial services, and by the late 1990s had more than 600 accounts with $48 million in assets and $422,000 in production. At that point he decided to concentrate on his best clients and pare down his business so that he could become a better all-around advisor, using separately managed accounts for investing. George did prune his client roster, then added investors who fit his revised profile; he now has well over $100 million under management. To help attain that level of business, he adopted a 12/4/2 client contact system that was based on findings from Merrill survey data. The firm found that clients feel most satisfied when they receive 12 personal contacts a year and four portfolio reviews, two of which are completed in person. George kept the 12 personal contacts, but makes four in-person visits instead of two. He believes so strongly in personal contact, in fact, that he has added one more personal contact—a full-day meeting—to the annual agenda for his best clients. Most top clients who started spending a full day with George thought such service was unusual at first. But after a few months of conducting full-day meetings, George found himself with three new multimillion-dollar clients as a result of referrals. The point: In-person meetings work.

A Better Client Review

A face-to-face meeting is the best way to reinforce your value with a top client. Too often, however, your hectic schedule precludes preparation that could transform what may be a tired ritual into an invigorating experience and an opportunity to attract additional assets. Consider these seven steps to optimize such a meeting:

1. *Pick a conducive setting.* Where can you best maintain control of the discussion? Your client's workplace is her turf and therefore a seat of power. A restaurant is neither private nor businesslike, and is fraught with interruptions. Your office may be the best place to hold court.
2. *Set an agenda.* It's a proven managerial tactic—he who has the agenda controls the meeting. One advisor I know faxes a written agenda to his top clients before the meeting to help set the stage. Agendas give you control and set the meeting's tone and pace.
3. *Review the last meeting.* What did you talk about? Refer to your notes and refresh your client's memory of what you've done since that meeting. He likely has forgotten what you discussed, as well as your efforts on his behalf.
4. *Review old business.* Talk about the investments and investment managers you chose together. What were the original objectives? How are the investments holding up? Though performance may be poor, is it understandable given the markets? What

alternatives are available, and do they match the client's objectives and time horizon?

5. *Consider new business.* What are your client's greatest concerns? They probably center on retirement planning, estate planning, income and asset protection, assisting children, and assisting parents. Does your client face risks in any of these areas? Should you adopt defensive strategies to reduce risks in the event the markets don't rebound? Are there weak spots in your client's plan? Your job is to help clients see the weaknesses and get protection. Remember, wealth is a balance sheet. Look for strategies to grow assets and minimize liabilities. Choose one item for immediate action and instill in your client a feeling of immediate control.

6. *Schedule a follow-up meeting.* Ever wonder why the dentist is so successful with repeat business? At the end of your meeting, schedule another session two to three weeks out in order to review the issues and the first action step taken. Scheduling a follow-up meeting signals to the client that you are actively on the case and focused on results.

7. *Vote to adjourn.* Make sure you have provided your client ample time to talk about her concerns. By pressing forward, you are moving her to action yet maintaining control. But don't steamroll. Leave plenty of time for discussion and venting, if necessary. And be sure to schedule your next review meeting, ideally one quarter out, to allow sufficient time for your current actions to settle.

The upside of all this? Your businesslike approach, combined with insightful strategies, could earn you additional assets and maybe a referral or two. There aren't too many advisors taking control these days. Be one of them.

Newsletters, Mail, and Other Contacts

While the in-person meeting is by far the most valued—and valuable—form of communication and interaction with top clients, you can leverage these contacts with supplemental communications via e-mail, regular mail, phone, and group meetings. Many advisors send clients quarterly newsletters provided by their firms or created on their own. (Before doing any outside communication, check with your firm's compliance department.)

I receive a number of newsletters every quarter and the variety is amazing. Most efforts have the obligatory market commentary, which typically reflects a consensus view—harmless and safe from a compliance perspective—as well as regulatory changes or Internal Revenue Service rulings that might affect a client household. There is often a specific topic of interest within the broader world of wealth management, such as a discussion of advance directives, charitable trusts, or hedge funds, and a suggestion for more information or a direct consultation. The more interesting letters include some personal information or news about the practice or a profile of one of the practice's professionals. This is a nice touch in that it makes your business more personal to the client and helps better position someone in your practice as a provider of assistance. Finally, I'm always drawn to the letters that include a review of a restaurant, hotel, recently read book, or even wine. These remind me of Steve Forbes' New York City restaurant reviews in his regular *Forbes* magazine column. Financial advice is not all about the markets, after all! Some advisors will also weigh in on charities and opportunities to give back. A very successful advisory practice, managed by Leon Levy in Philadelphia, highlights in its outgoing e-mails and on its web site the importance of supporting juvenile diabetes research—a longtime interest held by Leon and his team. All of these ideas provide clients with a more balanced view of you and your practice. They contribute to a sense of community around your practice because they reveal what you and your colleagues consider important enough to share with clients. You want your clients to talk about you, what you do, what you stand for, and, most important, what it's like to be a client of your practice.

Client Events

A more direct way to create community is to invite clients and key professional referral sources to join you and your team in events that convey the values and spirit of your practice. Properly structured, events personalize your practice, drive referrals, foster intergenerational relationships, and even draw media attention. The specifics that make client events great vary from advisor to advisor, but here are a few events that stand out from among my travels with financial advisors:

- *The picnic.* A Connecticut-based independent advisory practice holds a giant barbecue for more than 2,000 clients and colleagues every summer. A professional photographer is on hand to record the event, and a huge photo album is built and placed on display at each summer's party.
- *Advice on ice.* A Toronto-based advisor rents out the home arena of the Maple Leafs every year and invites the families of all clients. In a hockey-crazy town like Toronto, this event draws attention and is a source of fun for all ages.
- *Drink up!* Since the big client dinner has become too expensive and too much of a time burden for most clients these days, many advisor practices hold wine tastings in conjunction with seminars and other educational events. To make a wine tasting fun, different, and memorable, have a knowledgeable expert from a local shop provide color commentary and perhaps even a blind tasting. Other tips: Don't let attendees pour their own servings, and keep the event short so no one gets smashed.
- *The market guru.* John Rafal of Essex Financial Services holds an annual dessert and coffee affair for his top clients and invites a speaker from among his many national industry contacts. Adding his own thanks for the clients' support during the year, he kicks off the event by introducing his team and reinforcing their commitment to client solutions. The speaker is asked to hold forth on the current investing environment and provide context and perspective to the clients. With over 200 people in attendance, the event has become well known in the area. The editor of a regional radio broadcast—a longtime contact of John's—is an attendee, and his reviews of the meeting, John's practice, and the speaker's main points are aired on many business broadcasts the following day.
- *Investing perspectives.* Every January, advisor Kerry in Southern California holds a series of market strategy conferences for his clients. To accommodate their busy schedules, he offers identical sessions in the afternoon and evening of day one and in the morning and afternoon of day two. The format is professional

and practical. Three to four individual presentations comprise the meeting agenda, each addressing a topic of general interest to the affluent clients, who are encouraged to then follow up with individual strategy sessions to implement the ideas discussed in the larger forum.

- *The fishing trip.* An advisor in the Pacific Northwest sponsors a trip each year with several of his top clients. They rent a cabin and guide for a salmon fishing excursion that also serves as one of the group's advisory board meetings. The trip itself has become not only a unique bonding experience, but also a source of referrals as the clients return and explain to friends and colleagues how their financial advisor takes his board away for a retreat each year.

Receiving Ongoing Client Input

The advisor board event conducted by our colleague out in the Cascades reminds me how valuable regular input can be if it's coming from your best clients. No business can succeed without knowing what its best customers want and how competitors are trying to lure them away (just ask Ford or General Motors). Yet few financial advisors or their firms do effective market research. From advisor workshops we have conducted around the country, I have come away stunned by the lack of focus on top clients—and the paucity of knowledge about the competition. If you are serious about retaining your best clients in this competitive environment, you'd best get started by tuning in to those clients and boning up on the strategies of successful competitors.

Start by creating a venue conducive to learning more from these clients—a lunch or, even better, an intimate dinner. "I'd like to buy you dinner and ask your advice" is the line used by a great advisor team we know at a Wisconsin branch of a wirehouse. The team, which had successful business careers outside of financial services before becoming advisors, knows the value of market research and queries four or five top clients about their practice at least once a year.

"How are we doing?" is their lead question. They don't mention products or services because the dinner is totally focused on the client and the client's views of the practice. One of the advisors admits that asking that lead question wasn't easy at first. "We heard some things we didn't want to hear!"

But don't be squeamish. Ask your guests how you can improve your services to them, and press for specifics. Don't let them off the hook by accepting platitudes about your services. At the same time, don't cut them off or get defensive if they point out what they consider deficiencies. One advisor often asks, " 'If there is only one thing we could fix, what would it be?' That breaks the ice, and then we're off and running!"

If you believe ongoing input would be helpful—and it is—choose clients for your personal advisory board very carefully. Clients who have unique needs or use few services may not be the best sources of guidance. For example, one of the largest clients of a Midwestern advisor was a corporation that kept $3 million in a cash management account. The account was not especially profitable and it was unlike the bulk of the advisor's accounts, which were held by high net worth individuals. Business owners in general, however, make the best advisors, report our wealth management contacts, because they know the challenges of running a business and are familiar with issues such as technology and compensation.

If you are contemplating a shift in focus for your practice, such as moving toward more fee-based business or increasing account size, try out the idea on your advisory board. After meeting with its board, for example, the Wisconsin team began to reduce the number of clients it served. "They loved the idea, but we almost blew it when we explained how we planned to carve out 175 first-class clients from a book of well over 1,000," a team member said. "The board couldn't fathom how we would have the time to serve even 175 clients."

Another benefit of talking with top clients about your services is the opportunity to learn about the competition from those who are their targets.

"We learned the hard way that clients don't tell us everything," says Gerry, part of a $2 million team in Connecticut. "We brought a hedge fund to several top clients only to find out they already owned it!"

Do You Take Another Client's Call?

Here's an interesting question posed by a top advisor: "When meeting with a top client, do you take a call from another top client?"

Advisors I know are split on the correct response. One great advisor in Mississippi said the right thing to do is take the call. He then showed me his two business cards. One is for everyday use. The other is for his 30 top clients only; it includes his mobile phone number. "I tell them they can call me any day of the week—up to 10 P.M. my time."

Only one client has called him late in the evening—at 9:59 P.M.—just to make sure he would answer.

Other advisors say they wouldn't interrupt one client for another, generally because the private time with a top client should be respected. Geoff, in Western Canada, says he always includes at least one member of his team in meetings with top clients so that ducking out for an emergency call is doable. Clients, he says, seem to understand that they could be that caller with an emergency question someday.

SUMMING UP THE CLIENT EXPERIENCE

If you pull together all the services you offer and create a format for sharing them with clients, you should be able to explain your client experience with precision, confidence, and speed. Here's what an Advisor for Life might say if asked to describe the way in which his team interacts with prospects and clients:

- Before you become a client of our practice, you must invest at least two hours of your time in an interview and discussion about your current financial situation, your goals, and your concerns. This interview is part of a three-step process that gives us a chance to become familiar with each other, to discover areas in which we might assist you and your family, and, finally, to provide recommendations and take initial steps to fulfill your needs.

- As a client of our practice, you can expect monthly personal contacts. Of these monthly contacts, four will be in the form of in-person meetings in which we will discuss important aspects of your financial picture. These meetings are a cornerstone of our service to you and we value your attendance at all four sessions. We will also meet at least annually with other members of your family, business colleagues, accountants, attorneys, and other advisors in order to provide a more complete and current supervision of your financial needs.
- In order to fulfill our obligations to you, we require you to keep us updated as to any and all changes in your financial situation, as well as assets and investments held by other institutions.
- You will receive written and/or e-mail confirmation of all transactions as well as printed or electronic statements on a regular basis.
- Please join us for our annual golf event benefiting Hamilton House, a long-established shelter for homeless families in our area, and at our Client Conference, this year featuring the portfolio manager of the top-performing Success Fund and held at the City Yacht Club.

Master the process, and the client experience you offer should be a source of discussion among your clients that they can easily explain to others. In finance as in baseball movies, "If you build it, they will come."

Have Your Answers Ready

At your first meeting, a prospect is likely to want to learn more about you. To cement your image as a confident, knowledgeable advisor, be prepared with ready answers to perennials such as these:

- *How do you charge?* Today, your answer needn't be a black-and-white commissions-or-fees response. Clients today want a choice—and surveys of millionaire households in recent years have revealed that clients know they can use their fees and product purchases to obtain other services. For example, a

(Continued)

Have Your Answers Ready *(Continued)*

significant portion of respondents to a recent Phoenix Wealth Survey said that their financial plan was paid for by purchases of financial products, such as managed accounts. One successful advisor in Ohio suggests clients have a brokerage account for their personal trading, but keep their pension and "serious money" in fee-based accounts that he farms out to professional managers.

- *How many clients do you have?* Private schools and college admissions officers can tell you their enrollments at the drop of a mortarboard. Your answer conveys how busy you are and how likely you are to be available for a new client.

- *What kind of clients do you have?* I'm always amazed at the perceptions held by clients about the type of advisor they need given their situations. Some folks believe they must have the best, even if their temperaments and assets don't support their lofty expectations. By contrast, some quite wealthy people don't believe they have enough money to "be important" at a particular private bank or boutique advisory firm.

Exercise: Using Client Reviews to Revive Your Practice

- List your top 20 clients by trailing 12 months' revenues, not assets. These are the folks who are driving your current success.

- Note the last time you met for an in-depth discussion of their complete wealth situation. Set up a meeting immediately if it has been more than 60 days. Tell them a lot has been happening in the markets and you should meet to determine what steps, if any, are needed now.

- Think of their current concerns. A recent survey of affluent investors indicates their greatest fear is a decline in their living standards during retirement. Consider other wealth potholes. For business owners, what is the impact of the slowing economy? What about parents and older relatives—any medical worries there?

- Suggest new investments in specific sectors that have been battered, or that you think have real promise. Remind the clients that it is your job to bring up strategies that don't appear obvious. Your stature will rise, regardless of whether they are emotionally prepared to act.
- Lay out your thoughts about a more regular schedule to discuss wealth topics. Introduce the concept of scheduled conferences and put the next one on the calendar now. The dentist does it— why not you?
- Ask clients individually about how you and your team can increase your value. Are you overlooking any key services? Remember that these conversations are taking place with your very best clients. Go on the offensive to test your value and sharpen your services to fit. Do it now—don't become a statistic in the loss column!

CHAPTER 15

Driving Referrals

- *How can you earn your share of financial advice referrals—and not get stuck in the "investments" box?*
- *What is the driver of many boomer referrals—greed or need?*
- *What action steps should be on your referral list?*
- *How can you use case studies to create referrals from clients and centers of influence?*

As your business model changes, so too will the way you drive referrals. The Advisor for Life can draw from four distinct referral pools.

IT'S 10 A.M.—DO YOU KNOW WHAT YOUR CLIENTS ARE SAYING ABOUT YOU?

Consider this interaction between members of two affluent households:

Meg, a successful attorney, has just finished a tennis match with Sue, a full-time mom and wife of an attorney. The women and their husbands are friends.

"Meg, I need to ask your advice."

"Of course. Personal or professional?" Meg teases, with a smile.

"No, really," Sue pleads. "Tim and I have been considering our financial situation and we need to find a new advisor."

"What do you mean?" Meg responds. "I thought you worked with Wally [their mutual friend and a broker with a major national firm]. Is there a problem?"

"Well, I suppose so. Don't get me wrong—Wally has been a big help with our investments—and he helped us set up accounts for the kids. And of course he's such a nice guy," says Sue. "But recently we've had to work out Tim's mother's estate—and we had some issues about the retirement plan Tim set up for his employees. Wally couldn't answer most of our questions!"

"Hmm," Meg answers. "What are you saying?"

"All Wally seems to know about is investments," says Sue. "And our account performance lately is nothing to get excited about."

Exchanges like that between Meg and Sue may be happening more frequently than you think. Many clients think of their advisor as an "investments" guy rather than as something more. In the 2006 Phoenix Wealth Survey of millionaire households, more than 60 percent of respondents said the primary basis for their relationship with a financial advisor is for investments. But, as we know, investments are only part of the overall advice picture. At a certain point in the growth of a client household, the investments-only advisor becomes at risk if his expertise does not encompass areas of concern or interest to his clients, such as liability management, estate planning, and charitable giving—all areas identified earlier as key interests of affluent clients. The advisor who cannot rise to meet the planning challenges represented by these more complex issues will suddenly become expendable—even though the advisor may have performed competently in the relationship to date—and be well liked.

As boomers age and become increasingly aware of their vulnerability from underfunded retirement plans, the need to care for aging parents, and the necessity to fund their own longevity, they will outgrow their investments-only advisors. Faced with such important and immediate life issues, otherwise affluent households will be searching for help. This is of course the payoff for the Advisor for Life. As other advisors and brokers remained focused on investments, you will have created a practice based on providing solutions to real-life challenges—and the world will be looking for you. Much of your new business will be driven by prospects' feelings of vulnerability rather than desire for better investment returns. That shift is causing a fundamental change in the nature of client referrals, which now become based on the ability to solve problems and prevent and mitigate loss.

The old referral model based on performance helped most of today's financial advisors build their practices during the bull markets of the past 25 years, and with them much of the entire advice industry. Obviously, the investment-based referral is not dead; talented advisors always will be able to attract clients based on investing acumen. But the demographic wave of aging baby boomers is changing the rules of the game—and the rewards will go to the advisors who can make the shift.

GENERATING REFERRALS FROM FOUR SOURCES

In seeking referrals based on the ability to provide investment success, advisors focus on entrée to profit-seeking opportunists. If problem solving becomes your business, you must shift your focus and actively seek out people in trouble. Since the business of medicine is a lot like the business of financial advice giving, the methods doctors use to build their practices and employ referrals can be illustrative. A general, investment-oriented advice giver is much like the old-fashioned general practitioner. The model worked well in small towns or cohesive communities were everyone knew everyone else. But times are changing.

Today, advisors are more like medical specialists. High-end specialists in estate planning and concentrated stock positions are akin to cardiac surgeons and pediatric oncologists. In both worlds, the specialists stand far higher in esteem than the generalists, but both require the support of a bigger geographic area and a referral network in order for their practices to be economically viable. Medical specialists rely on their reputations for referrals from four principal sources: generalists, other specialists, promotion of their practice, and patients. In the financial realm, the referral sources are analogous.

Generalists

These are the journeymen stockbrokers, junior reps, and other advisors who are uncomfortable with the complexities of being an Advisor for Life. Since many advisors prefer to discuss only investments, they risk losing clients whose requirements exceed those of their limited focus. The potential for partnering with less sophisticated advisors is substantial—and one of the most significant growth opportunities for top advisors.

Tim, an advisor I've known for many years, works with several very sophisticated ultra-high-net-worth families and has been successful in creating innovative portfolio solutions. He shares his expertise with a number of advisors who each typically have only one such client. Tim supports the advisors with his portfolio solutions, while the advisors maintain the primary relationship. This account sharing trend is powerful, and I've seen versions in which advisors tap into the expertise of other advisors because of specialized knowledge in 401(k) and pension investments, estate planning, business succession, concentrated stock liquidation, and charitable giving strategies. Imagine the power of your practice if you became known for a particular strategy and were able to market yourself through other advisors; that is one of the highest-potential-impact strategies to boost your business to the next level of production.

Other Specialists

Talented professionals prefer the company of other professionals. The best accountants, lawyers, lenders, life agents, actuaries, family office directors, hedge fund managers, and private bankers all travel in the orbit of affluent clients and don't have time for marginal players. These colleagues are a significant source of potential referrals; cultivating them is time well spent. You will need to arm them with concrete examples of how you have helped your clients. The best way to provide this information is with a case study. Once these other professionals work with you, they will acquire their own insight into your skills and process. Until then, the case study can represent you well. (See later in the chapter.)

Direct Promotion of Your Practice and Your Firm

By promoting your team, your firm, and your knowledge, you will be able to drive business without seeming to be a self-promoter. Take the example of Clayton, a top wirehouse advisor and the lead principal of a team in a small Western city. As a fixture in his community for many years, he does little or no prospecting. Nevertheless, he pays for a prominent ad in the city's annual magazine and directory. The big ad stands as testimony to the reality that Clayton's practice is *the* financial advisory practice in town.

In his South Florida community, Bob makes sure that his team holds leadership positions in several major local charities. Most charities willingly publicize top givers, and Bob takes advantage of that fact. He reports that consistency is the key to reaping benefits from these efforts. Many advisors and business owners are short-term thinkers, he says. They will support a charity for a year or two in a big way, then lose their focus or reduce their commitment. Bob says that for a charitable involvement to work the commitment must be real, not just a public relations (PR) ploy, which is why he is actively involved in each of the charities he supports.

In affluent Beverly Hills, Jack and Tom (not their real names) head a successful financial advisory team that runs a charity golf tournament at a prestigious country club. The project is a major effort, requiring Jack's attention year-round. He solicits donations from business partners as well as local companies, and recruits a celebrity host as well as pro golf stars. His team does little else in the way of advertising because the tournament is so effective in raising the team's visibility.

Clients

People with money tend to associate with other affluent people. Some will refer a financial advisor so that a friend can gain access to a particular product or service such as a hedge fund or help with liquidating a concentrated stock position. To encourage a client or business acquaintance to make a "benevolent" referral—or one made out of concern for the needs of someone else—is more difficult. Aside from the purely selfish motive that a client may not want you to devote your finite time to someone else's problem, the client making the referral must be absolutely certain that you have the expertise necessary to solve the problem at hand.

A great way to solicit benevolent referrals is first to congratulate your client for having spent the time, energy, and money necessary to tackle a thorny planning issue. Consider estate planning. Since fewer than one in four millionaire households has a current estate plan, the risks to a millionaire family can be enormous if the primary income earner were to die prematurely without have done an estate plan. Protecting the family from such a risk—however remote—should be a top priority. But even the very best advisors struggle to bring clients to the estate planning table. Typically, a family addresses the issue after an advisor gets them to establish advance directives to ensure appropriate health care for their aging parents. The advisor then suggests that the clients do the same for themselves. This leads to other estate planning issues and often a full plan. When this occurs, congratulate your clients for their efforts, noting that only 25 percent of households of similar means have taken comparable steps to protect themselves. Then segue into referral mode by asking the next logical question: Do they have friends or colleagues who have similar good intentions but are in the 75 percent category of folks who have not yet gotten around to estate planning?

Remember, the key to creating the benevolent referral is your ability to confront clients with a point of vulnerability—and the need to protect themselves. That willingness to confront and challenge the client is often cited by top clients as a key attribute of a good advisor.

So now consider our earlier post-tennis conversation, but this time with a different twist:

"Sue, what are you saying?"

"Tim and I need more advice than Wally seems comfortable providing—I'm just very worried that some of our issues are beyond his expertise."

"Do you have specific concerns? You mentioned the estate—my firm has a couple of first-rate attorneys who specialize in estate issues. I would be happy to introduce you to them. And what about the retirement plan?"

"Thanks—that would be great. My mother-in-law's attorney retired long before she died and we don't know anyone at that firm. And the retirement plan is probably fine, but I overheard Tim and his controller talking the other day at the shop—something about an audit from the Department of Labor. I asked Tim about it and he said he had no idea what was going on. He and the controller have always picked the investments since the company was really small—but an audit is a big deal, Meg, isn't it?"

"Sue, this could be serious. We need to talk with a specialist. My advisors, Jan and Mike, are real pros with retirement plans. I'll call them right away."

REFERRAL ACTION PLAN

Referrals are not complicated, but even top advisors fail to maintain a conscious effort to generate them from their regular activities. Most experienced advisors with average-sized books of business probably have at their fingertips all the relationships they need to drive considerable referral business. The trick with referral generation, as with most business practices, is to make the effort creative and sustainable.

Consider your choices for referral generation. Of the four primary sources of referrals, which fit naturally with your practice? What can you do to increase the impact of these referral-generating concepts? Here is a checklist of requirements needed for each source of referrals:

Generalist Professional Referrals

- *Bio.* This is a professional biography that includes your background and experience. Your accomplishments should create confidence in another advisor and be superior to those of an advisor who would benefit from bringing you into a client solution.
- *Profile.* This is an overview of you and your team, further supporting your capability to assist another advisor and her client.
- *Your specialty.* This is an outline of your specific expertise, not a listing of the range of your services. You must have a particular specialty in order to position yourself relative to the generalist advisor.
- *An A list.* This is a list of the advisors who have a positive impression of you and your specialty, and who might consider bringing you into a case.
- *The prospect list.* These are names of advisors you don't know well who could be referral sources.
- *Contact plan.* This is a way to stay in touch with your list of advisor referral sources. How about a lunch meeting every quarter?

- *Collaboration plan.* Are there joint prospecting activities you can manage? Client seminars? Professional seminars for accounting professionals?
- *Prospecting plan.* How will you cultivate your list of prospective referring advisors? Do you have a newsletter or case studies of client solutions that you can share to keep your name in front of these advisors?

Specialist Professional Referrals

- All of the items listed for Generalist Professional Referrals. These constitute the basic components of your Referral Toolkit. However, modify specific elements as below.
- *The specialist A list.* Professionals with whom you share clients today: accounting professionals for sure, but also estate attorneys, mortgage lenders, insurance agents, benefits consultants, and record keepers for retirement plans. For handy reference, sort this list by profession and by client.
- *The specialist prospect list.* Professionals from the categories defined by the A list with whom you do not now share clients. Who do you want to meet and get to know? What do you know about their practices? Sort this list by profession.
- *Contact plan.* What is your plan for staying in touch with your A list? How often do you invite or include A list professionals in your client meetings? Each one of those activities is a reminder of your practice's value to other potential referrals. How often do you meet individually with each A list name without clients: a semiannual lunch or breakfast?
- *Collaboration plan.* How do work with your A list names to jointly prospect new clients? Do you use seminars, charitable events, and educational sessions such as estate-planning programs utilizing attorneys and accountants?
- *Prospecting plan.* How will you bring on new professional referral sources? Do you know enough about each target's practice? Can you invite the professional to a lunch or breakfast to learn more about his or her practice as a potential referral by you? Known as "priming the pump," it remains the easiest way to

meet top professionals. Who would turn down the opportunity to get new business from a top advisor like you?

Referrals from Promotion of Your Practice

- *Public relations.* What are the media opportunities in your community for your practice? Is there a specific target market with its own newsletter, such as building contractors, a country club, a medical group? Is there an opportunity to advertise or to contribute a regular column, such as that describing different advice issues? This is a potential use of your case studies as well.
- *Charitable activities.* What organizations and causes are most important to you and your team today? Can you improve your visibility and support to one or more specific organizations? Is there an annual event you can create or assume from someone else who wants to relinquish the job? What causes are most important to you and your top clients? Can they help to guide your mission?

Client Referrals

- *Client reviews.* This is the number one source of new client referrals. What new success stories have been created by your recent client solutions? Congratulate those clients and ask if there are other people they know suffering from or at risk from the same problem. You can help; would the client be comfortable introducing you? This is the benevolent referral.
- *Challenging clients.* Make a list of your top 50 clients and identify the number one concern of each client household. You should confirm the issue with each family, and to do so you may have to ask open-ended questions in some cases. Sort clients by issue type: estate planning, charitable giving, retirement planning, care of aging parents. Consider creating a batch of clients on each topic and creating a plan to address each topic in an organized way with the assistance of other professionals. For example, if among your top 50 clients, 12 need to complete current estate plans, brainstorm ideas with an attorney from your professional A list about how to help clients take up

the challenge of completing an estate plan. Can the two of you create an estate planning workshop for your clients? Offer two choices of location and time—one daytime and one evening. Make a list of the issues that will be solved in the seminar and send invitations to each client. Call clients yourself—don't delegate the phoning to an assistant—and follow up the invitation. Explain that the seminar was the result of your concern for the client and your interest in creating a simplified solution and an easy way to get started.

- *Client advisors.* This is a superb way to drive referrals when you have the chance to review your business with your "directors." Consistently reviewing your ideal client profile will remind these important advisors of your practice's unique value.

A FINAL THOUGHT ABOUT REFERRALS

Over the years, consultants and financial practice management experts have been exhorting advisors to ask clients for referrals. Advisors often feel sheepish about asking, fearing their clients will interpret the request as an imposition on the relationship, or, worse, turn them down because they don't believe the advisor is worthy of a recommendation.

Using Case Studies to Drive Referrals

The best way to capture new clients is to demonstrate how you've helped others.

Put yourself in the clients' shoes. They seldom know what help they need, what questions to ask, or how much the services should cost. And there is no shortage of financial firms claiming to have wealth management expertise. So how do you convince bewildered potential clients that you are their best choice?

I submit that you teach first. Selling complex services—and being paid well to provide them—often requires that you first explain the situation faced by the client. Would you let a surgeon dig into you without first making sure you understand exactly what is going to be done and how it will help you? Top wealth managers are constantly educating clients about risks and the strategies needed to overcome those risks, and often use the case method to do so. In its simplest form, a case study combines education about a specific financial problem with the solution created by that advisor or team for one of its clients. By clearly illustrating the issues and the steps to tackle the challenge, you enable prospects to get a more complete view of what will be involved should they go down the same financial path.

Here's how to build a case:

First, select a client for whom you solved a financial challenge and write down the story. Lay out all of the specific action steps that took place, including the process of discovering the problem and how you explained it to your client. Save the narrative. Properly edited, it can be submitted for publication.

Next, convert the words into pictures. Edit the narrative to bullet points of action steps. Draw boxes around each step in the process. Note points when you reached a crossroads and a key decision had to be made. The resulting graphic is now a flow chart with more powerful visual imagery for both prospects and centers of influence (such as CPAs) who want a clear view of your process.

Bring on the competition. Show how competing firms might respond at many points in your process. Smart clients talk to other people, so why not shorten the sales cycle by speaking directly to that competitive reality? This approach shows confidence and competence.

Finally, collect your cases. An album of successful case studies is better than a wall of diplomas. It shows that you have helped clients through difficult situations and that you were thorough enough to have chronicled the process. Try asking prospects how many advisors they've met who can match your attention to detail. And those details matter, whether in surgery or in wealth management. Wouldn't you prefer the pro with a proven process?

By focusing on your area of expertise and the problems you have solved for clients, you can offer demonstrable proof of your value and a clear example of what you might be able to accomplish for a new client. In this way, referrals can become an organic part of your practice.

Energizing Referrals

Kerry Bubb: "We have developed connections with a local utility company, a bank, and a credit union. These are important resources for building new clients, too. We have nurtured these relationships over the last 16 years and promote ourselves through these institutions. We recently worked with a power plant that was closing. We ran workshops for their employees on how to manage their retirement plans now that they were losing this job. You have to look for niches like this—they are tough to find but they are out there."

Mary Beth Emson: "To help grow our practice we try to capture the next-generation client—the new business is in the second-generation baby, as we call it. Only after you develop deep-rooted trust with your first-generation client can you begin to tackle the next."

Using Case Studies

Sam (not his real name) and his team have been very successful using case studies with both existing and prospective clients. Here are a few examples of the case summaries they share:

Investment Expertise

Issue:	Client desired to use options strategies to increase portfolio cash flow and limit downside risk.
Proposed Action:	Consider writing covered call options on certain stock positions and executing options "spreads" and "straddles" on other stock positions.
Outcome:	Client's cash flow was increased while limiting downside exposure to certain stocks.

Issue:	Client wanted advice on how to generate high investment returns without being "married" to the stock market.
Proposed Action:	Educate the client with respect to alternative asset classes, including hedge funds, private equity, venture capital, commodities, and floating rate debt.
Outcome:	Client allocated 15 percent of his investment assets to alternative investments that have little or no correlation to the stock market. This has allowed the client to achieve more consistent levels of return while reducing overall investment risk.
Issue:	Client received stock in a publicly traded Standard & Poor's 500 company upon the sale of his privately owned business. The newly acquired stock made up most of the client's net worth.
Proposed Action:	Review the myriad of strategies available to hedge single stock risk, convert the stock into investable cash, and gain access to a more diversified portfolio while minimizing income taxes.
Outcome:	Client implemented a prepaid forward contract and a cashless collar, and utilized an exchange-traded fund.
Issue:	Client funded a family foundation with $30 million of highly appreciated securities and asked for investment guidance.
Proposed Action:	Review goals of the foundation, discuss acceptable levels of investment risk, determine cash flow needs, and determine acceptable asset class utilization.

(Continued)

Using Case Studies *(Continued)*

Outcome: Prepared multiple asset allocations and determined best fit. Drafted Investment Policy Statement detailing both broad investment strategy and methodology for ongoing performance monitoring. Performed due diligence on multiple money managers and assisted with final implementation.

Wealth Management Approach

Issue: Client's private company was set to go public in six months and client wanted to know what planning strategies were available to him.

Proposed Action: Prepare multiple analyses and explain the various planning strategies available, incorporating income tax, estate tax, insurance, and investment considerations.

Outcome: Client implemented an installment sale to a defective grantor trust coupled with a family limited partnership and an irrevocable life insurance trust. On a present value basis, the client and his family saved approximately $80 million.

Issue: Client started a new technology company and wanted advice on corporation structure.

Proposed Action: Work with client's attorneys and accountants to compare and contrast C corporation status versus S corporation status versus limited liability company (LLC) status versus partnership status.

Outcome: Client chose to form an LLC and switch it to a C corporation about one year prior to going public. This enabled the client to save millions of dollars of income taxes while still effectuating all the estate planning strategies he desired.

Issue:	Client's will indicated $10 million would pass to various charities upon her death.
Proposed Action:	Form a family foundation and a charitable lead unitrust (CLUT). Subsequently, contribute $10 million of appreciated stock to the CLUT and allocate the client's generation-skipping transfer (GST) exemption to the CLUT.
Outcome:	Client's charitable legacy can now last forever, resulting in increased family unity. In addition, the client's GST exemption was utilized on a leveraged basis, resulting in millions of dollars of estate tax savings.
Issue:	Client was about to become CEO of a technology company and receive a substantial stock option grant, which would vest over four years. Client wanted wealth management advice.
Proposed Action:	Have employer amend stock option plan to allow for the exercise of unvested options. Client subsequently can exercise the unvested options (and convert them into restricted stock) and file a Section 83(b) election for the restricted stock.
Outcome:	Upon initial public offering (IPO), the client saved millions of dollars of income taxes.

CHAPTER **16**

Selling Yourself

- *How can you better position yourself in the crowded marketplace of financial advisors?*
- *How will you stand out?*
- *What are the important target markets for your services?*
- *What are the hot buttons to press when prospecting affluent households—and how can you best address their concerns?*
- *How can you use the media to promote your practice?*

THE NEW PROSPECTING

In the process of researching and writing this book, I made a number of discoveries. None was more surprising than finding that the majority of top advisors do not actively prospect for new clients. One reason top advisors don't prospect much is that most of their business is fee-based, providing them a comfortable annuitized income that does not require a steady infusion of new transaction-oriented clients. In addition, many top advisors are simply too busy taking care of their existing businesses to bother looking for new clients. In fact, top advisors say they spend just 2 percent of their time prospecting, making it the least significant of all their current activities. Many of the practices I visited in researching this book said that their new business efforts were confined to existing clients, but the vast majority of advisors admitted that no real prospecting is taking place at all. In addition, most advisors believe that trying to attract the business of baby boomers would be tantamount to "starting over." Said one advisor with nearly $2 million in fee-based revenues: "I have a pretty good business with clients I like. With the boomers, I'd have to start developing the clients from scratch, training and educating them, and I just don't have the energy for that. If someone comes along who is willing to let me do what I do, they can be a client."

So aside from being incredibly good news for those advisors who *do* want to prospect affluent households, what does this dearth of prospecting efforts mean for you? It means opportunity, but not if you merely seek "more affluent clients" or view your practice as a big bus with empty seats waiting to be filled with anyone wanting to hop on. Since your current clientele already defines much of what you are and what you do, your new clients should be very much like current clients so that your successful work practices can continue. Adding clients unlike your existing ones will crimp your productivity and divert your resources.

Prospective clients, of course, are totally unaware that you provide wonderful service to people just like them. In order to persuade potential newcomers that you can truly help them and are worthy of their trust (as mentioned before, trustworthiness is consistently the most desired trait in a primary advisor), you should run through the following checklist:

- Do you have a brochure that summarizes the background, experience, and expertise of you and your team? Do your best clients receive copies of this brochure at least once a year, and in the case of referral sources at least two or three times a year?
- Do you have a web site that supports your practice with the same information? Do your referral sources and top clients know about the site, and do you use it to inform both groups about developments at your practice?
- Do you have a newsletter or other client bulletin? Do you send it regularly to top clients, referral sources, and prospective clients? Is your mailing ever followed up by an invitation to a seminar or workshop hosted by your practice? Does anyone ever call the addressees to see if they have any questions about the content and ideas expressed in the newsletter?
- Do you have a "pitch book" that presents you and your practice as though you were in a formal competition for the client's ac-

count? Does each key professional referral source have a current copy, and are those people mailed a new edition when it is revised? Does each member of your advisory board have a copy?

■ Do you have ready-made case studies of important solutions you have created for clients? Do your top clients receive copies when you have solved a problem for another client involving a service that those clients have not addressed? Do you offer a workshop to top clients featuring the topic and invite them to tackle this thorny issue in the company of other folks facing the same issue? Do you invite specialist professionals to assist in the workshop and to work with your best clients? Do those professionals reciprocate with referrals for you?

The bottom-line requirements of this list of prospecting tools: Do they convey your expertise, experience, and value proposition to your existing clients, affluent prospects, and critical referral sources? You may not need all of these tools in order to chase down new clients, but make sure you have enough firepower before you wade into the next arena—your selected target markets.

HAVE TOOLKIT, SEEK TARGET

When meeting an advisor for the first time, I usually ask the advisor to tell me about her target market. The answer tells me a lot about that advisor's practice and whether she is actively prospecting. I hate to tell you how many times the answer has come back, "Target market? Sure—people with money." That's not target marketing.

Targeting requires defining and going after a very narrow slice of the broad, overall market—which in the case of the financial services business is "people with money." The general advertising done by the wirehouses is aimed at this general affluent market. But the Jane Doe advisory business must focus on something a little more precise. Consider these target markets:

■ Clients of a specific accounting firm, estate attorney, long-term care specialist, or pension accounting company. Are you the number one provider, or just one of three or four advisors on a list given to clients upon request?

- Membership of your country club, business club, social club, yacht club, beach club, or skiing group. I recently attended a dinner party at the invitation of a friend who is an acquaintance of a superb financial advisor—also in attendance. By the end of the evening, I realized that everyone at the party was also a client of the advisor, who is especially effective at creating a community of clients. If you are a friend of a client, he will track you down!

- Clients who are in the same business. George, a wirehouse advisor in Indiana, has been a creative thinker for many years as he built his successful practice. One of his best clients owns a manufacturing company and was impressed that George spent so much time learning about the client's business. He invited George to attend a national trade show for his industry. George took him up on the offer and has earned several significant clients as a result of the initial effort.

- An extended family. This niche might not be very lucrative unless the family is very wealthy, but it's another potential group of clients that can be secured from competition if you have a good relationship with the right family member.

- Members of the same medical or legal group. Steve in Boston was able to secure the account of a successful orthopedist, which led to the management of the physician's group pension, shared with more than 30 other professionals. Management of both accounts has led to other referrals from within the group.

- Executives of the same company. Especially effective for working with concentrated stock, retirement plans, rollovers, and executive benefits, this niche can be very lucrative if you are willing to work on behalf of the company and spend time with the top people.

- Parents of special needs or handicapped children. An extremely focused group with strong natural bonds, these families are constantly aware of financial challenges and are used to making difficult decisions. They speak openly and often about their concerns and needs.

- Employees of the same company. Primarily targeting the rollover market, a relationship with the human resources department or treasurer's office can help you develop an exceptional clientele. A wirehouse advisor in Philadelphia has been the main contact for virtually every new retiree at a major nearby petrochemical plant. Advisors in Cincinnati have worked with a well-known Fortune 500 company, providing countless retirement seminars featuring speakers from established investment management organizations available in their firms' managed account programs.

You probably have a considerable array of target markets right at the edge of your current practice. The secret to determining logical and available target markets is a review of your best clients. What groups do they represent? What relationships do they have? List just your top 20 client households one more time. To this list, add several columns for their affiliations. Look at the table in search of relationships and potential areas of common interest. Your goal is to begin building "pods" of clients in particular areas that can anchor a broader network of clients. These smaller niches can be protected from competitors because of the natural affinity of the members for each other. By infiltrating the group and becoming the advisor of choice, you can add to the group's sense of community—you are "their" advisor, just as they likely have "their" insurance agent, bank, accountant, restaurant, and golf course. In a simpler and less competitive time, you might have specialized in working with physicians or entrepreneurs, but the world has become smaller and markets more precise. Use each of these mini-niches like you would a toehold or fingerhold while scaling a rock wall. None of them is likely substantial enough to carry your book, but combined they get you to where you need to go.

Once you have defined a target market, you must employ a value proposition focused on the unique needs of that affinity group. For groups bonded by economic circumstances, it's a lot easier to create a particular approach based on a specific solution. For example, the retirees of a particular large company will all need to know their choices of retirement income options and will value anyone who can provide that information simply and clearly and with understandable, actionable choices. For adults with aging parents, the need for long-term care guidance and the use of advance directives can quickly unify an otherwise diverse group around specific topics addressed by your practice.

Small Accounts—The Debate

Nearly every securities firm has implored its advisors to seek larger accounts. The Securities Industry and Financial Markets Association (SIFMA) has reported that in 2005 the average brokerage book contained 538 accounts, and the average account value was $107,000. Consider the 80/20 rule, and it is not inconceivable that most accounts are much smaller than $100,000, the typical new minimum account size set by the firms. Is this majority truly unprofitable?

The counterargument is that many desirable clients lurk in these smaller accounts. Shaken by the collapse of retirement accounts, yet smart enough to know they must continue to invest, many investors have spread their assets across multiple relationships and may be in search of a single advisory home. But right now, they are looking for a real plan to get them back on the road to recovery. Your goal should be to develop strategies that get them moving and encourage them to consolidate their assets—and, in the process, bump off at least some of your competitors. So what can you offer?

- Asset allocation funds—especially those with automatic rebalancing.
- Multiple discipline accounts—separate account portfolios bundled together for better diversification and typically offering rebalancing.
- Mutual fund managed accounts—offering multiple funds across a variety of asset classes and manager styles. The automatic rebalancing feature, performance reporting, and tax lot record keeping are time-saving client service bonuses.

Although consulting purists first turned up their noses at the new packages, many eventually began to see the products' inherent appeal. One advisor I know has begun to use a fund of funds for his accounts under $250,000. "I get the diversification the clients need without the headaches of too many statements and fund oversight," he says, "and rebalancing is automatic—even the best clients balk at rebalancing in the heat of the moment." The advisor's team has raised over $40 million for the new strategy and is actively prospecting smaller accounts with very limited competition.

But target marketing need not be entirely reactive. You can create a niche if you can find an issue or service that draws people to you. In this *Field of Dreams* approach, find an area left open by other advisors, develop a convincing and eye-catching story, and then promote your idea with conviction and consistency for as long as it takes to draw a sustainable client base. A good example of this type of marketing is that used by law firms in the aftermath of specific events causing injury or loss—asbestos, securities fraud, tobacco. Law firms seeking clients appeal directly to the victim's desire for retribution—no dainty or passive approaches here. With a generation of aging boomers facing new awareness of their risks, you have many niches from which to choose in building affinity groups of clients. What hot buttons can you press to reach members of these groups without being drowned out by other financial providers and general advertising? Get personal and get loud. Not only must your idea strike a distinctive chord with your target, it must be a sustainable idea—one that you can use to anchor a campaign among affluent clients. You want people to start talking about your ideas to their friends and colleagues so you can leverage your impact. Don't underestimate how many times a prospective client may have to hear your message before taking action. Working for years with financial advisors, I've adopted the industry adage that any marketing message must be delivered at least seven times to a specific prospect for that person to take action—anything less is ineffective. You have to muster the energy to keep talking. Your conviction will make the sale more than logic, data, or a scary anecdote will.

MILLIONAIRE HOT BUTTONS—PRESS HERE

Establishing your target markets around key emotional issues is one of the best ways to ensure that your efforts resonate with prospective clients. Here are some hot-button issues and associated marketing strategies to consider:

Hot Button: Doubts about quality of advice

Strategy: The second opinion

Since many clients complain that the advisors are insufficiently proactive, step into that breach and offer your own suggestions. One of the best opportunities to acquire high net worth clients today is to offer a second opinion to prospects whose current advisor is inattentive. The goal is to demonstrate true financial consulting (asset allocation, manager selection, and other financial advice) so that disgruntled clients can come to understand that they have outgrown their less enlightened advisors. Most retirement plan wrecks are the result of violating one of the basic rules of intelligent investing. Don't assume a millionaire household fully understands why they have not succeeded or how they can recover. Offer your experience and perspective via a short, professional note with your card attached.

Hot Button: Fear of losing independence

Strategy: Writing a booklet

Surveys of baby boomers reveal that their primary concerns—a major illness, inability to afford health insurance, having to live in a nursing home—revolve around the fear of losing their independence. This is such a personal and emotional issue that pressing this hot button could traumatize a client. The trick is to turn the emotion into positive energy so that the problem can be addressed without getting wrapped up in a family's angst.

Remind clients that nursing home care and other long-term care needs can be funded with long-term care insurance and perhaps early purchase of arrangements at a continuing care retirement facility (see Chapter 11). In addition to reminding clients about long-term care options, make sure there are extensive advance directives in place to ensure that the client's wishes are carried out. This phase of your involvement is the most immediate and most impactful. A therapist's trick to help children address their fears is to have them write out a story or make a picture. Having clients complete a booklet about how they want to live in their older years—and the provisions they have made for the life they envision—can be very calming. Offer a workshop about preparing such a booklet to clients and prospects.

Hot Button: Aged parents

Strategy: Discussing a wide range of options

Baby boomers, on average, have more parents than children. This demographic reversal has shifted the economic burden of aging disproportionately to the boomers. Your target clients may be caught off guard by the need to provide care, both economic and emotional, to parents who may have underestimated their own longevity. Your strategy could be to provide a survival package of late-stage liquidity and expense-mitigating ideas. These include long-term care insurance, immediate annuities for income/longevity protection, and information about how to buy medical insurance and reverse mortgages. Consider sponsoring a discussion group of clients who have parental care challenges.

Hot Button: Too much debt

Strategy: Becoming a flexible lender

Wealth is a balance sheet, and huge inroads are possible if you can assist history's most accomplished debtors—the boomers—with their liabilities. Merrill Lynch and other firms have been very successful attracting boomer clients using interest-only mortgages. In addition, lines of credit can open doors to otherwise elusive business owners. Your compensation here is a referral fee, but it's also one of those benign referrals; clients can refer you to others without fearing you don't have the time to continue serving them.

Hot Button: Family's vulnerability should something happen to client

Strategy: Adding estate planning and insurance

Appeals to a client's fear of premature death are always iffy, especially among a boomer generation convinced of its longevity and vitality. Nevertheless, consider the hot button of this target market because only about one in four millionaire households has a current estate plan. In addition, the boomer generation shows signs of comprehending the enormity of its responsibilities; many boomers are coming to understand that an event as random as an illness or accident can completely destroy a life and lifestyle built on borrowing. Without adequate insurance in place, an unexpected reversal could wreak enormous dislocation and trauma. Ask the question again—"What would happen if something happened to you?"—and consider your top client house-holds. Maybe even consider your own. Suggestion: Broach this subject to a client household in the presence of both spouses and watch the body language of both parties. You'll get a sense of the receptivity and who feels more vulnerable.

Hot Button: Fear of incapacity

Strategy: A risk-prevention audit

Disability is more common than accidental death, but most affluent households do not carry adequate protection to maintain a lifestyle or a business should the chief breadwinner no longer be able to work. Even if an executive were covered through a policy at work, it is un-likely that the group policy would provide the income most affluent families require to meet current living expenses. And the likelihood of coverage for a nonworking spouse is almost nil, although the lost mo-bility of that person could be devastating to the household. To address the need, conduct a risk prevention/minimization audit. Where are the family's primary risks? What are the areas of each household's greatest economic vulnerability? What might happen if the household's income producer(s) could not work?

Hot Button: Divorce

Strategy: Offering sound, unemotional advice

Although a divorce may have been a long time coming and its specifics well known in advance, the full impact of the event usually is underestimated. Your empathy and compassion are required, as well as a "let's consider your options" discussion. Handled appropri-ately, this meeting is a listening session, prodded by the occasional simple question and followed by more listening. These are highly charged emotional events, and early actions are typically regretted later. Facilitated often by referral from accountants and attorneys, these cases can make you a valued ally of these important sources if you can provide a view of your strategy and approach to aiding such clients. For divorce cases, an affliction of over half of married couples, you can prepare. Do you have relationships with matrimonial attorneys? Ask around for the best. In many cases, one of the two parties in the divorce might not be entirely familiar with investments and finance. Prove to the centers of influence that you know the divorce-related issues and are sensitive to their needs. And understand that as an advocate—like the attorney—you will have to pick a side.

Hot Button: What do I do with the money?

Strategy: Developing a timing calendar

Few affluent executives or business owners earn their wealth through salaries. Most capture the bulk of their compensation from performance bonuses or profit sharing. Typically, these prospects and clients use those lump-sum payments to fund their investments and must decide what to do with a tidy lump sum once it is received. Since the vast majority of private and public companies pay bonuses in the first three months of a new year, you can work this idea from January through March with confidence that your message will resonate somewhere. Advertising, discussions with accountant contacts, and targeted letters to executives suggesting a discussion about what to do now in the markets all make sense because of the likelihood of activity. For your existing clients, do their distributions occur quarterly or annually? What are the formulas that determine the payouts? Important issue to note: Is business good enough to warrant a payout? Most payouts are made after the books are sorted out at year-end, providing insight into the current status of the business. Be alert to dips—reversals or slumps can impact the mental health of your clients.

MARKETING THROUGH THE MEDIA

There are few sales tools more powerful than having an impartial, influential third party endorse you as an expert. Sure, you can tell the world—or a segment of the world—that you're an expert by buying media space and paying for an advertisement. But while ads can raise awareness, they lack credibility. Being quoted in news and feature stories, however, positions you as a person whose comments and insights are worthy of note.

Joseph Finora, a Long Island, New York–based former Wall Street reporter and public relations executive (jfinora@optonline.net), says that it has never been easier to get quoted in the media because of all the financial web sites, talk shows, and publications regularly looking for financial experts. At the same time, it has never been more difficult to find the right place to say the kind of things that will position you as an expert. Joe suggests using a seasoned public relations (PR) professional to help you reap the benefits of a well-conceived media-relations program. Here are some pointers from Joe:

- Determine your PR objective. How will a comprehensive media-relations program help? Stick with one or two financial themes and areas of knowledge (retirement, municipal bonds, and options are just three examples), and be prepared to stay with the program for the long term. Offering yourself as an expert in one area only to change course a year or two later damages your credibility.

- There are no guarantees in media relations. That's why you should limit comments to subjects in which you're thoroughly knowledgeable. This reduces the possibility of error. If you are asked a question you feel uncomfortable answering, be honest and say you'd like to do some research. Offer to get back to the journalist or refer her to someone better qualified to respond. Providing an incorrect or misleading response can permanently damage your reputation.

- Seek professional PR help from someone who has worked successfully with other advisors or professionals such as attorneys and accountants. Ask at the chamber of commerce or speak with related professionals for a recommendation. Be sure the PR pro you're considering does not work for a direct or indirect competitor. Remember, bigger isn't necessarily better in PR; a small firm with experienced principals can be extremely effective. Before making a choice, check references and examine track records. If you're not ready for a long-term arrangement, ask about individual projects. These can be a good way to get to know each other; six months is a reasonable time frame.

- Although cultivating press relations can take time, after a few months you should be able to tell if your program is starting to work. If not, review what has and has not taken place on your behalf. Regular communication between client and media relations representative is key to success.

- Reporters crave news and timely insights, so make your comments newsworthy by being brief, making a point, and speaking plainly. Don't expect preferential editorial treatment (for example, having your picture taken or being quoted for saying something of little consequence) just because you advertise in the publication for which you're being interviewed. The editorial and advertising departments are separate; asking for editorial coverage because you advertise (or might advertise) is insulting to the editorial staff members who are trying to provide readers with unbiased reporting.

- Do not try to obtain favorable coverage by taking a reporter to lunch or sending a gift. Some media outlets have strict policies against such practices. Ask in advance if you can pay for lunch. At the end of an interview let the writer know you're available for follow-up questions and be sure she has your telephone number and e-mail address. Do not ask to review the story or use the meeting to promote other aspects of your practice. Usually there is no time for either of these, and the reporter may consider such behavior amateurish or insulting.

- Above all, never exaggerate, twist the truth, spin, or (let's use the plain old-fashioned word) lie. A responsible journalist will double- and triple-check information before submitting her story because people are known to be less than reliable when providing information—sometimes this is accidental, other times it's not. So stick to the facts.

Proving You're an Expert

How do you stand out in a marketplace flooded with financial advisors, all proclaiming retirement as their specialty? One way is by adding a specialty and a recognized designation. (See Table 16.1.)

Requirements for certifications vary widely. The Certified Financial Planner (CFP) designation from the Certified Financial Planner Board of Standards, Inc., based in Denver (www.cfp.net), requires three years of study in a variety of planning areas, while the other designations typically require only a few months or even days. Each designation also brings the potential to interact with the national body of members, many of whom are not in the financial advice field. For example, the Society of Certified Senior Advisors has more than 13,000 members, as well as a standards board to maintain professional integrity through supervision of the designees.

"I don't need a designation—my clients already value my expertise," you say. And you are likely correct—for now, because history suggests that the market leaders in any profession are well regarded and effective—right up until the time they lose out to more focused or capable competitors.

When my father and fellow columnist, Glen Gresham, graduated from medical school in the 1950s, rehabilitation medicine was a course of study, but not much of a specialty. Now entire hospitals are focused on the care of patients recovering from strokes, spinal cord injuries, and other ailments that formerly ended most often in death. And think of the growth during our lifetimes of the array of other medical specialists for every body part and affliction imaginable—heart, lungs, feet, hands, skin, and on and on.

With the population of senior Americans more than doubling over the next 40 years, advisors who plan to graduate from their careers with a degree in financial security had better get studying!

TABLE 16.1 Advanced Designations for Life Advisors, 2006

50,000+	Certified Financial Planners (CFPs)
3,500	Certified Senior Advisors
3,000+	Certified Investment Management Analysts (CIMA)
1,000	Chartered Advisors for Senior Living
260	Certified Retirement Financial Advisors
150	Registered Financial Gerontologists

No Time to Prospect? Hire a Rainmaker

Let me ask a blunt question: Are you an advisor or a salesperson? I know, everyone's a salesperson and the advisor/salesperson answer isn't necessarily either-or. But as the delivery of advice becomes more complex and requires more time for analysis and customer service, the time available for rainmaking shrinks. For many advisory practices, hiring a sales and marketing professional to promote and position the advisory practice with potential clients is a smart economic move. The move frees the advisor to spend more time with valued clients while at the same time enabling a sales professional to concentrate on prospecting—which we know is a low priority for most advisors. No matter how great a salesperson you are, someone else talking to others about what you do is more effective than you doing so on your own behalf. Many top advisors have hired full-time marketers to promote their practices. One advisor group on Florida's Gulf Coast was very impressed with a wholesaler from one of the team's investment companies. They took a deep breath, ponied up the cash from among the profits shared by the three principals, and took on the wholesaler. Used to working for a fairly low salary and sales-based incentive compensation, the wholesaler-turned-high-net-worth-practice-advocate got right down to business creating leads and following up both prospects and referrals. He had nearly paid for himself within a year of being hired.

How One Advisor Stumbled onto a Niche

During a recent meeting of a major firm's top advisors, I asked the audience to recall if they had ever found a product or service that was so important and so valuable that they proposed the idea to every single client. The resulting quiet was deafening. After a few moments, a gentleman raised his hand and declared that he had, in fact, offered one product to every client. In fact, he said that he now insists that every client endure his appeal. The audience was

(Continued)

How One Advisor Stumbled onto a Niche *(Continued)*

immediately attentive. What could the product be? A mutual fund? Shares of IBM? Writing covered call options? His answer: a long-term care policy.

Why long-term care? I probed for more information. His explanation was telling.

"I had a client who saved for many years to fund his retirement. One day, he became ill; he began to receive treatments for his condition, and the unexpected health-care costs depleted his retirement account. He was financially and emotionally devastated. I watched it happen, and I was powerless to do anything about it. I have since told that story to every one of my clients, and I demand they consider the risks of not having protection."

I asked, "Before that experience, had you ever sold long-term care insurance?"

"Never," he replied.

The Ideal Client

Greg in Florida avoids the "behavioral finance basket case" as a client. He protects his valued clients by not accepting new clients who will require too much time. "I'll take time on investment issues, but if someone is hiring an advisor to meet social needs, they should join a club. Clients hire us to manage money and preserve wealth, and that is what we do best."

Bill in New York City says, "Our ideal client is a family where you have a business owner and we provide a suite of services for that business—CMA [cash management account], credit functions, 401(k), other retirement plans. It's the multigenerational approach that we want to capture—a family with three or four generations. Our typical client has between $10 million and $30 million is assets and is about 55 years old."

Steve Grillo's ideal client is a self-employed business owner who started the firm. He (or she) is in his (or her) 50s and is married with children near college. Income range is about $150,000 to $200,000

The Ideal Client (*Continued*)

annually. Steve has about 200 clients on the investment side and about 750 on the insurance side. He is spending much time on client/market segmentation to identify the higher net worth prospect, saying, "$200k in assets or more is where we want to be. These are nutritious people whose goals and expectations are not all dollars and cents and who will accept advice. We nurture the clients because as they approach retirement they become bigger and better clients and our chances of retaining them increase."

Kerry Bubb says, "Our niche is really the client who has $400,000 to $1 million in their 401(k), own their home, and have a net worth of about $1.5 million. They have substantial assets in their retirement plan and we help them to efficiently manage it. We don't want the superrich client telling us what to do. Our minimum is $300,000. This is the client we are comfortable with—this is our zone."

His typical referral these days?

"This fellow was recommended to us by several clients. 'Rudolph,' they said, 'you should see Kerry—he can help you.' It goes to our point that your existing clients are your best resource pool. Here is some of the information we captured about Rudolph. It shows the depth and scope of our interviews and data capturing. Rudy is married and has been working for a utility company for 35 years. He and his wife have combined income of $150,000. They have a retirement portfolio that is now worth $2 million. Rudy wants to retire later this year. They want to sell their house and move to Mexico. They will need an income stream. They also need to set up an emergency fund. We know their hobbies, anniversaries, children's names, pet name—all of this personal data paints the picture. We use extensive data sheets to capture every iota of information about the client. They want to sell their home for $629,000, but we are suggesting that they lower the price. If Rudy needs to go back to work to generate income, he can do that by contracting. They have a bad taste for annuities. Rudy's mother is in a nursing home. We are educating them on inflation, what postponing retirement will mean financially, and the 5 percent rule of withdrawal on retirement plans."

(*Continued*)

The Ideal Client *(Continued)*

Sam (not his real name) says, "Our ideal client is a first-generation entrepreneur who sold his company for $50 million and received stock in a publicly traded company. Preferably there are multiple generations involved so they can capture future opportunities for the practice.

"Our clients think we are outstanding advisors and are a cut above the rest because we listen well and are always totally prepared when we meet with them; we are honest and smart, and we are investors ourselves, which we always make a point of telling them. Our clients really want us to make their lives simpler—and they do not want to lose money. Wealth preservation seems to be their biggest concern. Almost as important are cash flow issues for living well. High on the client list, too, is minimizing state taxes—net to heirs, net to philanthropy. Their expectations are reasonable rates of return and highflier avoidance."

CHAPTER 17

Valuing the Advisor for Life Practice

- *Could you monetize the value of your efforts by going to another firm?*
- *By going independent?*
- *By becoming a registered investment advisor?*
- *What about those advisors already operating independently?*

A t some point in their careers, advisors wonder how much their practice is worth.

Here's an answer to the value question.

Stephen Covey said, "Begin with the end in mind." He could have been referring, of course, to the journey an investor takes when entering into the financial planning process. His words have equal value to the practitioners and owners of financial planning and wealth management businesses.

One of the great ironies in our industry is that many advisors don't take the time to create a financial plan for themselves and their business. They rarely think through their goals as a business owner, much less the actual value they will need to realize from the sale or transition of the business in order to fund their own retirement dreams, hopes, and goals. There are many sad stories of advisors selling their firms for the wrong reasons, either because they lacked a plan or because they were forced into a sale due to unforeseen circumstances. So, with the help of Timothy D. Welsh, the founder of Nexus Strategy LLC of Larkspur,

California, and the former director of business consulting services for Schwab Institutional, let's focus on providing a framework to optimize value in an advisory practice and help prepare the Advisor for Life for his or her own future.

Value as a concept and as a hard number, says Tim, can have many meanings and definitions. Whether that value is defined in terms of current income, future sale price, or the ability to fund a lifestyle that enables the advisor to enjoy outside pursuits and interests, its true definition ultimately depends on the individual advisor. Practice valuation is really a discussion about an advisor's own financial planning. And since an advisor's business is most likely her biggest asset, the topic warrants a thorough discussion, whether the advisor is a wirehouse or regional broker or a fee-based independent Registered Investment Advisor (RIA), small or large. To optimize value and provide many choices, the advisor will want to create as many transition options as possible.

To illustrate one successful approach, let's begin with the story of Mike. Starting from scratch, Mike built a very successful investment advisory practice in Boulder, Colorado, eventually selling it to his employees on his terms and timing for a very nice valuation, freeing him to pursue the next chapter in his life. What did he do that is different from most advisors? He started with a plan.

Mike realized early on that he needed to create an organization with continuity that could eventually be run without him. As the academic and professional literature amply documents, the less dependent a business is on its owner, the more valuable and easier it is to transfer. In his first client—a young, motivated, intelligent, and enthusiastic professional—Mike found the qualities upon which he could build a business. So Mike convinced the client to become his first staff member, and then spent the next 10 years building the skills, experience, and wealth of this key employee so that when the time came, Mike's first client and first employee became his firm's second principal owner.

Of course, Mike's experience is unusual. But the process he used to build and realize value is not. That process, similar to the financial planning process, begins by asking a few key questions:

What is your definition of success?

Do you want to maximize the value you receive in a sale?

Do you want to eventually wind down your business and slowly shed clients as you retire?

Do you want to work less and play more?

Do you want to create a legacy and have the firm live beyond you?

Do you want to take care of your clients?

Do you want to take care of your employees?

The answers to these questions will dictate what you must do to define and optimize value for your particular situation. No matter what your desired outcome may be, a business that is systematized, efficient, and not dependent on the owner is the easiest to transition and monetize. Tim can help put some concrete numbers and analysis on this philosophical foundation, although he concedes that there are many ways to calculate and determine the value of a financial practice, with considerable misinformation surrounding the process. Using simple rules of thumb, such as a multiple of revenue, can lead to poor strategic decisions on the part of buyers and sellers, and even to transactions that ultimately fail and destroy business value and goodwill in the process. Consider, for example, an advisory firm in the South generating $3 million in revenue per year, whose two owners take home less than $75,000 each due to the firm's inefficient operation. Using the two-times-revenue multiple typically employed by transition web sites and business brokers, the firm would be valued at about $6 million. But who would want to pay that relatively hefty amount for the opportunity to earn $150,000 and work 60 to 80 hours a week? You'd be better off putting the money in certificates of deposit and playing golf!

The truth is, the value in any transaction resides largely in the down payment, earn-out provisions, tax treatment, and other seemingly ancillary elements—not in the negotiated price. Moreover, investment advisory firms—unlike tax preparation or restaurant franchises that have standardized pricing, technology, and service delivery models—often have vastly different economics, service models, and target markets, making them extremely difficult to compare.

Fortunately, there are some simple tools that can serve as a framework for determining underlying business value, such as the capital asset pricing model (CAPM), that old tool from accounting and finance classes. The formula is

$$V = \frac{CF}{r - g}$$

where value (V) is equal to cash flow (CF)—also known as operating profit; operating cash flow; earnings before interest, taxes, depreciation, and amortization (EBITDA); or other similar definition—divided by risk (r), a factor that is unique to each firm, minus growth (g), which is the long-term expected growth rate, not necessarily the historical rate at which the firm has grown. Why look at this formula in detail? By exploring each variable you can translate the implications of what impacts those variables into specific actions an advisor can take to maximize business value.

As its definition indicates, cash flow is determined by the underlying profitability of the firm. This measure can be simplified by taking an income statement approach and classifying firm expenses into direct expenses and overhead expenses. Direct expenses (the cost of goods sold in the accounting sense) may be defined as those costs incurred in the process of delivering advice to investors. Due to the people-intensive nature and personal touch of the industry, direct expenses consist of all advice-delivery and business-development activities and the direct compensation for people involved in those roles. Overhead expenses consist of the remaining expense items, such as rent, technology, insurance, advertising, and administrative and operational staff, which are necessary to operate the business. If a managing owner is also an advisor with client and business-development responsibilities, her compensation as an advisor and manager would be allocated to direct expenses based on the time spent working with clients and developing new business; the remaining compensation would be allocated to overhead expenses, reflecting her contributions to managing the firm's operations.

Continuing with the income statement approach, we arrive at cash flow by taking revenue and deducting direct expenses. That gives us gross profit, from which we subtract overhead to produce cash flow. Recent studies by the Financial Planning Association and the accounting and consulting firm Moss Adams, LLP, have yielded industry benchmarks based on the financial performance of several top-performing advisory firms. On average, efficient advisory firms spend roughly 40 percent of revenues on direct expenses and 35 percent on overhead expenses, leaving 25 percent of revenues as the operating cash flow of the business.

The next step in computing value is creating a proxy for the r in the calculation, or risk. In essence, we are trying to determine the rate of return required to compensate the owners for the business risk they are taking by owning a small investment advisory business. Risk is determined by several factors including firm size, concentration of the client base, overall client demographics, dependence on key employees, and types of revenue (recurring fees versus commissions). Clearly, firm size matters. A larger advisory firm with a diverse client base is less dependent on any one client as a percentage of total revenue; simply put, in a large firm there is less risk if any one client, no matter how significant, leaves. Similarly, a larger firm is less dependent on any one employee. If a key employee were to leave, the impact likely would be greater in a small firm than in a larger firm. Other risk areas involve business operations. Is the firm fully compliant with regulatory procedures? Are there any ticking time bombs in the client base in terms of potential litigation or regulatory fines? Even the kind of investing a firm encourages entails risk. If the firm is equities oriented, for example, its value is more at risk if equity markets were to turn down and the value of client assets were to fall.

So, what is a good proxy for risk in the formula? If we look at other asset classes and the rates of return required to compensate investors for the risks of investing in those, we can see that r for a closely held, illiquid, small business like an investment advisory firm is somewhere between the risk of a small-cap stock traded on NASDAQ (~15 percent) and that of an investment in venture capital (~50+ percent). For most established advisory firms with a history of profitability, industry experts agree that the risk figure usually is in the 20 percent to 35 percent range. Again, these numbers are merely guides, not necessarily what would be used when negotiating any specific deal.

This brings us to the last variable, growth (g). Growth in the CAPM formula is reflective of a long-term growth rate and is therefore theoretical in nature. It is not the historic growth rate of the firm; many advisory firms are less than 25 years old and have a high rate of growth due to their youth and the recent performance of the financial markets. They do not have a track record over a long enough time frame to compare performance over several market cycles. As a result, g is determined by the economy, expectations of the industry, investor demographics, and growth expectations of the specific business. It is therefore likely to be somewhere between 0 percent and 10 percent and can actually be negative in cases where a large portion of the client base would be likely to defect given an ownership transition. Again, this is a long-term growth rate for purposes of valuing the future cash flows of the business over many, many years.

What factors impact growth? From a buyer's point of view, the demographic makeup of the client base is extremely important. If an advisory firm has a large percentage of older clients receiving distributions from fixed-income investments, for example, growth would be slow (or even negative). Compare that to a client base consisting of young executives and professionals accumulating assets during their prime earning years. The aging of the baby boomers, in fact, will have a powerful impact on advisory firm valuation going forward, as more and more advisors focus on serving the distribution phase of wealth accumulation. Other factors that can influence g are operational efficiency and whether a firm can scale its existing infrastructure, whether a firm has a systematized sales and marketing capability that is proven to attract assets regardless of market conditions, and the area in which the firm is located (is it growing and economically vibrant?).

Now, let's look at a hypothetical efficient, long-established advisory firm having $1 million in revenue and good growth prospects. What would its value be? Returning to the formula

$$V = \frac{CF}{r - g}$$

we find that cash flow is $250,000, risk is 20 percent, and growth is 5 percent, producing a value of $250,000 divided by 15 percent, or $1.7 million.

Obviously, not all advisory firms are worth seven times cash flow or 1.7 times revenue, as in this hypothetical example. The key takeaway from this analysis is that there are several areas in the advisory business in which determined effort can build value. In essence, anything that increases cash flow, reduces risk, and increases growth is worth focusing on and investing time in. Specifically, infrastructure, systems, and good people are the keys to driving value.

From Table 17.1, it is clear that many of these tactics go hand in hand with developing a systematized, team-based service model that leverages technology. Doing so provides the business owner with the operational leverage to gain scale, better serve clients, develop employees, create career paths, and allow the business to function without the owner, as well as have clients who develop loyalties to the firm, not to one individual.

One growth strategy that is rapidly gaining acceptance is the building of an ensemble or team-based organizational structure. Pioneered by Moss Adams, this approach solves the business owner dependency issue by creating sets of teams led by a single senior advisor (or principal). (See Figure 17.1.) The senior advisor is responsible for overseeing the client relationship, setting the strategic direction of the relationship and the investment policy, as well as managing the team and new business development. Junior advisors are responsible for direct client contact and day-to-day servicing of the client along with financial and investment plan development. Each senior advisor manages three or four junior advisors and is supported by a pool of

TABLE 17.1 Focus Areas to Increase Business Value

Ways to Increase Cash Flow	*Ways to Reduce Risk*	*Ways to Increase Growth*
Efficient operations	Strong compliance culture	Systematized marketing strategy
Leverage technology	No one client or set of clients represents large percentage of revenues	Client base that is skewed toward contribution phase vs. withdrawal phase
Team-based service models	Client loyalty is to the firm and not to one individual or owner	Broad service offering
Gain scale	Experienced, skilled employee bench	Free up principal time for business development and strategic thinking

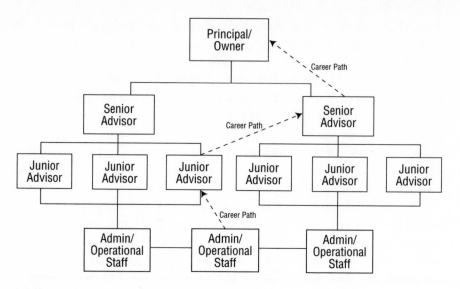

FIGURE 17.1 Team-Based Organization Chart

operational and administrative personnel shared by other teams. Benchmarks for the total number of relationships and assets under management (AUM) that can be handled per team, depending on service delivery (wealth management versus money management), vary, but roughly equate to about 100 relationships or $100 million in AUM per team. An added benefit to this approach is that the client works with a team and does not become attached to any one individual. Additionally, the team structure provides a career path for employees, who may be able to assume an ownership and/or managerial role in the firm one day. It also provides a scalable service platform that frees senior advisors to pursue new business development and to develop the firm and personnel.

One large gap apparent in advisory firms today is a dearth of managerial, entrepreneurial, and financially capable talent necessary to become future leaders and owners. Typically, advisory firms are created by entrepreneurs who add operational and administrative staff as they go along—not with any succession plan in mind. Once such firms enjoy success and reach critical mass, founders struggle to find people to take on more senior roles. Additionally, as founders look to their staff to eventually become owners, they realize that many staffers do not have the financial wherewithal to invest in a firm that may be worth several million dollars. As a result, founders' options often are limited to a small set of strategic buyers, such as banks or roll-up firms, that can afford to buy them out. This result may be very far from what they envisioned as a successful endgame.

This problem can be solved by creating an organization that has a career path and partner track. Also, creative long-term compensation plans can make partnership affordable. Mike, the Colorado advisor mentioned earlier, established a deferred compensation plan for his successor in which he retained a portion of his employee's bonus each year. This money was invested in an account owned by the firm in the name of the employee, who had discretion over how the money was invested. Over a decade, this account became quite substantial and was used as the down payment to buy the firm. Mike created not only an additional option for his exit strategy, but also a set of golden hand-cuffs that kept his employee interested and motivated in the long-term success of the firm. Additionally, he also created tax benefits for himself because when the account came due he paid it out as an expense, but the money he received as a down payment was considered a capital gain.

Mike's experience, like that of many other advisor firm owners, reveals that the bulk of an advisory's value is embedded in the success of its people. Like it or not, the advisory business is a people management business, and the more that is invested in excellent people, the better the return on assets. Whether that business is salable, and at what price, depends on the advisory owner's own goals and the steps taken to achieve them. Some advisors prefer to "stay small and keep it all," which in this industry can be a viable way to provide a healthy income stream. Such a course, however, is likely to impede the ability to transfer the business upon retirement.

For those wishing to create an enterprise that can go on without them and have value that can be monetized, it's best to create a business with that end clearly in mind. That requires working to attract the number, type, and size of clients needed to meet revenue and profitability targets; determining the organization needed to attract and service those clients; building teams of junior and senior advisors who can serve clients and grow with the business, treating them as an investment, not an expense; and leveraging technology to create efficiencies wherever possible, outsourcing that which is not core to the business.

By developing a solid team and operation, advisors can create an effective built-in transition plan. If that leads to a liquidity event, Tim Welsh suggests consulting the best legal, accounting, tax, and regulatory experts available. The devil—and the real payoff—of any transaction is in its details, not in the absolute numbers, he warns. So make sure you are guided expertly in that once-in-an-advisor-lifetime event.

CHAPTER 18

Taking Care of Number One

- *What about you, your goals, and your objectives?*
- *How concerned are you for the future of your practice and the industry?*
- *What can you do to protect your livelihood and value as the world gets "flatter"?*
- *What are compensation for the soul and compensation for the creative mind, and why is each so important?*
- *If you're busy taking care of affluent clients and their families, who's taking care of you?*

YOUR TURN

This entire book has focused where it should—on how to create advice so thorough and insightful that you, the provider of that advice, stand out in a crowded market of advice providers, drawing in affluent clients seeking your counsel because you truly understand their needs and can help them achieve their objectives. But what about you? Are you following the advice given in preflight warnings, at least metaphorically, and placing the oxygen mask on yourself before you assist others? Can you be effective on a sustained basis without first building a solid foundation to support yourself?

Top advisors are not unlike other high-performing professionals and athletes—you require years of preparation to achieve peak performance, a well-conceived practice schedule to keep your skills sharp, a personalized regimen of diet and exercise to keep your body well tuned and able to sustain your best efforts, and, most important, an emotional and spiritual program to maintain balance and meaning in all you do. Taking care of yourself is a tall order, and you can't do it alone. This chapter will frame your support needs and help you create a network of advisors, trainers, and coaches to keep you moving on the road to success—and help you stay engaged and happy once you arrive.

BEING THE ADVISOR FOR LIFE IS A CHALLENGE FOR *YOUR* LIFE

The often unspoken reality of providing a high level of personal service and advice to other people is that it is very difficult and demanding. Physicians like my father are entertained when financial advisors, admonishing clients to follow a recommendation, compare themselves to doctors: "If your doctor told you to do something, you'd do it—I'm like your financial doctor."

"Phooey," many doctors I know would say. "Have you seen some of our patients? They ignore issues of health at least as often as issues about money. Both are emotionally charged topics requiring—most likely—a change in personal preferences or lifestyle that they don't want to accept. Telling a lifelong smoker to quit is like asking a spendthrift to cut back and save for retirement. That's part of the reason the medical profession has evolved its pricing model. We get paid to examine, to test, to diagnose, and to prescribe—all before the patient decides if they will follow our advice. We can't depend on *that* happening!"

Giving personal advice is tricky. The irony is that the very best and very largest clients are typically high achievers themselves and require strong personalities to complement their intensity. I've addressed in previous chapters the need to show clients how they are at risk, and to challenge their preconceived notions and dreamy objectives. Injecting reality into someone's vision of the future can be incredibly valuable, lifesaving information—or an unwanted intrusion into a fantasy of affluence. Remember the advisor in Florida whose prospective client couple were stunned by his dire forecast for their retirement income— and the wife was indignant about wanting to dine out? Advising affluent families about *anything* is a tough job at times and financial matters may have more emotional pitfalls than any other type of interaction—even more so than health care.

Protecting Yourself from the Wrong Clients

Steve Grillo: "Do we ever fire clients? Not frequently, but sure. If a client is just too demanding or simply refuses to take our suggestions, we tell them they should find a new advisor. Some smaller clients that take a significant portion of your time can be a real challenge and can be damaging to your practice. You must evaluate your book of business, so we conduct time studies on our clients to see how much they generate in fees and how much time we spend with them. One client had $140,000 in an IRA, but it took the staff eight hours to complete the paperwork, not to mention my presentation time. The client is a friend of a friend so he is still with us, but the point is to manage your time wisely and, if need be, cut the client loose."

Sam (not his real name): "Building trust and confidence over a long time frame is how we have reached this level of success—with the patriarch, the spouse, and the children. And to accomplish this there are certain things that we don't do well by choice. We don't really entertain and we don't schmooze. We have our own family obligations, too, and we must allocate our time wisely to fulfill our personal responsibilities. It's all about finding balance in your practice. It's easy to lose sight of that if you are not careful."

YOUR ROLE: ADVISOR OR SERVICE PROVIDER?

Earlier, I discussed your potential role within the fabric of an affluent household. This is probably the most important place to start the mission of building your own foundation for personal support and growth. Are you a financial entrepreneur who aspires to mingle among a wealthy clientele as their peer, or will you assume a background role like Robert Duvall's Tom Hagen in *The Godfather*? Does your practice reflect a service model dedicated to "helping clients get organized," like a very successful advisor in South Florida, or are you the source of innovative alternative investment strategies? Are you known for your ability to quietly achieve consensus in difficult matters of family finance like Brian, Mary Beth, and their team, or are you an active stock picker with a passion for markets that can wow prospects with your insights? While there is value in all of these roles, the implications of each model have profound differences as to the advisor's needs for development and support. An advisor who seeks to lead clients and prospects with his big personality requires a very different type and level of emotional care than a more introverted and cautious advisor who prefers the view from behind the scenes.

You probably have a good sense of where you land in the service spectrum—from high-end peer of the affluent all the way to detail-dedicated support staff. But once you know your position, do you understand what you will need to maintain your professional edge? Just as the body requires certain vitamins, your professional and personal lives require attention and nourishment. To feed those needs appropriately, you must first be aware—and be truthful with yourself—of what they are. My observations of top advisors over the years have convinced me that most are not completely candid with themselves about their needs or concerns. In large part that is because they have few people in which they can confide issues that not all professionals or colleagues might understand. One of the great benefits of professional organizations like the Investment Management Consultants Association (IMCA), the Top of the Table, and other top advisor forums is the ability to connect with peers and share ideas. But how many advisors take the process to the emotional level and share common aspirations and concerns?

If you don't have an opportunity to share your professional problems, you may be flying solo right now while feeling agitated, frustrated, or simply bored. You are not alone. Many top advisors I know share these feelings:

- *Boredom.* Being a top advisor is great, but much of the work can be tedious. Developing asset allocations is not the work of nuclear physicists, and clients looking for get-rich-quick schemes can be annoying. Let's face it—working for affluent people in any capacity over time can be a challenge. So whether out of intellectual exhaustion or general fatigue, you would like to spice up your career, even though you are well paid, are well regarded, and have a great business.

- *Anxiety.* Fees are coming down, discounters are encroaching on your business, your clients are aging and dying off, and the baby boom generation is too irritating and demanding. What will become of your efforts? Are you going to make it? Areas within your control are responses involving better products and services, more complete staffing, and better technology. Areas out of your control include market performance and competition from better-financed players.
- *Frustration.* You think you're good at what you do, but many of your once-successful strategies don't seem to be working. Investing is more difficult, and marketing strategies that used to work wonders are not getting traction. Have you lost your touch?

The great challenge of working with creative, successful entrepreneurs is that each of their positive traits is matched by a drawback or demon. For example, the downside of creativity and daring is impatience and intolerance. Someone who is highly focused and driven can become inflexible. Wonderful insights into these life trade-offs abound in the pages of self-help texts. And, like you, I've read more than my fair share in order to learn more about myself, how to improve, and how to help others. My personal collection of these books fills a wall. But after plowing through all the books, tapes, and speeches, I have come to appreciate the simplest—and, I feel, most profound—messages. One of these comes from Laurie Skreslet, the first Canadian citizen to reach the summit of Mount Everest. When he was introduced to me by a business colleague, I heard firsthand from Laurie some of the wisdom he had drawn from years of living and working with Sherpas and the Tibetan people, who are well known for their writings on the nature of man. Laurie summarizes much of the Tibetan teachings by grouping them into three primary areas:

1. *Seven Dragons*—the fatal flaws based on lies or rationalizations you unconsciously or consciously tell yourself.
2. *Nine Needs*—those areas in which you require nourishment and care.
3. *Four Pillars of Vitality*—the foundation of your ongoing vitality.

My guess is that at one time or another most advisors, and perhaps you as well, have reached a growth plateau. Perhaps you are resting before another growth spurt or maybe you're burned out. Laurie believes a plateau may stem from one or more of your Seven Dragons draining your energy or from not honoring your Four Pillars of Vitality. Or maybe you're neglecting your Nine Needs, and not allowing these to resuscitate you. Let's examine in greater detail Laurie's interpretation of these centuries-old Tibetan insights.

The Seven Dragons

Lying in wait to sabotage your successes and positive actions are the Seven Dragons, or fatal flaws that consume your energy and detract from your best efforts. They are based, says Laurie, on lies you have told yourself—typically rationalizations based on fears you have about your life. Furthermore, each Dragon will manifest itself in a behavior based on the lie. For example, the Dragon of Stubbornness is based on the lie that if you modify your position on some topic you'll be seen as weak or unintelligent. The resulting negative behavior is to be inflexible. We all know someone like that! Here are the Seven Dragons, and the lies that sustain them:

1. *Arrogance*—you are better than others.
2. *Self-deprecation*—you are worse than others.
3. *Impatience*—there is not enough time.
4. *Martyrdom*—you are a victim.
5. *Greed*—you don't have enough.
6. *Self-destruction*—your life has no value.
7. *Stubbornness*—you cannot be flexible or change.

Dragons, says Laurie, are as smart as you. The smarter you are, the smarter they are. Dragons are the product of rationalizations, but ultimately emanate from fear. Fear distorts reality. Climbing Mount Everest, Laurie has learned the hard way that when fear takes over, people make bad decisions and behave irrationally. Fear prevents you from making good decisions and behaving appropriately and effectively in the moment. When you are aware of your fears, you can address them, channel your energy, and adjust your behavior. In this way you reacquire the power over your fears. By knowing your Dragons, you can catch them in action—effectively "photograph" them at work. If you know which Dragons are prone to attack, you can starve them of nourishment. Some Dragons match up well, such as Arrogance and Self-deprecation. Arrogance is based on the fear of being judged, whereas Self-deprecation is based on the related fear that you are inadequate or not up to the task at hand.

The fears behind the Seven Dragons are:

1. *Arrogance*—being judged.
2. *Self-deprecation*—being inadequate.
3. *Impatience*—missing out.
4. *Martyrdom*—being a victim.
5. *Greed*—not having enough.
6. *Self-destruction*—life is not worth living.
7. *Stubbornness*—change.

As a result of these Dragons, you might overcompensate to show you are better than other people. The negative pull of these dragons is ego, and the positive pull is pride. Your overcompensating behavior and your arrogance may make you feel better (the positive pull), but you can easily become obnoxious if you don't manage the negative pull. The seductively good feeling of a positive pull is a lure that you must recognize and be wary of, because it is being generated by a Dragon. The illusion created by the positive pull is that you are taking care of yourself—such as speaking boastfully or with unnecessary arrogance—but your behavior is really based on the fear that you are not as good.

Consider the positive and negative pulls of the Seven Dragons, listed in Table 18.1.

Managing your Dragons means recognizing and understanding your Dragons' positive pull as well as the destructive potential of their negative pull. If you know your Dragons, you can catch them as they affect you and starve them of attention before you are drawn too far by the negative pull.

TABLE 18.1 The Seven Dragons

Dragon	Positive Pull	Negative Pull
Arrogance	Pride	Vanity, ego
Self-deprecation	Humility	Abasement
Impatience	Daring, audacity	Intolerance
Martyrdom	Selflessness	Victimization
Greed	Appetite, lust for life	Insatiability
Self-destruction	Sacrifice	Suicidal tendency
Stubbornness	Determination	Obstinacy, inflexibility

The Nine Needs

Working from the acronym SAFEPEACE, Laurie outlines these components of an active human existence:

1. *Security*—the need to have everything in order, to feel safe and connected. For someone with high needs for security, not having control can be scary. People with high security needs might tend to pay off their debts, save a lot, and maintain their health more carefully than others. Consider your clients with security needs who are easily drawn to estate planning and life insurance. The positive pull of security is to feel safe and secure, while the negative pull (the lack of security) is to be fearful or indecisive. The negative pull comes from the feeling that things aren't in order.

2. *Adventure*—the need for new experiences and a feeling of drama and anticipation. Laurie's well-developed need for adventure has taken him to the top of the world's highest mountain. Adventure is involvement in activities with no certainty of a safe outcome. People requiring adventure can be innovators, seeking new ways to do things and to be first. Many entrepreneurs and salespeople have high needs for adventure. The positive pull of adventure is enthusiasm for the situation, and people with adventure needs typically have great presence. The negative pull of adventure is reckless behavior and what Laurie

terms "destructive drama" (for example, having an affair or taking unnecessary physical risks), in which the need for adventure supersedes appropriate conduct.

3. *Freedom*—the need for spontaneity and independence. Freedom is about having choices and the ability to make choices. Freedom drives you to keep your options open, seek out answers, and oppose unreasonable rules. People with a high need for freedom typically excel at new projects in which independent thinking will shine. They are often good teachers. Many financial advisors and wholesalers have a well-developed need for freedom. The positive pull of freedom is based on independence—self-confidence, high self-esteem, the ability to see options everywhere. You don't see too many freedom people worried about being trapped or suffering from martyrdom. The negative pull of freedom is the fear of commitment. The negative pull can also result in seeking separation and distance from others, and perhaps the inability to understand other people.

4. *Exchange*—the need to communicate with others on an equal and fair basis, and to receive as much as one contributes. In fair exchanges, both sides win. People with high needs for exchange have a good sense of balance; they enjoy working with contracts and agreements. They are excellent communicators and enjoy participating in discussions, teams, clubs, committees, and boards. Good exchange is critical to relationships. The positive pull of exchange is maintaining appropriate communication, as well as balanced sharing of value and knowledge with others. The negative pull is generated by unbalanced exchange—secretive or inappropriate communication, gossip, or criticism. The negative pull can also create cynicism.

5. *Power*—the need to have authority, to be in a position of power, and to explore the uses of power. Power needs drive people to easily accept responsibility and take charge in a crisis. The positive pull of power is leadership, self-empowerment, and success. The negative pull is the abuse of power—viciousness, authoritarianism, and dictatorship.

6. *Expansion*—the need for intelligent growth. The need for expansion is the need to broaden your horizons and create new empires. Expansionists like to go where no one has gone before.

These people like to create and build. They find it energizing to find new ways to do things. They are likely seen creating or expanding their personal fortunes, adding to their knowledge, creating new products, and collecting art and other objects of interest. The positive pull of expansion is an ability to see the big picture and the ability to perceive and benefit from the impact of ideas and products. The negative pull is inappropriate growth or expansion, hoarding, taking from others, excessive gregariousness, weight gain. Uncontrolled growth is a negative pull.

7. *Acceptance*—the need to be accepted by others, to have a sense of belonging. Acceptance is a need that has many positive attributes, including the tendency to exhibit behaviors you think will lead to your acceptance by others. These include being easygoing, having a willingness to accept others, being nice to everyone you meet, and tolerance. Acceptors are valuable members of a group because they go with the flow. They are typically peacemakers as well. The positive pull of acceptance is acting in a way so that people want to accept you—the tendency to be humanitarian, likable. The negative pull is denying your true nature, going along with the crowd, being a doormat.

8. *Community*—the need to be involved, to create a web of relationships, and to be social and amid gatherings of people. Community is a need that manifests itself in group activities of all kinds—parties, organizations, events—for the sake of the interaction in a group. In contrast to exchange, which is based on an equal sharing of value, those with a need for community need just the crowd alone, not any specific information or value from its members. The positive pull of community is the love of people and family, to be very social. The negative pull is indiscriminate contact, contact for contact's sake, neediness, clinging on to others, and dependence.

9. *Expression*—communication that is both internal and external, the need to be seen, heard, felt, and noticed by others. Expression shows up in people who engage in attention-getting activities, such as writing books! Opinions can be expressed in speeches, letters to the editor, paintings, or design. Most artists would have expression as one of their three most heartfelt needs. Expressives may dress to be noticed versus simply dressing for success. The

positive pull here is creativity and a willingness to show it. The negative pull of expression is to be *too* self-expressive, show too much, be so wrapped up in yourself that you don't notice how expressive you are! Think of my grandfather, who was a prolific writer and speaker but who convinced himself at one point in his later years that he was also a singer. He was wrong!

Applying the Nine Needs to determine your own nurturance requirements requires introspection. Laurie asks you to imagine three concentric circles drawn around your heart. Which three needs do you hold closest for fulfillment? These needs in the innermost circle are the most important components of your being. Laurie explains that you will find a way to fulfill these needs, even if you have to take dramatic steps. In fact, the best way to identify your innermost circle of three needs is to think about the times in your life when you have acted against reason and logic to make sure one or more of these needs was met. Was there any time when you acted out of intense feeling while other people around you cried, "Are you crazy? What are you doing??!"

Needs have both positive and negative pulls, and dimensions of each can affect the way we react. For example, since the need for Security has the positive pull of feeling safe and connected, and the negative pull of fear and indecisiveness, failure to manage the balance can prevent you from functioning. The impact of these needs is up to you. If you are aware of your innermost needs, you must honor them, because ultimately they will be satisfied one way or another. The key is to understand and appreciate your needs, and to manage the negative pull. For example, if you have a well-developed need for adventure, you value new experiences, drama, change, and the anticipation of new challenges. You will enjoy the positive pull of presence and enthusiasm, but you must remain aware of and be willing to manage the negative pull of reckless behavior and destructive drama. Changing jobs or mates just for the adventure is not managing your negative pull. Buying that Porsche may be termed an act of indulgence whereas it is really a way of satisfying your need for adventure and breaking free. Again, consider times in your life when you have acted against reason and logic—what need were you fulfilling by your actions? Now, about that Porsche . . .

The next three needs, in the middle circle, are of lesser importance in determining your level of fulfillment, and again less so with the outermost group. Considering these needs within your own world, what areas jump out at you? Listening to Laurie, I immediately grabbed the importance to me of Freedom, Expression, and Expansion. My efforts on this book reflect those needs, as have my 25+ years in wealth management and product development. Security, Adventure, and Exchange have driven most of my career choices and the way I execute the required tasks. Power, Acceptance, and Community float around the edges of my world, but are not as conscious needs as the other six.

If the Nine Needs provide you with food for thought, now contemplate again the list of Seven Dragons with a view to matching up your primary needs with the personal foibles that can stand in your way. For example, if you have a strong need for Expression, are you prone to the Dragon of Arrogance? If you have a strong sense of adventure or freedom, are you impatient or—much worse—haunted by a self-destructive Dragon? The latter example might be that of a mountain climber like Laurie!

Ultimately, the value of the Nine Needs is to help guide your interactions with other people. To the extent you are aware of your needs, you can better manage your behavior to be more effective. For example, if you know that you have a well-developed need for Freedom, your embrace of spontaneity might be intimidating or downright off-putting for someone with high needs for security. The two of you may never connect until you realize that your needs are at odds with each other. Contemplate the risks of being the senior partner of your financial advisory practice with a high need for freedom or adventure and having a staff with high needs for security or acceptance. You probably scare the daylights out of your team from time to time. Understanding of others creates tolerance, and considering your needs and identifying the needs of those people closest to you will make you a better communicator, as well as a better mate, partner, and parent.

I'm certainly not qualified to play psychotherapist for you and your successful practice, but I do observe a lot of similar actions and issues among top advisors. And most of those issues can be addressed within the confines of your advisory practice and propel you on to a more satisfying career.

The key is to be aware—acutely aware—of your strengths, your vulnerabilities, your professional needs, your personal needs, and the Dragons that stand in your way. Armed with an accurate view of yourself, you can seek out people and activities that nourish your sense of well-being; acquire relationships, colleagues, and clients that complement your strengths and skills; and—most important—avoid people, situations, business relationships, and other life events that can harm you in some way.

With three very active children, numerous interests, and a busy travel schedule, I have struggled with life balance. I constantly marvel at people who have achieved what appears to be balance in their lives. But oftentimes, when digging deeper, I've found that the "balance" I perceived is actually just a better success in one of the areas that I've neglected or at which I don't excel relative to that person. As a result, and by watching many top performers in different lines of work and sport, I've developed a theory of life as a sandbox, in which success in one area is a higher pile of sand. Given a finite amount of sand in a sandbox, the success was taken at the expense of another area within the sandbox. As a metaphor for life, success at work might be taking away from the "sand" of your personal life. Many of us suffer not from

Opposites Attract—and Make Money Together

Jim, a physically imposing and gregarious advisor I met early in my career, was a scratch golfer and club champion who drew the light in every room he entered. When he first visited my advisory office more than 25 years ago during a ski trip, he was sitting in *my* chair behind *my* desk within moments of his arrival. He knew he was a power player and made no apologies. He liked talking about stocks and options and how his clients liked to make risky bets that often paid off well. His down time was spent with clients on the golf course and on trips to golf venues. He was not burdened by late nights studying charts or combing through trust documents. As his business evolved to a stage where the clients began to get more serious about their long-term goals, Jim had to choose whether he would adapt to their needs or continue on as The Player. He became partners with a successful corporate executive client who preferred the yacht club to the golf club and who was as reserved as Jim was outgoing. Their partnership of complementary personalities and interests gave them virtual command of their community's affluent clients. Everyone knew one or the other member of this team.

lack of determination, but from lack of perspective for how to deal with the imbalances. Looking more deeply into our personal mirror can be revealing, but you have to be willing to look.

YOUR MAINTENANCE PLAN: THE FOUR PILLARS OF VITALITY

With the benefit of honest introspection and candor about your Needs and Dragons, what are the strategies to manage both aspects of your life? Consider Laurie's Four Pillars of Vitality. First imagine a four-legged bar stool. If all the legs are balanced, the stool stands firm. If even one of the legs is weak or too short, the stool wobbles and falls. The Four Pillars represent balance, and the failure to honor all four equally can topple the chair. Here are the four:

1. *True Work*—the tasks and efforts that make a positive difference in your vocation.
2. *True Study*—that which feeds your pool of knowledge and enhances your success within your vocation.
3. *True Play*—what you do to reconnect with joy.
4. *True Rest*—that which allows you to disconnect.

True Work

Which work tasks produce the greatest results? For my money, the time you spend directly with clients is the highest and best use of your time. It is 39 percent of the total time spent by top advisors, according to Advisor Impact. The more time you can spend with clients, the greater return to your business. That of course means creating time to be with clients at the expense of your time now devoted elsewhere. This trade-off is truly the "sandbox" I referred to earlier. Client service time, time spent marketing your services directly to prospects, and time spent with referral sources are the three most valuable uses of time among top advisors. Other duties can be farmed out more profitably to other people. Perhaps it is a no-brainer, but still the most common opportunity to reclaim time I find among top advisors: time spent on projects and duties that are not the highest and best use of the advisor's time. True Work touches your heart, says Laurie. It is that work that proves your existence makes a positive difference.

Advisor Advice

John Rafal, whose firm now manages over $1.6 billion, has more than 30 years' experience as an advisor. He offers the following advice for advisors of all ages:

- Treat yourself as your own best client—make sure you have a will and appropriate trusts in place. Fully fund your retirement plans, and arrange all your gifting and charitable bequests. And rebalance your own portfolio!
- Set goals for your practice that are measurable—and a stretch. Don't pick a goal that is easy to achieve. Your goal could be revenue, new assets, new accounts, or the number of complete financial plans. Whatever the goal, monitor it monthly and make it a stretch to achieve.
- Educate yourself. Attend a few advisor conferences each year. Meet people, get ideas, and keep yourself sharp.

True Study

True Study has become a passion for top advisors who seek to perfect their craft. Laurie says that True Study fills the pool of knowledge that feeds your True Work. IMCA and other industry organizations tap into this desire for more information and the pursuit of innovative and differentiating strategies for investing and solving client problems. I suggest a broader view than simply technical or even practice management concepts. Perspective is a valuable asset for any advisor, and more scholarly approaches may be for you to include a history or a biography from time to time. Leadership books are fine, but what about following the development of a leader through the words of a talented historian? To better understand your target market, read the stories of successful entrepreneurs and business leaders. What makes them tick? What would they value in an advisor? Many independent advisors I know gather in specific study groups to share ideas and often use their assembled assets as clout to attract a knowledgeable speaker. Some of my favorite experiences over the years have been as a participant in

Sharpening the Saw in Southern California

Kerry Bubb stays educated by reading—a lot. He subscribes to eight publications including *Fortune, Forbes, Worth, Barron's*, and a boating magazine, but not the *Wall Street Journal*. Every night, he reads from 7:45 to about 9. Kerry also reads lots of history books and gets ideas from them; Lewis and Clark are a favorite subject. He listens to audiobooks, too—there's plenty of time for that when you are driving through the Mojave Desert! He speaks highly of *Raving Fans*. He attends many conferences, believing that if he walks away from a conference with one real takeaway that he can put into practice, the conference was worth the investment. And he works hard to keep the dialogue open with other strategic thinkers at conferences. Be humble and stay so, he says, because there is always more to learn.

these gatherings. Finally, the achievement of a specific professional designation is a visible enhancement of your professional stature and evidence of expertise. *Study* may also be a misnomer for an educational passion that manifests itself in writing. Try a column or feature for a local paper or magazine. Chronicle one of your client successes as suggested in Chapter 15 about referrals—the case study. Be forewarned, you might get hooked like I did!

True Play

True Play for many advisors may be the famous 18-hole "open-air conference" with friends or clients. But that might not be the total departure required to recharge your batteries. Contemplate Laurie's characterization of True Play as reconnecting with joy. Is that a fair description of your golf round with a few clients or a referral source? Instead, consider the run you take alone on a wooded trail or the time spent fishing with your child. Lori, one of the nation's top advisors, from upstate New York, is a marathon runner—not exactly a client event! Scott, another top advisor, lives in the California wine country and has exchanged his love of rock climbing and extreme sports for a fanatical passion for golf. My longtime friend Frank Campanale has

> ## Compensation for the Creative Mind
>
> One of the challenges of providing advice to affluent households is that much of the work can be repetitive. A creative advisor can become stifled unless there is an outlet for that creativity. Bill in New York City has helped many families with estate planning and charitable giving issues. He took his efforts one step further by working with his church, where he is an elder, and helped create an innovative booklet to capture the innermost thoughts and most important directions required to help a family achieve their objectives in planning for their final days.
>
> How do you want to be remembered within your profession? As a top advisor with a legacy of helping affluent families, I cannot believe your job is simply a way to finance your lifestyle. What can you do to have a lasting impact? Will you use your stature in the community to promote a political change? Will you use your wealth to fund an important cause or endow an educational opportunity for children?

flown hot-air balloons in international championships for over 20 years. The focus required for a night flight over mountains precludes any thoughts of business or clients. I'm not too concerned about this particular issue among the top advisors I know—most seem to have found something fun to do when they are not serving affluent clients.

True Rest

True Rest is perhaps the most elusive strategy, because it is not an extended time in bed on a weekend or a day off doing chores. I had to look a long way through my life to find something I could do that would allow Laurie's guidance to disconnect. A long, solitary walk on the beach sans BlackBerry and mobile phone probably comes closest for me, although I've tried to create a similar feeling with a book on an airplane, but to no avail. I know several advisors who depend on physical removal from their circumstances to fully disconnect—and I have to agree there is something very liberating about being in a place where circumstances prevent you from communicating with ease. An investment

True Rest Is a True Disconnect

Kerry Bubb: "For me, rest is defined as total disconnect: no newspapers, no calls, no magazines, no cell phone, and no laptop. And True Rest does not mean sitting in the house. What it does mean is taking my boat to Catalina or going dirt biking in the desert with my son, daughter, and wife. If the staff wants to reach me they can, but I am not worried. Another thing that the disconnect does is instill pride and responsibility in the staff. They like the fact that I have enough confidence in them to run the shop. Another point on free time—don't make plans to do it at the last minute. Plan well in advance. I am marking my calendar for next August right now!"

Leon Levy: "True Rest is defined as taking off Fridays, cutting down on the workweek, spending time at the summer home at the shore, having financial independence, and being a philanthropic citizen. I also achieve True Rest from observing and practicing my religious beliefs."

banker I have known for many years lives a long way from his office in New York City—at the very end of the suburban train line. He does so in part to create a physical space between himself and his work. His family appreciates the separation as well. Another banker is not so removed, but her family religiously retreats to a rented home in Hawaii for one week every February, no matter how pressing her business demands.

MAINTAINING YOUR GUARDRAILS

If you've built a personal advisory board for your practice, consider creating an executive committee of that board that works directly with you on the sole topic of *you.* Such a board's input can directly impact your growth and development, and make candid, even brutally honest, observations about how you are working and living. For many advisors, the best advice comes from a spouse. That is certainly true in my case. My wife Jane has proven time and again her value in assessing situations and providing an objective opinion. Sometimes your intensity may intimidate people, making them reluctant to share their true thoughts out of fear of upsetting you or losing you as a friend. I've come to value those people who will give themselves permission to intrude at an appropriate time and place. You may know such people. Value them because by being privy to certain aspects of your life that others don't see, they can make an enormous contribution.

What about help in the workplace? Who is watching out for you there? Who in your office would know whether you are doing a good job or how you could improve? Even the best golfer benefits from having a coach who can see what the golfer does not—the swing from an outsider's vantage point. Who watches what you do? Most top performers can handle constructive advice, but not as many will actually create the opportunity for someone to have the proper perspective to give it. I know countless advisors who have spent thousands of dollars on coaches and improvement seminars only to later realize that they were expecting the coach to tell them what to do. Unless someone actually sees you in action and gets the true story, they cannot provide the most important advice you may need.

This perception/reality issue is the reason I use the painfully simple document referred to earlier as the Top 20 Client Analysis. Created out of frustration when working with 180 ultra-high-net-worth advisors at an international private bank—based in locations around the globe—I needed a format to reveal their businesses. When I asked what services they provide to top clients, I got a "yes" to every entry on a long list of services. Knowing they could not be that good across the board, I worked with their firm's headquarters to determine exactly which clients of those advisors truly owned the products and services claimed by the advisors. You can guess the results of that survey: Advisors provided an average of three services per client household, most of which were asset allocation, investments, and retirement planning. Estate planning and charitable giving were offered, but only sporadically. Other services, such as business succession planning and asset protection planning, were rarely seen. The perception of the top advisors was that they were providing these services, certainly talking about them, but that, for whatever reason, these services were not actually in place among their top clients. This observation, of course, is the basis for my contention that even the very best practices can improve their profitability without acquiring a single additional client household by making each relationship more complete—and eliminating those that do not have the potential to be more complete. (See the Top 20 Client Analysis, Appendix C.)

THE END OF THE ROAD

Where will your practice be when you decide to enjoy your own retirement? The old saw from my years as a brokerage firm executive
was that no one had ever attended a broker's retirement party. I sus-
pect you may have retirement plans, but what are they? More important, what is the disposition of your practice? Succession planning for
the practice is not entirely a topic for discussion in the three weeks before your retirement—it is an important issue for your current clientele.
Who wants to save and plan for retirement and have their advisor go
first? Chuck is a great friend and advisor in North Carolina who lost
one of his largest client families when the husband passed away and
the wife informed Chuck that all of their assets were now to be trans-
ferred to a bank trust department. Stunned, Chuck was told that her
deceased spouse had set up the trust in the event something happened
because he was afraid Chuck might not be around. Chuck and his
client were the same age! Working on a plan for your practice today
can become part of your legacy, but also directly boost its current success. Continuity of your efforts is an admirable future goal, but greater
clarity will benefit everyone in your world today. Give consideration to
Tim Welsh's observations in the preceding chapter about valuation.

PARTING THOUGHTS

There are very few jobs in the world whose potential economic and
social impact is greater than that of an effective financial advisor. If you
are truly skilled at what you do, the ripple effect of your work extends
far beyond protecting the wealth of the already wealthy. Because of
the social hierarchy that is capitalism, the professionals and business
owners you assist can spend more, hire more people, bequeath more
assets, fund more employee retirement plans, and live longer and more
productive lives to the benefit of others as well as themselves. Your influence on charitable board members, retirement plan directors, and
endowment trustees ripples through the economy's layers in a giant
wave of prosperity. Your personal success can be deployed through
your community for current and lasting effect. Your teachings about intelligent investing, diversification, planning, and preparation can help
other professionals such as accountants and attorneys in their efforts to

help clients. With so much potential to help so many people, you are in a rare and exciting role that transcends that of a mere investment broker or life insurance salesperson.

The Advisor for Life is really an advisor *about* life, and yours can be a wonderfully fulfilling career with lasting value for a wide variety of people. Take up the challenge to become more than you are today—no matter how good you may be—because no one will ever apply as much pressure to succeed as you can yourself. Congratulations for your success to date, but I'm even more excited about what you can do in the future. Good luck!

Practice Analysis

Team: _____

Participant: _____

Completion Date: _____

Welcome to the Practice Analysis!

The goal of the Practice Analysis is to provide you with a way to capture the most important information about your business—and in a format that can be readily referenced by you for future refinements. Too often I observe advisors struggle with a practice management issue because they do not have the data necessary to properly analyze the issue and create potential solutions. Completing the Practice Analysis ensures that critical information about your practice will be maintained in the electronic file, where it can be used at your convenience.

The immediate benefit of the Practice Analysis is the introspective exercise of completing the Analysis. Top advisors and teams who have used the Practice Analysis confirm that simply responding to the questions makes them think more about their practice and helps sharpen their focus. Used in conjunction with an advisory team, the Practice Analysis can pull together different team member perspectives and create a more unified view of your business.

This Appendix is a tool available for download at www.greshamcompany.com.

I A. Practice Basic Information

A. Location of practice: _____

B. Establishment date: _____

C. History of practice: _____

_____

_____

D. What are your current assets under management? _____

What were your assets 1 year ago? _____

What were your assets 5 years ago? _____

1. What percentage of your AUM is:

_____% Managed   _____% Mutual
         accounts   funds

_____% Individual   _____% Alternative   _____% Other
         securities   investments

_____% Equities   _____% Fixed income

_____% Alternatives   _____% Other

2. What was your practice's gross revenue last year? _____

3. What was your practice's gross revenue 1 year ago? _____

4. What was your practice's gross revenue 5 years ago? _____

E. What percentage of those revenues is from:

_____% Fees—**Today**   _____% Commissions—**Today**

_____% Fees—**5 years ago**   _____% Commissions—**5 years ago**

_____% Other

F. Tell me about your client base:

1. What is the total number of accounts in your practice today? ____

a. What was the total number of accounts in your practice 1 year ago?
    ____

b. What was the total number of accounts in your practice 5 years ago?
    ____

2. What is the total number of households in your practice today? ____

a. What was the total number of households in your practice 1 year ago?
    ____

b. What was the total number of households in your practice 5 years ago?
    ____

G. What percentage of the practice's AUM is tax exempt?   _____%

H. What percentage of the practice's AUM is taxable?   _____%

I. What is the number of "A" households (top clients) in your practice? ____

    1. What percentage of the practice's AUM do "A" households represent? ____%

    2. What percentage of the practice's total revenues do "A" households represent? ____%

J. What percentage of the practice's AUM is tax exempt? ____%

    1. What percentage of the practice's AUM is taxable? ____%

K. What is the number of "B" households (OK clients) in your practice? ____

    1. What percentage of the practice's AUM do "B" households represent? ____%

    2. What percentage of the practice's total revenues do "B" households represent? ____%

L. What is the number of "C" households (product accounts) in your practice? ____

    1. What percentage of the practice's AUM do "C" households represent? ____%

    2. What percentage of the practice's total revenues do "C" households represent? ____%

M. Top 20 client household inventory:

    1. What is their most common source of wealth? _____

    2. What are their average investable assets? _____

    3. What percentage of their investable assets does your practice typically manage? ____%

    4. Which of these primary services or strategies does your practice offer to your top 20 clients?

Cash management accounts	_____	Securities	_____
Mutual fund managed accounts	_____	Mutual funds	_____
Separately managed accounts	_____	Variable annuities	_____
Life insurance	_____	Asset allocation	_____
Asset protection planning	_____	Estate planning	_____
College funding	_____	Disability protection	_____
Charitable giving	_____	Long-term care	_____
Retirement planning	_____		

    5. How many of your top 20 clients provided a referral last year? ____

        a. How many new clients did you receive in total from these referrals? ____

        b. Where did their assets transfer from? _____

        _____

        _____

    6. How many of your top 20 clients added money into their accounts last year? ____

    7. How many of your top 20 clients took away money last year? ____

8. Did your practice lose any of your top 20 clients last year?

Yes _____   No _____

a. If yes, where did they go and why did they leave? _____

_____

_____

I B. Team Composition and Roles: Who are the members of your team and what roles do they play?

A. Name: _____

Background: _____

_____

Position scope: _____

_____

Primary responsibilities: _____

_____

_____

Secondary responsibilities: _____

_____

_____

B. Name: _____

Background: _____

_____

Position scope: _____

_____

Primary responsibilities: _____

_____

_____

Secondary responsibilities: _____

_____

_____

C. Name: _____

Background: _____

_____

Position scope: _____

_____

Primary responsibilities: _____

_____

_____

Secondary responsibilities: _____

_____

_____

D. Name: _____

Background: _____

_____

Position scope: _____

_____

Primary responsibilities: _____

_____

_____

Secondary responsibilities: _____

_____

_____

E. Name: _____

Background: _____

_____

Position scope: _____

_____

Primary responsibilities: _____

_____

_____

Secondary responsibilities: _____

_____

_____

F. Name: _____

Background: _____

_____

Position scope: _____

_____

Primary responsibilities: _____

_____

_____

Secondary responsibilities: _____

_____

_____

II. New Business Development: What is your marketing process?

A. Marketing and positioning:

1. When a client asks you, "What do you do?," what is your answer?_____
   _____
   _____
   _____

2. What value does the team bring to your clients? (Value Proposition) _____
   _____
   _____
   _____
   _____
   _____

3. How do you do what you do? What is your process?_____
   _____
   _____
   _____
   _____

4. Who do you do it for?

   a. Target market:

      1. Describe your primary target market and explain why it is your
         primary target market. _____
         _____
         _____
         _____
         _____

      2. What is your appeal to that market?_____
         _____
         _____
         _____
         _____

      3. What are your tactics for reaching that market? _____
         _____
         _____
         _____

b. Secondary market:

1. Describe your secondary target market and explain why it is your secondary target market. _____

_____

_____

_____

2. What is your appeal to that market?_____

_____

_____

_____

3. What are your tactics for reaching that market? _____

_____

_____

_____

4. Why do you do what you do? What are your business beliefs?

_____

_____

_____

_____

5. What makes you different? _____

_____

_____

_____

_____

6. Who is your toughest competition and why?_____

_____

_____

_____

_____

7. Who is your toughest local competition and why?_____

_____

_____

_____

_____

8. How do you package yourself?

   a. Do you use a presentation book? (If yes, provide a copy)
      Yes _____ No _____

      1. What is the focus of the presentation book? _____

         _____

         _____

      2. Who is your target audience? _____

         _____

      3. What are the contents of the presentation book? _____

         _____

         _____

      4. What is the flow of the presentation book?_____

         _____

         _____

      5. What is the presentation book's message? _____

         _____

         _____

   b. Does your firm have a brochure? (If yes, provide a copy)
      Yes _____ No _____

   c. Do you advertise? Yes _____ No _____

      1. Where and how do you advertise? _____

         _____

         _____

9. How does your practice position itself with centers of influence? Tell
   me about your strategy and tactics. _____

   _____

   _____

   _____

   _____

10. Client referrals: What is your strategy and your tactics for obtaining
    client referrals?_____

    _____

    _____

    _____

    a. Does your practice have a formal advisory board?

       Yes _____ No _____

b. Do you interview your clients about your services and their satisfaction?
Yes _____ No _____ How often?_____

11. Who is your competition? _____

_____

_____

a. How do you keep current about competitors? _____

_____

b. Do you interview your clients about competition?
Yes _____ No _____

12. Meeting with prospective clients:

a. What is the typical agenda? _____

_____

_____

_____

b. Information gathering: _____

_____

_____

c. How do you present your team capabilities? _____

_____

_____

d. Presenting the solution: _____

_____

_____

e. How do you establish roles for the advisor and the client? _____

_____

_____

f. How is the team integrated into the process?_____

_____

_____

g. What is your follow-up process? _____

_____

_____

_____

III. Wealth Analysis and Management

A. Setting the investment goal:

  1. How do you gather the information needed for establishing a viable investment goal? _____

  _____

  _____

  _____

  _____

  _____

  2. How is the investment goal articulated? Quantified? _____

  _____

  _____

  _____

  _____

  3. What tools do you use?

  a. Strategic tools—help provide direction (e.g., WM life cycle, WM picture)

  _____

  _____

  b. Tactical tools—help guide solutions

  _____

B. The Investment Policy Statement and asset allocation:

  1. What are the inputs for the IPS? _____

  _____

  _____

  2. What is the format for the IPS and what are the key components? _____

  _____

  _____

  3. How is the IPS related to clients? _____

  _____

  _____

  4. What educational tools are used (e.g., Elements chart)? _____

  _____

  _____

C. How do you create IPSs for your clients? _____

  _____

  _____

  _____

D. Investment process:

   1. What is your investment philosophy? _____

      _____

      _____

      _____

      a. How is it articulated to clients? _____

        _____

        _____

        _____

      b. How is it articulated to prospects? _____

        _____

        _____

        _____

        _____

      c. How is it articulated to centers of influence? _____

        _____

        _____

        _____

   2. What are the primary products used to manage assets? Rank by importance, 1 to 5, with 5 being the most important.

      Managed accounts _____ Mutual funds _____ Individual securities _____

      Alternative investments _____ Platforms (e.g., mutual fund wrap) _____

   3. Investment selection process:

      a. Product lineup: What products do you use and why? _____

        _____

        _____

        _____

      b. What is your selection process for products? _____

        _____

        _____

        _____

      c. What is your review process to track effectiveness of products?_____

        _____

        _____

        _____

    d. What are your termination criteria? _____

_____

_____

_____

4. Investment models:

    a. What are your asset allocation parameters? _____

_____

_____

_____

    b. What are your risk/return parameters? _____

_____

_____

_____

    c. What types of analysis do you use? What are the most important
       measures? _____

_____

_____

_____

    d. Role of taxes in your investment process: _____

_____

_____

_____

    e. How do you assess liabilities? _____

_____

_____

_____

5. Monitoring:

    a. What benchmarks do you use for portfolio monitoring? _____

_____

_____

    b. Do you track by absolute return or relative return? Both? _____

_____

_____

    c. What role does the client play in monitoring? _____

_____

_____

      d. What is your review process? _____

_____

_____

6. Your team's rebalancing philosophy:

      a. What is your rebalancing process? _____

_____

_____

      b. How do you communicate with clients when rebalancing portfolios?

_____

_____

      c. How do you model for tax implications? _____

_____

_____

      d. What method of reporting do you use? _____

_____

_____

E. Wealth management process:

1. What is your definition of "wealth management"?_____

_____

_____

2. What is your wealth management philosophy? _____

_____

_____

3. Approach: What need or service do you most often lead with?_____

_____

_____

4. What wealth management services does your practice offer?

Retirement planning	Yes ____	No ____
Estate planning	Yes ____	No ____
Family dynamics	Yes ____	No ____
Asset protection planning	Yes ____	No ____
Income protection planning	Yes ____	No ____
Education planning	Yes ____	No ____
Long-term care planning	Yes ____	No ____
Other services	Yes ____	No ____

5. How do you work the funding of a wealth management need into the
   process? _____
   _____
   _____
   _____
   _____

6. Implementation:
   a. What tools do you use? _____
      _____
      _____
      _____

   b. Do you have strategic alliances? _____
      _____
      _____
      _____

   c. Do you use internal cross selling? _____
      _____
      _____

IV. Client Service

A. How often do you meet with your top 20 clients for a detailed review? _____
   _____
   _____

B. What is the agenda for your client reviews? _____
   _____
   _____
   _____

C. Do you provide a written agenda? If yes, please attach a sample.
   Yes _____   No _____
D. How long are these review meetings? _____
   _____
   _____

E. Does the structure of your meetings vary? If yes, tell me why._____
   _____
   _____

F. Who attends your review meetings? _____
   _____
   _____

    G. What reports and information do you include in these meetings? _____

   _____

   _____

    H. Describe a recent successful client review meeting. _____

   _____

   _____

   _____

   _____

    I. What is the optimal number of client households? ____

V. Business Management

    A. What is the single biggest challenge to your practice today?_____

   _____

   _____

      1. What actions are you taking now to address this challenge? _____

   _____

   _____

    B. What will be the single biggest challenge to your practice in the future?

   _____

   _____

      1. What actions are you taking to address this future challenge? _____

   _____

   _____

    C. How do you see competition in the future? During the next five years, who are the winners and who are the losers? _____

   _____

   _____

    D. What do think will happen to client fees over the next five years? _____

   _____

   _____

   _____

E. What risks confront the advice industry over the next five years? _____

_____

_____

_____

F. Does your practice have a written business plan? What are your primary goals?

_____

_____

1. Who is the author of the business plan? _____

_____

2. How often do you update the plan and what is the process used?_____

_____

G. Benchmarks:
    1. What are your important success benchmarks?
       Growth ____   Assets ____   Client accounts ____   Revenues ____
    2. What goals do you seek for your benchmarks? _____

    _____

    3. What additional benchmarks would you like to have? _____

    _____

    _____

H. Team management:
    1. Who in your team defines the roles? _____
    2. Who does reviews of key personnel?_____
    3. Do you have job descriptions?   Yes ____   No ____
    4. How often does your team meet and what is the format of that meeting?

    _____

    _____

    5. Hiring:
       a. Who handles the hiring for your practice? _____
       b. What is the hiring process for the practice?_____

       _____

       c. How do you pay? _____

       _____

I. Practice communications:
    1. Do you have a Client Relationship Management system? Yes ____   No ____
    2. How do you maintain client files?_____

    _____

    _____

3. How do you share client information? _____

_____

_____

4. How do you handle compliance issues? _____

_____

_____

J. Technology: What role does technology play in your practice?

1. Does your Client Relationship Management link account values and information?   Yes _____   No _____

2. How do you track accounts? _____

_____

_____

3. How does technology support:

a. Sales: _____

_____

_____

b. Marketing: _____

_____

_____

c. How is each person supported? _____

_____

K. Succession plans:

1. Does your practice have a written plan? Yes _____ No _____

2. How has this plan been articulated to team members? _____

_____

_____

3. How has it been articulated to clients, prospects, and centers of influence?

_____

_____

4. Have you had an evaluation of the value of your practice?
Yes _____   No _____

5. How would the value of your practice be established? _____

_____

_____

_____

VI. After-Action Review

A. What did you learn about yourself and team? _____

_____

_____

_____

B. What is the best way to share best practices information to gain maximum utility?

_____

_____

_____

C. What observations/recommendations would you like?

_____

_____

_____

D. Are there any areas of sensitivity you would like me to avoid?

_____

_____

_____

APPENDIX

Organizational Chart

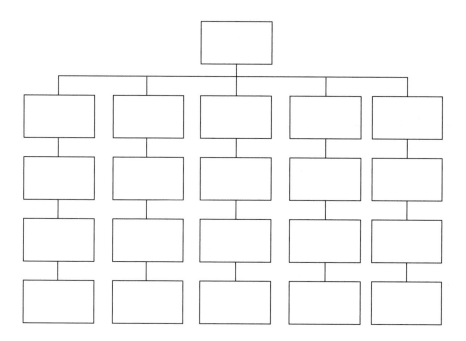

Use this chart to plot your current organization, with individual roles and responsibilities. Refer to it in regular meetings to review relationships and roles and to determine areas of potential change.

Investment Policy Statement

High Net Worth Individual/Family Wealth

(Client)

Approved on (Date)

This investment policy statement should be reviewed
and updated at least annually. Any change to this
policy should be communicated in writing on a
timely basis to all interested parties.

*This Investment Policy Statement (IPS) has been prepared
by **Fiduciary360**. It is intended to serve as an example of
the type of information that would be included in a
comprehensive IPS. Investment Advisors are advised to
have legal counsel review their IPS before it is approved.*

Special thanks to Don Trone of Fiduciary360 (www.fi360.com).

We would like to give a special thanks to Don Trone, an influential leader in
the investment advisory industry and true innovator in defining the evolving roles
of fiduciaries, for his generosity in supplying to us the Investment Policy Statement.

EXECUTIVE SUMMARY

Type of Client: Taxable, Individual

Current Assets: $650,000

Time Horizon: Greater than 5 years

Modeled Return: 8.0%

Modeled Loss: −9.4% (Probability level of 5%)

Asset Allocation:

	Lower Limit	Strategic Allocation	Upper Limit
Domestic Large-Cap Equity			
Blend	5%	10%	15%
Growth	5	10	15
Value	5	10	15
Mid-Cap Equity	5	10	15
Small-Cap Equity	5	10	15
International Equity	5	10	15
Intermediate-Term Fixed Income	30	35	40
Cash Equivalent	0	5	10

PURPOSE

The purpose of this Investment Policy Statement (IPS) is to assist the Client and Investment Advisor (Advisor) in effectively supervising, monitoring, and evaluating the investment of the Client's Portfolio (Portfolio). The Client's investment program is defined in the various sections of the IPS by:

1. Stating in a written document the Client's attitudes, expectations, objectives, and guidelines for the investment of all assets.
2. Setting forth an investment structure for managing the Client's Portfolio. This structure includes various asset classes, investment management styles, asset allocations, and acceptable ranges that, in total, are expected to produce an appropriate level of overall diversification and total investment return over the investment time horizon.

3. Encouraging effective communications between the Client and the Advisor.
4. Establishing formal criteria to select, monitor, evaluate, and compare the performance of money managers on a regular basis.
5. Complying with all applicable fiduciary, prudence, and due diligence requirements experienced investment professionals would utilize; and with all applicable laws, rules, and regulations from various local, state, federal, and international political entities that may impact the Client's assets.

BACKGROUND

This IPS has been prepared for John and Mary HNW Client (Client), a taxable entity. The assets covered by this IPS currently total approximately $650,000 in market value, but the Client's net worth is estimated to be $1,225,000. Assets not covered by this IPS include:

1. Corporate-sponsored defined contribution programs, where both the husband and wife participate (combined, valued at $350,000); and
2. A vacation condo valued at $225,000.

STATEMENT OF OBJECTIVES

This IPS describes the prudent investment process the Advisor deems appropriate for the Client's situation. The Client desires to maximize returns within prudent levels of risk, and to meet the following stated investment objectives:

Advisor lists investment objectives:

1. Retire with sufficient assets to support a lifestyle of _____.
2. Provide college tuition to grandchildren, etc.

Time Horizon

The investment guidelines are based upon an investment horizon of greater than five years; therefore, interim fluctuations should be viewed with appropriate perspective. Short-term liquidity requirements are anticipated to be minimal.

Risk Tolerances

The Client recognizes and acknowledges some risk must be assumed in order to achieve long-term investment objectives, and there are uncertainties and complexities associated with contemporary investment markets.

In establishing the risk tolerances for this IPS, the Client's ability to withstand short- and intermediate-term variability was considered. The Client's prospects for the future, current financial condition, and several other factors suggest collectively some interim fluctuations in market value and rates of return may be tolerated in order to achieve the longer-term objectives.

Expected Return

In general, the Client would like the assets to earn at least a targeted return of 8.0%. It is understood that an average return of 8.0% will require superior manager performance to retain: (1) principal value and (2) purchasing power. Furthermore, the objective is to earn a long-term rate of return at least 5.5% greater than the rate of inflation as measured by the Consumer Price Index (CPI).

Asset Class Preferences

The Client understands long-term investment performance, in large part, is primarily a function of asset class mix. The Client has reviewed the long-term performance characteristics of the broad asset classes, focusing on balancing the risks and rewards.

History shows that while interest-generating investments such as bond portfolios have the advantage of relative stability of principal value, they provide little opportunity for real long-term capital growth due to their susceptibility to inflation. On the other hand, equity investments, such as common stocks, clearly have a significantly higher expected return, but have the disadvantage of much greater year-by-year variability of return. From an investment decision-making point of view, this year-by-year variability may be worth accepting, provided the time horizon for the equity portion of the portfolio is sufficiently long (five years or greater).

The following eight asset classes were selected and ranked in ascending order of "risk" (least to most).

Money Market (MM)

Intermediate Bond (IB)

Large Cap Value (LCV)

Large Cap Blend (LCB)

Large Cap Growth (LCG)

Mid Cap Blend (MCB)

Small Cap Blend (SCB)

International Equity (IE)

The Client has considered the following asset classes for inclusion in the asset mix, but has decided to exclude these asset classes at the present time:

Global Fixed Income

Real Estate

Rebalancing of Strategic Allocation

The percentage allocation to each asset class may vary as much as plus or minus 5% depending upon market conditions. When necessary and/or available, cash inflows/outflows will be deployed in a manner consistent with the strategic asset allocation of the Portfolio. If there are no cash flows, the allocation of the Portfolio will be reviewed quarterly.

If the Advisor judges cash flows to be insufficient to bring the Portfolio within the strategic allocation ranges, the Client shall decide whether to effect transactions to bring the strategic allocation within the threshold ranges (**Strategic Allocation**).

DUTIES AND RESPONSIBILITIES

Investment Advisor

The Client has retained an objective, third-party Advisor to assist the Client in managing the investments. The Advisor will be responsible for guiding the Client through a disciplined and rigorous investment process. As a fiduciary to the Client, the primary responsibilities of the Advisor are:

1. Prepare and maintain this investment policy statement.
2. Provide sufficient asset classes with different and distinct risk/return profiles so that the Client can prudently diversify the Portfolio.
3. Prudently select investment options.
4. Control and account for all investment expenses.
5. Monitor and supervise all service vendors and investment options.
6. Avoid prohibited transactions and conflicts of interest.

Investment Managers

As distinguished from the Advisor, who is responsible for *managing* the investment process, investment managers are responsible for *making* investment decisions (security selection and price decisions). The specific duties and responsibilities of each investment manager are:

1. Manage the assets under their supervision in accordance with the guidelines and objectives outlined in their respective Service Agreements, Prospectus, or Trust Agreement.
2. Exercise full investment discretion with regard to buying, managing, and selling assets held in the portfolios.
3. If managing a separate account (as opposed to a mutual fund or a commingled account), seek approval from the Client prior to purchasing and/or implementing the following securities and transactions:
   - Letter stock and other unregistered securities; commodities and other commodity contracts; and short sales or margin transactions.
   - Securities lending; pledging or hypothecating securities.

- Investments in the equity securities of any company with a record of less than three years of continuous operation, including the operation of any predecessor.
- Investments for the purpose of exercising control of management.

4. Vote promptly all proxies and related actions in a manner consistent with the long-term interests and objectives of the Portfolio as described in this IPS. Each investment manager shall keep detailed records of the voting of proxies and related actions and will comply with all applicable regulatory obligations.

5. Communicate to the Client all significant changes pertaining to the fund it manages or the firm itself. Changes in ownership, organizational structure, financial condition, and professional staff are examples of changes to the firm of interest to the Client.

6. Effect all transactions for the Portfolio subject "to best price and execution." If a manager utilizes brokerage from the Portfolio assets to effect "soft dollar" transactions, detailed records will be kept and communicated to the Client.

7. Use the same care, skill, prudence, and due diligence under the circumstances then prevailing that experienced investment professionals—acting in a like capacity and fully familiar with such matters—would use in like activities for like Portfolios with like aims in accordance and compliance with the Uniform Prudent Investor Act and all applicable laws, rules, and regulations.

8. If managing a separate account (as opposed to a mutual fund or a commingled account), acknowledge co-fiduciary responsibility by signing and returning a copy of this IPS.

Custodian

Custodians are responsible for the safekeeping of the Portfolio's assets. The specific duties and responsibilities of the custodian are:

1. Maintain separate accounts by legal registration.
2. Value the holdings.
3. Collect all income and dividends owed to the Portfolio.

4. Settle all transactions (buy-sell orders) initiated by the Investment Manager.
5. Provide monthly reports that detail transactions, cash flows, securities held and their current value, and change in value of each security and the overall portfolio since the previous report.

INVESTMENT MANAGER SELECTION

The Advisor will apply the following due diligence criteria in selecting each money manager or mutual fund.

1. *Regulatory Oversight:* Each investment manager should be a regulated bank, an insurance company, a mutual fund organization, or a registered Investment Advisor.
2. *Correlation to Style or Peer Group:* The product should be highly correlated to the asset class of the investment option. This is one of the most critical parts of the analysis, since most of the remaining due diligence involves comparisons of the manager to the appropriate peer group.
3. *Performance Relative to a Peer Group:* The product's performance should be evaluated against the peer group's median manager return, for 1-, 3-, and 5-year cumulative periods.
4. *Performance Relative to Assumed Risk:* The product's risk-adjusted performance (Alpha and/or Sharpe Ratio) should be evaluated against the peer group's median manager's risk-adjusted performance.
5. *Minimum Track Record:* The product's inception date should be greater than three years.
6. *Assets Under Management:* The product should have at least $75 million under management.
7. *Holdings Consistent with Style:* The screened product should have no more than 20% of the portfolio invested in "unrelated" asset class securities. For example, a Large-Cap Growth product should not hold more than 20% in cash, fixed income, and/or international securities.
8. *Expense Ratios/Fees:* The product's fees should not be in the bottom quartile (most expensive) of their peer group.

9. *Stability of the Organization:* There should be no perceived organizational problems—the same portfolio management team should be in place for at least two years.

CONTROL PROCEDURES

Performance Objectives

The Client acknowledges fluctuating rates of return characterize the securities markets, particularly during short-term time periods. Recognizing that short-term fluctuations may cause variations in performance, the Advisor intends to evaluate manager performance from a long-term perspective.

The Client is aware the ongoing review and analysis of the investment managers is just as important as the due diligence implemented during the manager selection process. The performance of the investment managers will be monitored on an ongoing basis and it is at the Client's discretion to take corrective action by replacing a manager if they deem it appropriate at any time.

On a timely basis, but not less than quarterly, the Advisor will meet with the Client to review whether each manager continues to conform to the search criteria outlined in the previous section; specifically:

1. The manager's adherence to the Portfolio's investment guidelines;
2. Material changes in the manager's organization, investment philosophy, and/or personnel; and,
3. Any legal, SEC, and/or other regulatory agency proceedings affecting the manager.

The Advisor has determined that it is in the best interest of the Client that performance objectives be established for each investment manager. Manager performance will be evaluated in terms of an appropriate market index (e.g., the S&P 500 stock index for a large-cap domestic equity manager) and the relevant peer group (e.g., the large-cap growth mutual fund universe for a large-cap growth mutual fund).

Asset Class	*Index*	*Peer Group*
Large-Cap Equity		
Blend	S&P 500	Large-Cap Blend
Growth	Russell 200 Growth	Large-Cap Growth
Value	Russell 200 Value	Large-Cap Value
Mid-Cap Equity	S&P 400	Mid-Cap Blend
Small-Cap Equity	Russell 2000	Small-Cap Blend
International Equity	MSCI EAFE	Foreign Stock
Fixed Income		
Intermediate-Term Bond	Lehman Brothers Gov't/Credit Intermediate	Intermediate-Term Bond
Money Market	90-day T-Bills	Money Market Database

A manager may be placed on a "Watch List" and a thorough *review* and *analysis* of the investment manager may be conducted, when:

1. A manager performs below median for their peer group over a 1-, 3-, and/or 5-year cumulative period.
2. A manager's 3-year risk-adjusted return (Alpha and/or Sharpe Ratio) falls below the peer group's median risk-adjusted return.
3. There is a change in the professionals managing the portfolio.
4. There is a significant decrease in the product's assets.
5. There is an indication the manager is deviating from his/her stated style and/or strategy.
6. There is an increase in the product's fees and expenses.
7. Any extraordinary event occurs that may interfere with the manager's ability to fulfill their role in the future.

A manager evaluation may include the following steps:

1. A letter to the manager asking for an analysis of their underperformance.

2. An analysis of recent transactions, holdings, and portfolio characteristics to determine the cause for underperformance or to check for a change in style.
3. A meeting with the manager, which may be conducted on-site, to gain insight into organizational changes and any changes in strategy or discipline.

The decision to retain or terminate a manager cannot be made by a formula. It is the Client's confidence in the manager's ability to perform in the future that ultimately determines the retention of a manager.

Measuring Costs

The Advisor will review with the Client, at least annually, all costs associated with the management of the Portfolio's investment program, including:

1. Expense ratios of each investment option against the appropriate peer group.
2. Custody fees: The holding of the assets, collection of the income, and disbursement of payments.
3. Whether the manager is demonstrating attention to "best execution" in trading securities.

INVESTMENT POLICY REVIEW

The Advisor will review this IPS with the Client at least annually to determine whether stated investment objectives are still relevant, and the continued feasibility of achieving the same. It is not expected that the IPS will change frequently. In particular, short-term changes in the financial markets should not require adjustments to the IPS.

Prepared: Approved:

_____   _____
Advisor   Client

Date _____   Date _____

Top 20 Client Analysis

Use the following charts to plot your products and services and financial strategies.

What products and services do you offer? Where can you gain productivity and new assets?

Products/Services
(*Check all that apply*)

	Client's Name																							Number of Clients
Cash Management Account																								
Securities																								
Mutual Funds																								
Mutual Fund Managed Account																								
Separately Managed Account																								
Variable Annuities																								
Life Insurance																								

Financial Strategies
(*Check all that apply*)

	Client's Name																							Number of Clients
Asset Allocation																								
Retirement Planning																								
College Funding																								
Estate Planning																								
Charitable Giving																								
Disability Protection																								
Asset Protection Planning																								
Long-Term Care																								

Source: Stephen D. Gresham, *Attract and Retain the Affluent Investor* (Dearborn Trade, 2001).

Here is a working sample of the charts, filled in.

What products and services do you offer? Where can you gain productivity and new assets?

Products/Services
(*Check all that apply*)

Client's Name	B. Johnson	T. Smith	J. Shapiro	R. Kelly	M. Lynch	C. Edwards	W. Brown	K. Woodward	A. Nelson	N. Murray	R. Harris	C. Jones	T. Davis	S. Miller	D. Parker	H. Mullen	P. Carter	F. Allen	L. Bradley	B. Taylor	Number of Clients
Cash Management Account	✓	✓		✓	✓		✓	✓	✓	✓			✓		✓		✓	✓	✓	✓	14
Securities	✓	✓		✓	✓		✓	✓	✓	✓	✓	✓	✓			✓	✓		✓		14
Mutual Funds		✓		✓		✓			✓				✓				✓	✓	✓		8
Mutual Fund Managed Account		✓			✓		✓		✓			✓		✓			✓	✓			8
Separately Managed Account			✓				✓		✓			✓		✓			✓	✓	✓		8
Variable Annuities		✓										✓									2
Life Insurance													✓								1

Financial Strategies
(*Check all that apply*)

Client's Name	B. Johnson	T. Smith	J. Shapiro	R. Kelly	M. Lynch	C. Edwards	W. Brown	K. Woodward	A. Nelson	N. Murray	R. Harris	C. Jones	T. Davis	S. Miller	D. Parker	H. Mullen	P. Carter	F. Allen	L. Bradley	B. Taylor	Number of Clients
Asset Allocation	✓	✓	✓	✓	✓		✓	✓	✓	✓	✓		✓	✓	✓		✓			✓	15
Retirement Planning	✓	✓	✓	✓			✓		✓	✓	✓	✓	✓		✓			✓	✓		13
College Funding					✓	✓	✓		✓	✓				✓	✓		✓			✓	9
Estate Planning		✓				✓	✓					✓	✓				✓				6
Charitable Giving		✓				✓											✓				3
Disability Protection																					0
Asset Protection Planning		✓															✓				2
Long-Term Care		✓																			1

Bibliography

Anthony, Mitch. *Selling with Emotional Intelligence*. Chicago: Kaplan Business, 2003.

Anthony, Mitch, and Scott West. *Storyselling for Financial Advisors*. Chicago: Kaplan Business, 2000.

Bernstein, Peter L. *Against the Gods*. New York: John Wiley & Sons, 1998.

Blanchard, Ken, and Sheldon Bowles. *Raving Fans*. New York: William Morrow, 1993.

Chhabra, Ashvin. "Beyond Markowitz." *Journal of Wealth Management* (Spring 2005).

Clason, George S. *The Richest Man in Babylon*. New York: Penguin Books, 1926.

Covey, Stephen. *The Seven Habits of Highly Effective People*. New York: Simon & Schuster, 1989.

Dychtwald, Ken. *Age Power*. New York: Tarcher Putnam, 1999.

Dychtwald, Ken, and Joe Flower. *Age Wave*. New York: Bantam, 1990.

Dychtwald, Ken, and Daniel Kadlec. *The Power Years*. Hoboken, NJ: John Wiley & Sons, 2006.

Eisenberg, Lee. *The Number: A Completely Different Way to Think about the Rest of Your Life*. New York: Free Press, 2006.

Ellis, Charles D. *Investment Policy*. Homewood, IL: Dow Jones-Irwin, 1985.

Gordon, Ken. *Winning with Integrity*. British Columbia, Canada: Gordon Financial Group, 2005.

Gordon, Ken, and Rachel Orr. *Tomorrow Never Lies*. Los Altos, CA: TNL Press, 2000.

Gresham, Stephen D. *The Managed Account Handbook*. Hartford, CT: Phoenix Investment Partners, 2002.

Gresham, Stephen, and Evan Cooper. *Attract and Retain the Affluent Investor: Winning Tactics for Today's Financial Advisors.* Chicago: Dearborn Trade, 2001.

Halberstam, David. *The Education of a Coach.* New York: Hyperion, 2005.

Halberstam, David. *The Reckoning.* New York: William Morrow, 1986.

Krzyzewski, Mike, and Donald Phillips. *Leading with the Heart.* New York: Warner Books, 2000.

Krzyzewski, Mike, and Jamie Spatola. *Beyond Basketball.* New York: Warner Books, 2006.

Levin, Ross. *The Wealth Management Index.* New York: Irwin/McGraw-Hill, 1997.

Malkiel, Burton G. *A Random Walk Down Wall Street.* New York: W.W. Norton & Company, 1985.

Murray, Nick. *On Becoming a Great Wholesaler.* Mattituck, NY: Nick Murray, 1995.

Murray, Nick. *Simple Wealth, Inevitable Wealth.* Mattituck, NY: Nick Murray, 2004.

Murray, Nick. *The Value-Added Wholesaler in the 21st Century.* Mattituck, NY: Nick Murray, 2005.

Peterson, Peter G. *Gray Dawn.* New York: Random House, 1999.

Peterson, Peter G. *Running on Empty.* New York: Farrar, Straus and Giroux, 2004.

Prince, Russ Alan, and Karen Maru File. *High-Net-Worth Psychology.* Fairfield, CT: HNW Press, 1999.

Prince, Russ Alan, and David Geracioti. *Cultivating the Middle Class Millionaire.* Overland Park, KS: Wealth Management Press, 2005.

Prince, Russ Alan, and Hannah Shaw Grove. *Inside the Family Office.* Overland Park, KS: Wealth Management Press, 2004.

Pusateri, Leo J. *Mirror Mirror on the Wall Am I the Most Valued of Them All?* Buffalo, NY: Pusateri Consulting and Training, 2001.

Rouwenhorst, K. Geert, and Gary Gorton. "Facts and Fantasies about Commodity Futures." Yale ICF Working Paper 04-20, New Haven, CT, February 2005.

Skreslet, Laurie, and Elizabeth MacLeod. *To the Top of Everest.* Tonawanda, NY: Kids Can Press, Ltd., 2001.

Stanley, Thomas J. *Marketing to the Affluent.* New York: McGraw-Hill, 1988.

Stanley, Thomas J. *The Millionaire Mind.* Kansas City, MO: Andrews McMeel Publishing, 2000.

Stanley, Thomas J. *Networking with the Affluent and Their Advisors.* Burr Ridge, IL: Irwin Professional Publishing, 1993.

Stanley, Thomas J. *Selling to the Affluent.* Burr Ridge, IL: Irwin Professional Publishing, 1991.

Stanley, Thomas J., and William D. Danko. *The Millionaire Next Door.* Athens, GA: Longstreet Press, 1996.

About the Author

Steve Gresham is executive vice president and director of retail markets for Phoenix Investment Partners, Ltd., the $37 billion asset-management division of The Phoenix Companies, Inc. (NYSE—PNX). From 2001 to 2006 he led the successful turnaround of Phoenix's retail asset management business, and in 2007 was nominated by *Institutional Investor* as Fund Marketer of the Year. Prior to joining Phoenix, he managed his own wealth management consulting firm—The Gresham Company, LLC—serving over 50 organizations in the United States and around the globe.

He began his career in 1980 as a security analyst and portfolio manager for the U.S. advisor to The Central Group of Canada, Ltd. (ASE—CEF). After building a successful investment advisory practice at Advest, Inc., he managed Advest's mutual fund and managed account businesses through 1991, developing some of the industry's first fee-based accounts, including separately managed accounts, advisor-managed portfolios, and nondiscretionary, fee-based brokerage. He then returned to Wall Street to lead retail asset management distribution for Systematic Financial Management, Inc. (1991–1994) and Weiss, Peck & Greer, LLC (1994–97). In 1995 at WPG, he created and launched The Tomorrow Funds, a life cycle mutual fund series offering target maturities.

Mr. Gresham is active in industry media, having appeared on CNN, CNNfn, Bloomberg Radio and Television, USA Network and PBS, and in *BusinessWeek*, *Fortune*, and the *New York Times*. He is the author of *The Managed Account Handbook* (Connecticut River Press, 2002 and in Japan by Nikko Cordial Advisors, 2006) and *Attract and Retain the Affluent Investor* (Dearborn Trade, 2001), which have together sold in excess of 20,000 copies. A longtime industry magazine columnist, he currently writes a monthly column, "Retirement Doctor," with his father, retired physician Dr. Glen E. Gresham, appearing in *Registered Rep.*

Mr. Gresham serves on the board of governors at the Money Management Institute and is a founding board member of the International Money Management Institute. He was formerly a director of The Institute for Certified Investment Management Consultants and a member of the advisory board of the Association for Professional Investment Consultants (APIC). He is an independent director of Chase Investment Counsel Corporation in Charlottesville, Virginia. Mr. Gresham is a graduate of Brown University.

About the Contributors

Peter Burton is a graduate of Auburn University, receiving a Bachelor of Science degree in Finance. Prior to founding the Burton/Enright Group with Robert D. Enright in 1989, he served in a management capacity with Union Carbide. He entered the financial services industry in 1986 and earned the Chartered Financial Consultant designation from the American College. Peter is an investment advisor representative and holds the Series 7, 22, 63, and 65 licenses from the National Association of Securities Dealers (NASD); he is also a member of the Financial Planning Association (FPA).

He currently resides in Danville, CA with his wife Tammara and their two children, Alexandra and Peter Jr.

Evan Cooper is Director, Wealth Management News at Thomson Financial in New York, where he is part of the Thomson Financial News management team. Before joining Thomson, Evan was research editor at *Institutional Investor* magazine, where he was responsible for *II*'s signature surveys, including the All-America Research Team and similar surveys covering equity and fixed-income research in Europe, Asia, Latin America, Brazil, Japan, and Russia. He also directed the magazine's coverage of financial technology.

Earlier, Evan was editor-in-chief of the monthly magazines *On Wall Street* and *Bank Investment Consultant*. Evan also served as Senior Vice President and Director of Communications of the Securities Industry and Financial Markets Association (SIFMA); Vice President of Communications at Drexel Burnham Lambert; News Bureau Manager of the New York Stock Exchange; and as a Vice President at Rubenstein Associates, a large New York public relations firm, where he directed the PR activities of financial-firm clients.

A former reporter at Fairchild Publications and the *Miami Herald*, Evan has a BBA from Baruch College of the City University of New York and holds a Master of Science degree in Journalism (MSJ) from The Medill School of Northwestern University. He is co-author, with Stephen D. Gresham, of *Attract and Retain the Affluent Investor: Winning Tactics for Today's Financial Advisor.*

Joseph Finora has worked on Wall Street as a communications executive, and earlier in his career as a financial journalist. Joe has helped financial services firms of all sizes create communications as well as press policies and crisis-communications plans. He is at:jfinora@optonline.net.

Giles Kavanaugh, as chief operating officer of Pusateri Consulting and Training, challenges financial advisors, branch managers, and financial services firms in the United States, Canada, and the United Kingdom to discover and articulate their unique value. Giles also directs Pusateri's strategy, creates new programs and offerings, and writes articles for advisors. Prior to partnering with Leo Pusateri in 2002, he launched and led Sustained Learning group for Horsesmouth, a New York City–based online resource for advisors. Giles began his career in 1995 at Zephyr Management, where he helped raise and manage a $117 million South African private equity fund. Giles was a research assistant to currency expert Barbara Rockefeller on her book, *CNBC 24/7: Trading Around the Clock, Around the Globe.*

Michael Lynch is a vice president at Twenty-First Securities and is responsible for developing and maintaining working relationships with professional investors. Since joining the firm in 2004, he has introduced innovative stock concentration risk management techniques and cash management strategies to professional investors for use in their client portfolios.

Mr. Lynch began his career at Hennion and Walsh, a full-service brokerage firm specializing in municipal bonds. He spent four years at Phoenix Investment Partners, where he was senior internal investment consultant and a sales technology specialist. While at Phoenix, he developed relationships with top advisors at leading firms and acted as a portfolio liaison for an assortment of world-class equity, fixed income, REIT, and market neutral money managers and their respective roles in a diversified portfolio by incorporating modern portfolio theory and quantitative and qualitative analysis.

Mr. Lynch attended the University of Scranton, graduating in 1998 with a BS in Finance and a minor in history. He is currently a candidate in the

CFA program, having successfully completed Level II of the program in 2006, and is planning to sit for the Level III exam in June 2007.

Mr. Lynch is a member of the CFA Institute (formerly AIMR), the New York Society of Securities Analysts (NYSSA), and NYSSA's private wealth management committee.

Jeff Marsden, of PriceMetrix, works with investment firms to enhance the productivity and revenues of their financial advisors, who leverage the PriceMetrix Productivity Program to become better CEOs of their businesses. Users access a business performance dashboard with practical intelligence highlighting opportunities and potential actions. This is complemented by personalized user field support and an exchange of top performer best practices. The Productivity Program drives effective decisions and actions related to client selection and management, product and service offerings, and revenue and pricing strategies.

Arlen Oransky has over 25 years' experience in the financial services industry and is currently Vice President of Member Development for the Money Management Institute (MMI), the national organization representing the managed account solutions industry. Prior to MMI, Arlen has held executive level positions with Phoenix Investment Partners Private Client Group, TIAA-CREF, and Weiss Peck and Greer Investments. He is a graduate of the State University of New York at Stony Brook and earned a Master's Degree from Loyola College. Arlen has collaborated with Steve Gresham for *Attract and Retain the Affluent Investor* and was co-editor for *The Managed Account Handbook.*

Leo Pusateri is president of Pusateri Consulting and Training, a Buffalo, New York–based sales consulting and training firm he founded in 1992. The firm provides counsel based on the philosophies of value in the financial services industry, serving leading advisors and firms. Leo is the author of *Mirror, Mirror, on the Wall, Am I the Most Valued of Them All?*, a book that helps financial entrepreneurs explore the concept of discovering their value. Leo has over 29 years of sales and marketing experience, including nine years as a sales consultant with Learning International—formerly Xerox Learning Systems—and three years as the vice president of marketing for Elias Asset Management, prior to founding Pusateri Consulting and Training in 1992. Leo received his BBA degree in Marketing from St. Bonaventure University in 1977. He resides in East Amherst, New York, with his wife Ann and their four children.

Laurie Skreslet has been a professional mountaineer for over three decades with extensive experience in the North American Rockies, South American Andes, and Asian Himalayas. His expertise spans technical ice climbing, rock climbing, and alpine and high-altitude mountaineering. During his career Laurie achieved the distinction (in 1982) of becoming the First Canadian to climb Mount Everest.

Laurie is a certified Association of Canadian Mountain Guides (ACMG) guide, with over 32 high-altitude expeditions to his credit. He has also been an instructor at the Colorado and Canadian Outward Bound Mountain Schools, teaching over 45 courses.

Laurie has led 21 guided trips to climb Aconcagua, the highest mountain in the Western Hemisphere and one of the Seven Summits.

Laurie has written a children's book, *To the Top of Everest*, which was nominated for both the Hackmatack Children's Choice Book Award and the Canadian Library Association Book of the Year for Children Award. It has also been added to the Children's Literature Choice List.

Tim Welsh is president and founder of Nexus Strategy, LLC, a strategic marketing consulting firm to the wealth management industry. Prior to founding Nexus Strategy, Tim was Director of Business Consulting Services for Schwab Institutional, where he led the development and marketing of practice management resources for independent Registered Investment Advisors (RIAs), including an award-winning suite of business succession, financing, and M&A services along with the industry's leading platform for referral marketing. While at Schwab, Tim also held senior roles in marketing, advertising, PR, and event strategy and content development.

Prior to joining Schwab, Tim was vice president at Merrill Lynch, where he was responsible for marketing, product development, and financial advisor training for the financial planning group.

Tim is the author of a number of industry white papers and articles and is frequent speaker at industry conferences and events. Tim earned a bachelor's degree in economics from the University of California, Berkeley, and a master's in business from the University of Colorado. He holds the Certified Financial Planner (CFP) designation and currently serves on the national board of directors for th Financial Planning Association (FPA).

Index